# Daniel Unplugged

A COMMENTARY & TRANSLATION

# Daniel Unplugged

A COMMENTARY & TRANSLATION

SAMUEL M. FROST, TH.M.

McGahan

*Daniel Unplugged: A Commentary & Translation*

Copyright © 2021 by Samuel M. Frost

All rights reserved. No part of this publication may be reproduced, stored in a retrieval system, or transmitted in any form or by any means—electronic, mechanical, photocopy, recording, or any other—except for brief quotations in printed reviews, without the prior permission of the publisher.

McGahan Publishing House | Lynchburg, TN
www.mphbooks.com
Requests for information should be sent to:
info@mphbooks.com

---

ISBN 978-1-951252-13-7

## Contents

Introduction ................................................................. 7

Outline of Daniel ...................................................... 13

Chapter One ............................................................. 17

Chapter Two ............................................................. 31

Chapter Three .......................................................... 61

Chapter Four ............................................................ 75

Chapter Five ............................................................. 93

Chapter Six ............................................................. 119

Chapter Seven ....................................................... 139

Chapter Eight ........................................................ 165

Chapter Nine ......................................................... 181

Chapter Ten ........................................................... 211

Chapter Eleven ...................................................... 221

Chapter Twelve ..................................................... 265

Bibliography .......................................................... 291

# Introduction

MY INTENT WAS not to write an extensive commentary on the Book of Daniel. The material on this Book as anyone knows who has studied it is vast. Daniel has been subjected to every type of scrutiny and analysis that can be imagined, so it seems. Who can blame those who wander into its inviting pages for becoming frustrated? Its allure in spite of this is that it proclaims to tell the future, and we all would like to know what is going to happen to us. On that score, Daniel has been subjected to massive criticism, being found a fraud, a forgery, a made-up story to appease the fears of the faithful. This commentary, if it can be called a commentary in the normal sense, does not engage in these academic polemics. As the author, I am familiar with them, having studied Daniel for well over twenty-five years. I have read the critics as well as the defenders – in depth. I am up to date, so to speak, on the current issues of this work. For me, and for the reader to know, the text as we have it is what it is. It says what it says. It is up to us to decipher it, interpret it, as best as we can.

Two major polar opposites of the Book, each having an arsenal of material for their defense, is that Daniel was written in the second century B.C.E., or that it was written, as it appears to be written, in the sixth century B.C.E. during the rise of the Neo-Babylonian Empire. This is a centuries old debate. I side with the text and leave the other stuff alone. The text itself purports that it was written during the time of the King, Nebuchadnezzar, to the first few years of the King, Cyrus of Persia. It is best to simply let the text say *what* it does *when* it says what it says. As for the matter of faith, of actually *believing* the text as it stands, that is another matter altogether. The reader will have to take that up with their God.

This commentary is not exhaustive. There are no footnotes. There are no quotations from scholars. I do not engage in any extensive discussion on Ancient Near Eastern religion(s), or the cuneiform texts from that period. I have, and I want the reader to understand this, weighed neck deep into that material for many years. I have read virtually all the important passages of the classic historical works, the great and respected Commentaries, and the little ones and not so well-known ones. The arguments for the interpretations of world empires, for and against, are not found in this work, either. Most readers of Daniel want to immediately go to Daniel chapter two, or seven and nine. What I concentrate on is that there are chapters one, three, four, five, six and so on. These chapters, when read closely, *inform* us of the Book as a whole. I approach Daniel as a literary work and the author has strategically arranged each division and section for a purpose. Daniel interprets, I believe, itself. Thus, although I do quote Scripture outside of Daniel a bit, I even try to refrain from that as well. Of course, where there are overt references to the Scriptures, I admit them (Jeremiah, for example).

It is, of course, entirely impossible of not mentioning any outside information. We are dealing with an ancient world. Much of it is lost to us. We are dealing with Kings and Kingdoms. We have, on the face value, a work that is written with the idea that God has decreed the future of Daniel and his people, Israel. This decree is divine causation of very real future events; epoch events. The point is simple: God calls the shots, his angels cue up their sticks, and the billiard balls fall into their destined pockets. He runs the table, and he cannot be beaten.

From a personal point of view, I have been in "church" all of my life. I remember the names of my earliest Sunday School teachers. I remember Daniel in the Lions' Den, the Story of Shadrach, Meshach, and Abed-Nego and the great Gold Statue of Nebuchadnezzar (and that God turned him into a wild animal for seven years). I came from a Dispensationalist background in the Scofield Bible tradition. My step-father, may he rest in His arms, was a Seventh Day Adventist, and anyone that knows them knows that Daniel is critical to their establishment as an organization. In Bible College I learned that Daniel nine was the "fall of Jerusalem" in 70 A.D. I also begin to understand that there was another alternative to the largely Futurist school I was raised in. That brought me to the culture of the Second Century B.C.E. and one named Antiochus IV, King of Seleucia. I am starting my fifties in life so needless to say, Daniel has been a large part of my upbringing. I have been reading and writing on Daniel for quite some time. I have thrown away a lot, also.

There were many parts in Daniel that never squared with the paradigms I held to. There were always those problem issues that appeared to contradict my interpretations. They were either dismissed or simply "explained away" as not really crucial to the "overall" scheme I had adopted. But there they were, and they wouldn't go away. Of course, it could be accepted that Daniel is the product of many hands and that in the end an editor simply slapped all of these strands together completely unaware of the contradictions, or simply not caring about them. That, to me, was unacceptable. Daniel is a literary work, a composite book with a purposed design from its opening to its last words. It begins with the Exile of Israel in its first verse and ends with the hope of resurrection in its last verse. The "lot of inheritance" was lost in the Exile. It is received at the resurrection. Daniel transcends the historical and the mundane and is entirely immersed in a perspective that has to be revealed to him. If he just simply saw the world and the unfolding of history, Israel, the people of God, is nothing more than a speck in the world. It would not make sense. Israel's God would be just as feeble.

This is, then, a cumulative effort on my part, my notes, and simply, my thoughts as I read this wondrous Book. I can say this: for the first time in my life this Book makes sense. Thus, this study is a *personal commentary*. I hope you enjoy it and where you may disagree at least ponder what feeble insight I may have.

I do have to add one very important disclaimer. Every reader of any Daniel Commentary will immediately go to chapters 2, 7 and 9 to find out the "really important" parts. If you do this in my book, you will be disappointed. *This commentary was deliberately written as a book. The reader is to start at the first page and read each page in order until the last.* As the revelations in the book are progressive, so also is the material as I bring it out (as it is brought out in the texts). In other words, if you jump right in to Daniel 9, you will miss a good deal of material that *leads up* to that chapter. You will also miss out on the continuing matters that relate to chapter 9 in chapters 10-12. In short, *this commentary is to be read as a whole*. It is a book-commentary. A commentary in the form of a novel. It is my hope that you will enjoy it. That it will challenge you.

[A further note: the translation of Daniel I have rendered is to the best of my abilities in Hebrew and Aramaic. There are some verses that are notoriously difficult to translate. My translation is not "smooth English" in many places. I have consulted many "helps" as they are called in doing the work of translation, and am aware of many of the critical issues involved, and have equally consulted, as a rule, as least ten of the better, well known and well received Versions].

**Samuel M. Frost, Th.M.**
7th Week of Trinity, 2018.

# Outline of Daniel

I. Introduction to who Daniel is and his gifts. Outline of the Seventy Years of Jeremiah, from Exile (1.1) to Cyrus (1.21).

II. Dream-Image of King Nebuchadnezzar's Dominion and the succession of his Dominion to his offspring. The announcement of its end, marking the end of the Seventy Years. The remnant ("rock") will be established by Cyrus. Jerusalem and the sanctuary will be rebuilt and the people restored.

III. III. The reaction of King Nebuchadnezzar to the Dream-Image. Instead of just a head of gold, his whole Dominion and his successors will be gold as well. His dominion will have no end. The three sons of Judah refuse to acknowledge what God has revealed: The Babylonian Dominion will end. The "rock" will be established and the Image will be destroyed.

IV. IV. In the King's continued quest to establish his greatness, another dream is given to him, announcing that he himself will be cut down and made into a stump. The King confesses that God is correct. His Dominion is the only Dominion that lasts forever.

V.     V. The fulfillment of the Dream-Image of chapter 2. A weak and divided Dominion under the rule of a divided Father and son is found wanting in the balances of God. Cyrus, under the name Daniel gives him, Darius, is made King of Babylon (1.21).

VI.     VI. Cyrus/Darius realizes the power of Daniel's God in that Daniel is unjustly condemned by conspirators against him. Like a sheep to the slaughter, Daniel utters no defense. God rescues him, and Cyrus issues one of many Edicts afterwards that would lead to the fulfillment of the Dream-Image of chapter 2.

Chapters 1-6 is an entire block or unit that is completed during the Seventy Years of Jeremiah's word. It is from the First year of Nebuchadnezzar's rule (1.1) to the First year of Cyrus (1.21; 6.1).

VII.     VII. This begins a new set of visions and words of what is to come to the people of Israel who have returned to their country in the land of Judah. Four beasts/Dominions are seen as rising from the tidal wave of the four winds of the heavens and are made to stand on the visionary land together. The fourth beast is a monster and a little horn will arise from it that will cause great terror to the people and the city. However, this is according to the judgment of God who has decreed to hand them over for a brief time. Judgment will be decided against the little horn (a King) and in favor of the saints.

| | |
|---|---|
| VIII. | VIII. Daniel is foretold that the Dominion of the Medes and Persians will fall. The ancient people of Javan will arise. Its King will fall and be replaced by Four Dominions that arise from the four winds of the heavens. The little horn will come from one of those Dominions and cause great terror to the people and the city. But their city and sanctuary will be restored. |
| IX. | IX. Studying the word of Jeremiah concerning the Seventy Years, Daniel is informed by a mighty angel that God has decreed not just those Seventy Years, but Seventy Sevens for the city and the people. A Ruler will come and bring great terror to the people and the city, but his days will end. |
| X. | X-XII. Daniel is again visited by a great and mighty angel and is told the details that lead up to the coming King who brings terror to the people and the city. He will come to his end. The people and the city will be delivered. Resurrection is promised to those who overcome by their faith in God. |

Chapters 7-12 form the second half or unit of the Book. They are progressive in nature in that the first vision (chapter 7) has no identifying interpretation of the Dominions. Chapter 8 identifies that the Medes and Persians and the Dominion of Javan will be followed by the Four Dominions of chapter 7. They are only identified as standing in the place of the King of Javan (Greece). Further detail is given of what the little horn of chapter 7 will do to the people and the city.

Chapter nine adds more detail in terms of "how long" it will be until this little horn arises. Chapters 10-12 form one setting of the mighty angel showing Daniel what is written in the book of truth. This forms the events of chapter 11 leading to a further identification of the little horn; he is a King of the northern Dominion that will rise from the Four Dominions that come from the four winds of the heavens (11.4; 8.8; 7.2). Thus, working from chapter 11 with the greatest amount of detail to the first vision of chapter 7, the entire combination of two visions and two appearances of an angel who speaks "words" to Daniel are formed and are to be interpreted together.

The first section of Daniel is the Seventy Years (1-6) and its fulfillment. The second section is the Seventy Sevens (7-12) and its fulfillment. The Book was written and compiled to be an encouragement to those who truly love their God. It is given to Daniel from the God who truly loves those who love him. Their names are written in the book and they are promised resurrection at the last day (far removed from the time of fulfillment for these visions and revealed words) when they will receive their full inheritance.

## Chapter One

*In the third year of the Dominion of Jehoiakim, King of Judah, Nebuchadnezzar, King of Babylon came to Jerusalem and laid siege upon it. Adonai (The Lord) gave Jehoiakim, King of Judah, into Nebuchadnezzar's hand. Adonai also gave out of many vessels of the House of the Elohim (God) into his hand. Nebuchadnezzar brought these to the land of Shinar, to the House of his elohim, even the vessels he brought into the Treasury of his elohim.*

The writings of Daniel do not begin with a joyful sound. It is a horrible catastrophe. Yet, Adonai (Lord) has done this. Adonai gave Judah over to the "hand" of the King. Not only that, but to add insult to injury, the items that belong to Adonai, the items of His House, are given to the "hand" (often translated, *power*) of an invader. Further, to add even more sorrow, these holy items of the Temple of Adonai, the House of The Elohim – items used in worship to the glory of His Name – are now in the House of a foreign, pagan "god" (Marduk, who was also Bel, "lord"). The prosperity and wealth that were at one time the blessings of the God of Judah, the temple vessels that once were used in holy convocations, worship and atonement are now found in the most blasphemous of settings. Adonai did this. He is the Supreme Judge over all the affairs of wo/mankind. He takes away, and he gives to whomsoever he wills.

The date of this siege is roughly 605 B.C.E., Jehoiakim's third year (fourth year according to Jeremiah, using the Judean year-date). It is the year of the announcement of Jeremiah's "word of the LORD" that Babylon would be the superior Dominion "for seventy years" (Jeremiah 25.1-ff; 29.10, which reads, "for

Babylon." Israel's Exile and her desolations would be *included* in these seventy years. Babylon rose to supreme power in 609/8 B.C.E. and ended in 538/539 B.C.E – seventy years). This is crucial to the author for he will come back to this very fact in chapter nine (and here in 1.21). That the Prophets, particularly Jeremiah, are known allow for the readers to understand the fuller historical context to which I will hopefully bring out. Nebuchadnezzar actually orchestrated a series of raids against Jerusalem from 605 B.C.E. onwards (597, 589-586 B.C.E. when the city and temple were finally destroyed and burned. Thus, from 587/6 to 539/538 Israel was desolate for forty-nine years). Daniel is taken captive with the first raid. Jehoiakim was, then, still King of Judah. It is necessary to read the passages in 2 Kings and 2 Chronicles, as well as Jeremiah (and Ezekiel) that deal with this era.

These writings record the very actions that the book of Daniel is centered upon. It is not my intention to elaborate upon the differing calendar dates, suffice it to say that the "solutions" worked out do not alter the text as it stands. There is no error proven in them as some would speculate. Daniel's dating abilities, as he saw it when he wrote it, is spot on. We must ever keep in mind that the author is writing from *his* standpoint in time based on *his* methods of calculation in terms of calendar-time(s).

As already alluded to, the Exile of Judah (and previously Northern Israel under the Assyrians – 722 B.C.E.), is due to their sin. They broke the covenant. "I prayed to the LORD my God and confessed: "O Lord, the great and awesome God, who keeps his covenant of love with all who love him and obey his commands" (Daniel 9.4) is contrasted with, "we have sinned and done wrong. We have been wicked and have rebelled; we have turned away from your commands and laws" (9.5). The covenant God made with Israel through Moses had been broken. The curses of the broken covenant have come upon them as a result. With this in mind, Daniel's story (and his friends) takes on a different tone. *Daniel is living as a follower of his Lord during the time of a broken covenant.* The Exile is not a sign that God has forever left Israel, but that God has judged Israel for breaking the covenant. Israel is now treated as any other nation under the wrath of God. Yet, as already noted in 9.5, God "keeps his *covenant of love* to those who *love Him*." The wrath of God upon Israel *is* God keeping *his* covenant with them.

The use of the name for Babylon is telling here. Shinar is the ancient name. It is only used seven times in the Scriptures. It is a city founded by Nimrod (Genesis 10.10, 11, who founded "the Great City"). Nimrod also built Nineveh, capitol of Assyria (which is also called, "the Great City" – Jonah 1.2, 3.2,3, 4.11). It is also the place where the LORD confounded the languages of man and scattered them (Genesis 11.2-ff). Ironically, then, the author employs this term. The Lord has given Jerusalem over to Shinar, the ancient place of Nimrod, who also founded Assyria, where the Northern Kingdom of Israel was scattered (722 B.C.E.). Judah is now scattered along with Israel where the first "scattering" of man took place. Daniel, who will predict the rise and fall of many kings, kingdoms and nations, is at the very place where the scattering of the nations originated. Judah is now "scattered" by the "hand" of the King. Israel has become "one of the nations" scattered – just like all the rest.

*And the King said to Ashpenaz, Chief of the King's Eunuchs, to bring from the sons of Israel who were of royal offspring and nobility, boys who were without defect, good looking, educated in all wisdom, knowledgeable, able to teach and stand in the palace of the King to teach them books and the language of the Chaldeans.*

It is to be understood here that Daniel and his friends were of noble stock, already trained to a degree perhaps within the Royal households of Israel. They were most likely between the ages of 12-15 years old at this point. They were to be thoroughly trained in the cuneiform alphabet of Akkadian, and the various socio-religious tablets of the day. It was customary to orient captured youths into the new way of life and religion, showing complete dominance of the victorious kingdom.

Again, Shinar is in the land of the Chaldeans. Chaldeans are first mentioned in Genesis 11.28, where we find Abram. He is called out from the land of the Chaldeans to the land of Canaan. Daniel is taken from Canaan and placed in Chaldea, specifically, Shinar. It certainly would call attention to one knowledgeable of these things. Daniel, a son of Abraham, is in exile in the very place where the promises were made to Abraham and his seed; that he should become a great nation *and be a blessing to the nations*. The promises of God, in other words, do not look too promising. Yet, Adonai is the one who has given Nebuchadnezzar, King of Shinar over the land of the Chaldeans those whose origins in Abraham are from there as well. And, as the book unfolds, Daniel and his fellows are a blessing to the Gentile King.

*So the King apportioned a daily food allowance for them from his own, and from his own wine to drink for three years in order to make them great. Then they would be able to stand before the face of the King.*

It is difficult not to see the continuing allusions to Abraham's own life here. We have already seen that Daniel is in the ancient land of the Chaldeans, in Shinar. In Genesis, Abraham defeats the King of Shinar, and the King of Sodom comes out to offer him goods for payment. Abraham does not take the offer so that it cannot be said that he made him "rich" (Genesis 14.21-ff).

The absence of any nomenclature such as "the God of Israel" and the like are not here in the story in Genesis in that the nation in Abraham's time had not been formed. The lofty names, God of Heaven, Creator of Heaven and Earth are used, and these designations we find throughout the book of Daniel as well. I might also add that Abraham's name in this text is still, Abram, and has not been changed. Daniel's name is, in the next verse, changed. Daniel refuses the King's portions. Like Abram, Daniel stands before the King on his own terms, in his own integrity on the basis of his sole devotion to his God. Abram, too, stood in covenant with God as does Daniel — even though with Abram, Moses' covenant had not yet been made – and in Daniel's case, was broken. God is a covenant keeping God in spite of the absence, or in the breaking of the covenant of Moses. *What other covenant was there that God kept with those who loved Him? How was it kept by those who loved Him?* Faith?

*Among these were of the sons of Judah, Daniel, Hananiah, Mishael, and Azariah . The Chief of the Eunuchs set names on them. He set Daniel with Bel-teshazzar; on Hananiah with Shadrach; on Mishael, Meshach; and to Azariah with Abed-Nebo. Now Daniel had set upon his heart that he would not defile himself with the King's food, and with his wine for drinking. He sought the Chief of the Eunuchs; that he would not defile himself.*

In Sirach 40.29 we read, "When one looks to the table of another, one's way of life cannot be considered a life. One loses self-respect with another person's food, but one who is intelligent and well instructed guards against that." Now was not the time of feasting. Now was not the time to enjoy the spoils of the King over Daniel's people, Judah, sons of Israel, sons of Abraham, the Chaldean-made-Hebrew. Besides, the King's table would have undoubtedly served unclean meats, and here Daniel reflects on what is often a missed point: the law of God is "upon his heart." He does not say, "the King's food is defiled." He says that he wishes "not to defile *himself*." His own *conscience* would have been violated, and this would not put Daniel in a place where he could serve the King well. Is it better to defile one's conscience and serve, or attempt to keep one's dignity in place and serve? If service was going to be the road ahead, then Daniel wants to offer his best. Can a son of Abraham serve a pagan King with a clean heart? Without being defiled? As for food, *conscience* becomes the norm (one's heart), for we find that Daniel does, eventually, eat from the best of food (10.3).

This raises another question. Can the servants of Israel here remain faithful to their God without a priesthood? Without a temple? Without atonement and the feasts? Daniel is not in any sacred assembly here. He is fully in the world, but he is not of this world. This is why, I suggest, that Daniel hints at Shinar and the father of Israel, Abram who was also without the land, without priest and without a temple. Yet, at the defeat of the King of Shinar, Abram *is* greeted by a priest of Salem: Melchizadek. And, as we shall see throughout Daniel, the lofty names of God and his lofty attributes are uttered by both this priest and Abram. *Faith* works in the heart, "upon the heart" of Daniel. He "sets" his heart on this, and he "seeks out" accordingly. As a foreign name was "set" on him, Daniel "sets" his heart: I may be given a foreign name, but I am *Dani-El,* God is my Judge, and my heart is set on Him. This allegiance of the heart for God has possible consequences leading to death. Daniel's "heart" – the very phrase, "upon his heart" – is exactly that spoken of by Jeremiah, "I will put my law upon their heart" (Jeremiah 31.31). This is the carrying out of the "law upon the heart" for young Daniel. *This is true covenant life. It has no temple, no sacrifices, no city. It is a new beginning, at the very beginning of what becomes of Israel in the land of the Chaldeans.*

*Now, The Elohim gave Daniel over to loving kindness and tender mercies from the Chief of the Eunuchs.*

I have already quoted Daniel 9.4 above, and there we find "loving kindness" also used here. "Loving kindness" and "tender mercies" are *covenantal* terms. The Greek translation of Daniel has "grace and mercy" – two very common terms in the New Testament Bible. God's "covenant" is a covenant of loving kindness to those who love Him. Daniel is shown covenantal kindness among his enemies (for God is able to make enemies be at peace with His loved ones, the saints). God's covenantal blessings continue on Daniel, even when he is apart from Temple, apart from the priesthood, and apart from the feasts and sacrifices and in Exile. In other words, in spite of a broken covenant, there are covenantal aspects that remain *apart* from the one made with Moses. How can Daniel maintain covenantal favor from God when clearly the things required of Moses' covenant were now in ruins? It is to be noted, too, that God "gave" (same as 1.1) Daniel this favor. It is never to be missed in Daniel that "The God" runs the affairs. In the midst of an unholy people, Daniel and his companions "shine".

The answer to the question raised above is found in the Psalms, "The law of his God is in his heart; his feet do not slip" (37.31). "I delight to do your will, O my God; your law is within my heart" (40.8). And in Isaiah, ""Hear me, you who know what is right, you people who have my law in your hearts: Do not fear the reproach of men or be terrified by their insults" (51.7, and many other like verses). Daniel followed the LORD and "set his heart" on his ways. The law was written on his heart.

This is, then, an important theme, for the Prophets, like Jeremiah, speak of a time of a new covenant, a new thing when God will write his Law on the heart (Jeremiah 31.31-ff). In other words, Daniel is demonstrating the very heart of covenantal faith and love. It is not that it is a "new" covenant, but *the* covenant, the *heart* of the covenant as it was supposed to be all along. Daniel, then, is demonstrating "new" covenant life – covenant life *apart* from the works required by the details of the sacrificial system (which are demolished at this time, and were not in function in Abram's time). Daniel is demonstrative of true, inward, covenant life ("circumcision of the heart") that was not frequent or common in Israel (but was demonstrated among those often called, "the remnant" – Daniel will use this term as well). This is the projected future of the Prophets however: what is uncommon in their day will become very common in future days. I will continue to come back to these themes in Daniel.

*And the Chief of the Eunuchs said to Daniel, "I am one who fears my Adonai, the King who has appointed your banquet food and drink. Will he not see your faces jaunt from the other boys who are in your group? Then you would make my head guilty before the King!*

The King ruled by fear. Daniel does not wish to defile his heart. The Chief does not want to defile his head. He has been commanded by the King, who he fears, to give them the portions of food. This is an interesting exchange between Daniel's heart and the Chief's head, for they mean the same thing. A defiled heart/head is a defiled, guilty conscience which has done something that it knows should not be done. Far be it from Daniel to cause another to defile himself on his behalf. Therefore:

*So, Daniel said to the Guard, the one the Chief of the Eunuchs appointed over Daniel, Hananiah, Mishael, and Azariah, "I implore you, test your servants ten days and let us be given sown foods to eat, and water to drink. Then you can compare our appearance with the others who are eating the King's food and do what you wish with your servants. So, the Guard listened to this word and did as they asked for ten days.*

Rather than Daniel getting the Chief in any trouble, he went to the lower Guard. If the "word" failed, the Guard would be guilty. But why would the Guard run the risk? Perhaps in the chain of command, the lads would simply look worse than the others, and he could punish them however he wished, and this would be motive enough. If they did look worse, he would have had to give an account to the Chief, who would have had to give an account to the King. The LORD had not told Daniel to eat foods from the soil (fruits and vegetables). This was something on Daniel's heart. It was a strong impulse of conscience to take such a risk. However, the Chief "feared" the King, but Daniel "feared" the LORD. If the plan failed at least he was not defiled, even if he ran the risk of being humiliated.

*At the end of the ten days their appearance was healthier and fatter in flesh than all the other boys that had eaten from the King's table.*

That we should see here the hand of God upon their physical appearance as miraculous does no injustice to the text. It is not because of their diet. It is because they obeyed their heart in their devotion to the Lord. The term in the Hebrew is "flesh" – their flesh was made "fat" by eating *less* than the portions of the King's table (which would have undoubtedly contained meats). One does not gain weight by eating vegetables and water only! Nor is this text advocating that Daniel continued throughout his life eating only vegetables and water. Daniel 10.3 lets us know this.

*And so it was. The Guard would remove portions of food and wine of their feast and served them planted food.*

The picture we have here is that the feast of the King, a daily affair whether he was there or not, would have all sorts of food available. There would be a variety of meats, cooked foods, what have you. There would also be fruits, vegetables ("sown food" "seed food"). The text appears to say that when serving the boys their portions, the Guard would "lift" the meats and serve them only the vegetables and water. Undoubtedly, as we should be, the Guard would have marveled somewhat in doing this, watching these four lads remaining not only healthy, but healthier than the others! It would not have added up. We are not told that the Chief of the Eunuchs (the Den Master over these boys) was ever told about the matter, or whether anyone else knew or saw what the Guard was doing.

*To the four boys the God gave to them knowledge and comprehension in all books and wisdom, but Daniel he gave discernment in all visions and dreams. Now, the end of the days the King ordered arrived. The Chief of the Eunuchs brought them before the face of Nebuchadnezzar. The King had word with them. He found none among all them like Daniel, Hananiah, Mishael, and Azariah. So they stood before the face of the King. And every word of wisdom, of understanding which the King sought from them he found ten hands better than all the Magicians and Conjurers who were in his Dominion. And so Daniel was until year one of Koresh (Cyrus), the King.*

One may have already noticed how many times that "God gives" occurs throughout this chapter. He gave the King of Judah into the hand of the King of Shinar. He gave Daniel favor. He gives wisdom and knowledge to the four boys. Through this, the Guard gave the four boys their food. God's blessings are upon them.

It is by design that this section, 1.1-21, begins with the Exile (605 B.C.E.) and ends with "year one" of Cyrus (539/538 B.C.E.). That Cyrus, the King of Persia is also called, "the King" let us know that the previous "the King" (Nebuchadnezzar) does not remain and thus the seventy years decreed for the nations to serve Babylon ended. This includes the times of the Exiles according to the word of the Lord given to the Prophet Jeremiah, and will come into direct focus in Daniel nine. "All the vessels of the House of the God, large and small, and the treasures of the House of the LORD and the treasures of the king and his officers were all brought to Babylon. They burned the House of the God and tore down the wall of Jerusalem, burned down all its mansions, and consigned all its precious objects to destruction. Those who survived the sword he exiled to Babylon, and they became his and his sons' servants till the rise of the Persian kingdom (Septuagint has 'Medes'), in fulfillment of the word of the LORD spoken by Jeremiah, until the land paid back its sabbaths; as long as it lay desolate it kept sabbath, till seventy years were completed. And in the first year of King Cyrus of Persia, when the word of the LORD spoken by Jeremiah was fulfilled, the LORD roused the spirit of King Cyrus of Persia to issue a proclamation throughout his realm by word of mouth and in writing, as follows…" (2 Chronicles 36.19-22).

It is also critical to note, as an author myself, that the "book" as a whole and its visions have already been "seen" by Daniel (that is, Daniel wrote his visions when he saw them, but towards the end of his life finally compiles them and his life stories into the book we now have before us). They are finally "compiled" together with added segues that, like a knitting thread sew the "words", "visions" and "events" together into one literary piece ready for public consumption. Thus, the vocabulary is picked (key phrases and words) that link together the stories of the four lads and the visions and "word of the Lord" to Daniel. The opening chapter, from Nebuchadnezzar to Cyrus (70 years), that God is with Daniel in terms of "loving kindness", that Daniel is able to understand and interpret visions, words of wisdom is never to be forgotten as the composition unfolds. These boys are "sons of Israel", "sons of Judah" exiled from the Land. Their God goes with them. In this light, another key phrase, "at the end of the days" occurs here. They endure for a period of "three years" and emerge "at the end of the days" healthy and full. However, and this is critical, the end of this period of three years *is not* the end of their trials! More trials come after "the end of the days" of this period. Daniel has placed this first episode of being threatened with possible death, and enduring under the threat until "the end of the days" period was over. However, as we shall see, in the visions there is coming a period for Israel called the "end of the days", but it is not to be taken to mean that Israel's trials would be over at that time. The first chapter was a "ten day" period within the "three years" that concludes with "the end of the days" for Daniel. Because he remained loyal to the covenant of God upon his heart, he emerged victorious.

This, then, is the setting wherein Daniel and his three friends are found. This also sets up the next section, 'The King's Dream'. According to the Prophet Jeremiah, after the seventy years of Babylonian Dominion over the whole earth God would set up a kingdom which would never be destroyed (Jeremiah 31.40). Or so it appears…

## Chapter Two

*In the Second Year of Nebuchadnezzar's reign he dreamed dreams. His spirit was disturbed all the while he slept.*

It is to our advantage that we learn from Daniel the nature of our makeup (anthropology). Daniel's "heart" (his conscience) sought not to be defiled, and here the King's "spirit" is active, even though his body was overcome with sleep. There are other phrases throughout Daniel that intimate man's nature. Of course, if God speaks in dreams and visions, man is more than a collection of substance. God speaks not only to the bodily features (eyes, ears) but also to the heart and spirit. It is the body that sleeps. The spirit is disturbed sometimes with dreams. During his second year (or from another angle his third year, depending on what calendar Daniel used, or from what point he started his count. It is left unsaid in the text) Nebuchadnezzar had a powerful set of dreams so much that he was fully able when awake to recall it.

*So the King said, "Call for the Magicians, and to the Conjurers, and to the Sorcerers, and to the Chaldeans so that they may declare to the King his dreams!" And they came and stood before the King's face.*

The first two titles were found in 1.20. The Chaldeans were mentioned in 1.4 and probably refer to the highly educated. Sorcerers are a new title. Daniel and the three boys, who are now three years older, but probably eighteen or nineteen years old, do not assemble before the King. Even though they have undergone the three year training, it appears that they were not yet mature enough by Babylonian standards to be awakened. This was an emergency meeting at night. The line up here is the experienced veterans of Nebuchadnezzar's father, Nabopolassar. Even though Daniel and the three far exceeded the others, it is hinted at that they were in their houses along with other enchanters, thus not all assembled before the King.

*And the King said to them, "A dream I have dreamed! My spirit is disturbed until I understand this dream!" And the Chaldeans spoke Aramaen to the King, "King! Live for ages! Speak the dream and we will give pesher (interpretation)." And the King answered and said to the Chaldeans, "The word goes out from me: Behold! If you do not tell me the dream and its pesher, you will become limbs! Your houses will be made rubble!"*

It is at this point that Aramaic is used to the end of chapter seven. Certain key words show themselves here with "interpretation", "dreams" and the like. Dreams, by themselves, have no meaning until they are interpreted. Nebuchadnezzar utters his word that they must not only interpret the dream, but tell him what the dream is, too. It is here that we might find (and many have) a parallel with another young lad, Joseph (Genesis 41.1-ff). The theme between these two stories is obvious. However, in that story Pharaoh tells the dream to his court. Here Nebuchadnezzar does not. It may be saying that Daniel is even greater than Joseph in this respect. Nonetheless, God, who is the giver of dreams and can disturb a person's sleep, causes whole situations to change on a dime for both Daniel and Joseph. One day they are simply young boys doing whatever they were doing, and the next day they find themselves in an extraordinary situation that changes and alters their entire lives. Such is God.

## Chapter Two

Dreams were very important to the religious King, who worshipped Marduk and other gods. Having a dream with clarity, one that disturbed him (to the point of his irrational word to the court to kill the Chaldeans, Magicians and the like), meant the gods were saying something to him. It was a message. He must know it. It could be that his Kingdom is at stake. He must know his fate so that he can make his decisions wisely, either to avert them, or comply. Since we already know the dream that shows a statue being destroyed it may be hard for us to appreciate the force of disturbance here. This would have been disturbing to a King. What does it mean? Is he going to be ruined? Is he to ruin others? From history of the culture we know that Kings took vivid dreams as omens from the gods.

*"But if you tell me the dream and its pesher, a gift and a reward and much honor you will receive from me. Now, tell me the dream and the pesher!" And they answered and said, "Tell us the dream and your servants will declare its pesher." And the King answered and said to them, "I know from truth that you are attempting to gain time because of that which you saw that was gone out from me: the word. So, if you do not make known to me the dream there is only one result: your Decree (of death). You will agree together to come up with a word, a lie and a corruption to speak before me, gaining the time. Thus, tell me the dream and I will know that you have its pesher as well."*

The word went out from the King in 2.5, using the same Aramaic expression here. This word is "seen", which is of interest to us because of the similar expression in Daniel 9.23 (in Hebrew). A word goes out and is received by the Angel Gabriel and is given to Daniel. Daniel is told to understand this word and this "appearance". That is, the "seeing" of the word that has gone out from above. Here, the King speaks a word that has gone out from him and is "seen". This is different from "your decree". The decree is death. The word is "tell me the dream and its interpretation." They "saw" this (understood it). It's kind of like the expression, "I see what you mean."

*And the Chaledeans answered before the King and said, "There is not a man upon the dry ground who is able to declare the word of the King. All before – whether a great king and ruler – a word like this has not been asked – not to any Magician, or Conjurer, or Chaldean! The word which the King asks is serious. There is not another which can declare this before the King. As for this, gods who dwell with the flesh there are not!" All of this exchange before the King angered him. He was greatly angered and said, "To destruction for all the Wise Ones of Babel!"*

From my last comment, "the word" of the King is, "tell me the dream and its interpretation". That is brought out clearer here. The "decree" then, is the death penalty, and they understood that! They also "saw" (understood) the word. The negatives used here sets up the greatness of Daniel (rather, Daniel's God). The situation is rendered impossible. Historically, the ridiculous claim of the King has never been asked. Even in the parallel story of Joseph, the dream was at least told. There is no man who can do such a thing. We should note a tone of sarcasm (perhaps ridicule) towards the King in their last statement. "What you ask, O' King, perhaps a god who dwells with the flesh can answer, but unfortunately, Your Highness, there aren't any of them around" (much laughter).

Might we suspect, however, with the rather drawn out exchange of dialogue here that a "god with the flesh" is the only

## Chapter Two

solution? The Septuagint has "angel". Are they imagining here a god(s) that dwells "with" flesh in the sense of "among", or a god who has flesh? A god who dwells on the dry ground, who is not a man, but nonetheless dwells on earth with a covering of flesh? Such an idea is not farfetched. Some Kings thought themselves to be gods "with flesh" or "dwelling amongst the mortals." Perhaps, then, they are with great tongue in cheek pointing out that Nebuchadnezzar is asking something to be done which cannot be done, and has placed a decree (death) upon an impossible demand is the sign that he is losing it. To compare him with past "great rulers" and "kings" would seem to suggest this.

Well, regardless, this does not sit well with the King at all. The Aramaic is greatly animated here. He was angered already at all of this, and when they said this last line, he became even angrier (if that were possible). The King is now so enraged (and this is an idea later used in Daniel for Kings, see also, Zechariah 1.15) that he makes good on his decree, senseless as it is. And, perhaps, we should have quotation marks around the "Wise Ones" for they are not so "wise" after all. They are not inspired. They do not have the gods at their requests. What, then, is the point of having such a class around if they are not even able to carry out a simple request that a Magician or Conjurer is supposed to do (is paid to do)? [We should understand the story of Bel and The Dragon, found in the Apocrypha, where the young Daniel shows that the "conjuring" of the Magicians is, actually, a trick].

This passage is the first time we encounter the word, or title, "Wise Ones", denoting an umbrella term for the Chaldeans, Magicians, Sorcerers and Conjurers. Daniel does not (and was not called before the King) appear to be either of these other offices, but is constituted as one of the Wise Ones (who were not present before the King). This further shows the total irrationality of the King. His decree is to be carried out on those who are not even present before his face! This madness, then, brings young Daniel and his other recent graduates into the malaise. That the others were experienced (they recounted the history of such "dream-interpretation" requests) and of a certain class which Daniel was not is for certain. But let us continue.

*And so the Decree was issued that the Wise Ones be killed. And they sought for Daniel and his companions to be killed. Upon this, Daniel restored counsel and discretion to Arioch, the King's Chief of Guard, who came forth to kill the Wise Ones of Babel. He answered and said to Arioch, the Captain of the King, "Why is the Decree so urgent from before the King?" Then Arioch made known the word to Daniel. So Daniel rushed in and petitioned from the King to give him an appointed time and he would declare the pesher to the King.*

We do not know, nor are we told, that anyone of the Wise guild were killed. Some of the ones standing before the King may have been struck down, but we are not told. It is more probable that the Decree was uttered and preparation by the execution squad was made ready. They then went out to gather together the Wise caste from their houses (who were not present before the King). Daniel settles down the Chief guard, Arioch and "restores" order. Again, we should continue to notice the difference between the Decree and the word here.

Daniel and his companions (and others most likely) who were not present did not even know the Decree went forth since it had to be explained to him. And, Daniel, having impressed the King before as noted in chapter one, goes in to personally meet with him. He does not mention that he would tell the king the dream, but that he would make known what the King was really after: the interpretation. What does this dream mean and does it affect his Dominion? Is it an omen? If the gods have given him this dream, then the gods can also give the interpretation through the proper mediums and incantations that have worked before. Daniel asks for specific time, not to "gain time" (a longer duration). The Chaldeans sought to "gain time" and the word for "time" there is different from the one here (the Septuagint renders them both with the same word). Daniel simply asks for one night (the rest of that night). Knowing that his Decree could not even spare Daniel and his companions, the King relents for the rest of that night. If even Daniel cannot make known the dream and its interpretation, then they are not worthy to live, either. It was a tense situation. Life and death were at stake. Even the lives of the Sorcerers, Magicians, and Conjurers, blasphemous enemies of God as they are, and liable to the death penalty under the Law of Moses, were spared for one night in order to see the display of Daniel's God.

We may also note that Arioch, having seen the word that went forth from the King, has now been sent to go out and deliver the word to the Wise Ones. Daniel is to consider the made known word. The Decree has been made. But can it be changed?

*Then Daniel went off to his house. He made known the word to his companions, Hananiah, Mishael, and Azariah…*

Here is a detail that helps understand that after their graduation they received a house. The dream apparently took place in the night, so we would assume. The King urgently calls for the assembly of the more experienced Wise caste, those that had served his father. He does not bring out the freshmen. They remained asleep in their houses. While going through these homes, they are awakened. Daniel had undoubtedly known Arioch and was able to settle him down long enough to personally go into the King's chamber (which he could do since the King had already found him in favor). Daniel does not play around and gets right to the point: 'I will make known the interpretation you desire. Give me a night. Sleep on it. Don't make such a rash decision as this without giving me a chance.' He is allowed to go back home and inform his friends the King's 'word': tell me the dream and the interpretation. He also relates the 'decree': we will all die together if we don't.

*...and to ask for compassion from, before the God of the heavens, concerning this mystery so that Daniel and his companions would not be destroyed together with the rest of the Wise ones of Babel.*

If my reading is correct, Daniel is relating here that the Wise had not yet been killed. Daniel's own religion is on the line. It would be entirely sacrilegious to be killed with the blasphemers, counted with them as being unable to reveal mysteries. This would have been a blemish on God's name. Daniel would not have it. He asks God for compassion. Because of their love for the true God, he is asked to spare them the shame of going down with those pagans who blaspheme his name. And the LORD heard their request. We should also note that "the rest of" denotes that Daniel and his companions were youths of that guild, or class, but were not so experienced as to be called in the middle of the night for such an emergency as this.

*So to Daniel, in the vision, which was at night, the mystery was revealed. Daniel then blessed the God in the Heavens.*

Here we have, twice now, "the God of the heavens" as the more common designated title. 'Adonai' and 'the God' have been used in chapter 1, but the more frequent phrase, the God of the heavens, carries a far more universal ring than the God of Israel would. Gods were local. Babel was regarded as the center of the land. Tribal deities were to be placated and religious indoctrination was practiced, as it was with Daniel. Their names are changed and they now live among the pagans. Yet, their God goes with them where they go. The God of Israel doesn't stay in Israel even though his own house has been burned (1.1). He is with Daniel and his companions. Daniel's God "dwells with the flesh" of his people! And this is precisely the point of the impossibility of the Chaldeans when they exclaimed that no gods dwell with the flesh. Well, Daniel's does! The God of the heavens dwells with the flesh of *ish* (Aramaic for humankind). We may note also that their "gods" (plural) is contrasted with Daniel's God (singular). "There is no man on the dry ground that can do this!" Well, there is!

*And Daniel responded and said, "Let the Name of the God be blessed for ages and to ages for the wisdom and the power belong to Him. He changes the appointed times and the times in general, passing away Kings and he causes Kings to rise. He gives the wisdom to the wise and the knowledge to those knowing discernment. He reveals the deep, the hiding things. He knows what is in the darkness and with Him the light is let loose. To You, God of my fathers, I praise and adore, for you have given me the wisdom and the power so that now you have let me know that which we petitioned from you, for the King's word you have made known to us."*

Needless to say, this passage before us is holy. It explores every possible facet of knowledge that can be called knowledge. God is all knowing and there is absolutely nothing that is not known to him, including even a simple dream given on a particular night to an individual King. Not only does this God know everything that can be known, he directs the affairs of times, small times and epoch times and everything in between. He changes them at will. He causes Kings to rise, and brings them down.

It is of interest to me, however, that the Chaldeans sought to gain "time" or, the Septuagint uses the word here as well, "change" time. The King, perhaps, already suspected that his dream had to do with the future (what else is the benefit of a dream?). He states that the Chaldeans may be trying to "buy time" – awaiting his downfall. Maybe they know something he doesn't. Paranoia and rage both grip the King. Daniel's praise is after the fact of his dream in the night. He now knows what it means. His praise reflects the contents of the dream and its interpretation: God changes times and seasons for the rise of Kings and their fall. The wisdom and discernment to the wise is that they, too, would be able to "discern the times" – if they were paying attention. God brought about the downfall of King Jehoiakim. He "gave" him into another King's "hand". He has set up Nebuchadnezzar. Knowledge and wisdom and discernment have to do with knowing what the LORD is doing – and that means knowing Who is doing it! When He is known as the One Who does these things, praise erupts out of the sheer awe of His power and wisdom.

In an astounding phrase, wisdom and power belong to God and He has given to Daniel the same. Daniel, a "son of man" (8.17), is "given wisdom and power" (compare 7.14). Daniel has wisdom (in knowing how to conduct himself in light of his current surroundings), and the power (knowing who is in charge) to carry that out. Daniel has impressed the King, found favor with the Chief of Eunuchs, convinced the guard of the Eunuchs to give him vegetables, and has settled the nerves of Arioch, the Chief of the Court, and has averted death (and the deaths of others). That's power! Daniel is ruling in the midst of his enemies with the God who rules all things because he adores Him "upon his heart."

We must also notice the Daniel identifies the God of the heavens with the "God of our fathers." We do not know Daniel's parents. Some have supposed that these boys belonged to a King of Judah, like Hezekiah's sons (Isaiah 39.7), and this is not to be immediately rejected. Nonetheless, that Daniel in chapter 1 shows "upon his heart" considerable knowledge and nobility indicates an early training in the Law and other writings by his time. Jeremiah and Ezekiel are contemporaries (that Ezekiel mentions Daniel is to be noted as well, Ezekiel 14.14,20). Daniel's praise exemplifies a typical psalmistry of the Hebrews. His theology, in other words, is that of a son of Judah; a devout Israelite. The Lord has not forsaken his people and because of Daniel's presence, even the heathen are spared.

*Upon all of this, Daniel went to Arioch, who the King appointed to destroy the Wise Ones of Babel. He went and said thus to him, "Do not destroy the Wise Ones of Babel. Bring me before the King and the pesher*

*I will declare to him." Then Arioch quickly brought Daniel before the King and said to him, "I have found a great man from the sons of the Exile, of the Judeans who can declare the pesher to the King!" And the King replied and said to Daniel, whose name is Belteshazzar, "Are you able to make known the dream I have seen, and its pesher?" Daniel answered before the King and said, "The mystery which the King enquires of no Wise One, Conjurer, Magician, Astrologer is able to declare to the King. However, there is a God in the heavens who reveals mysteries to the King, Nebuchadnezzar, that which is to be in afterwards of the days. Your dream and visions of your head upon your bed, it is this: You, the King, your thought upon your bed, they have come up, and were what is to be afterwards. The One who reveals mysteries has made known to you what is to be. As for I, it is not because my wisdom is greater than all the living that this mystery has been revealed to me, but by reason of the pesher to the King – thoughts of your heart – you should know."*

There is a literary building up to the actual announcement of the dream itself. The death sentence was uttered, the King was troubled, lives were held in the balance during the night. The sword was at their throats. An enraged King must know the answer to the dream and visions! And now it has come. There are many items here that all come running together.

First, it is fairly clear that none had yet been put to death. Arioch stood down the order until the night was spent. In a sort of comical way, Arioch takes the credit in that he states that he has found a man, a great man, who has the answer (Nimrod, in Genesis 10.8 is called a "mighty man" – he founded Shinar, mentioned in Daniel 1.1). In actuality, and unbeknownst to Arioch, young Daniel went in to the King and convinced him to hold off on the order.

Nebuchadnezzar knows this and immediately asked Daniel a single question. That Nebuchadnezzar phrases this question in the same terms as the jesting of the Chaldeans (who are undoubtedly present) which enraged him is to be noted. They said, "No man on the dry ground is able to do what the King asks!" And here, the King says, "Are you able to do what I ask?" Yes, he is.

However, Daniel is not one to take the credit. No man is able unless God enables him. This is all in accords with Babylonian theology. The gods do dwell with the flesh of men, and the paid staff of the Wise Ones has simply failed. This Wise One, this Belteshazzar, who has come from the Exile, and whose name reflects the conquering might of the power of Marduk/Bel in the hands of the King is now in the King's palace and service!

It is to be understood that Daniel's hymn of praise and his prologue to the dream here inform us already a bit concerning the dream. The dream and visions in the mind of the King (his "head") concern what is to become of his Kingdom. Daniel, in other words, not only tells the King the dream and the interpretation, but actually tells him his thoughts as he lay upon his bed. His thoughts were consumed with what would be after his reign (Kings are obsessed with their lineage). How is his Kingdom to fare in the hands of the gods? Are they angry with him? Have they deserted him? If we understand that in Nebuchadnezzar's reign, which is among the longest in history, lasting forty-three years, his thoughts would naturally be on sustaining his Dominion. Daniel is in the early years of his reign when this dream took place. So, what is to be "after this"? What are the latter days going to be concerning the King's Dominion?

Nebuchadnezzar finally is "overcome with sleep" while thinking these things, and God gives him a dream that greatly disturbs him. What does it mean? Is it an omen? It is the King himself? This, then, underscores the reasoning behind the unusual request of the King to the Chaldeans. He cannot rely on trickery or lies. The only solution to truly understanding this dream is if the dream itself is declared together with its interpretation. That way the King can be totally assured as to the meaning, for no one, save the gods, would be able to answer such a puzzle, and it is the gods that the King seeks concerning his future, "what is to be in the latter days". Daniel, by telling the King his thoughts before he slept and dreamed, secures his attention.

Finally, the thought of the King's heart, Daniel adds, becoming quite intimate in his manner and showing personal respect, should be known and should not trouble him any longer. In effect, Daniel is saying that God has given him a right to know by revealing this mystery, relieving him of his disturbed state. It is not for every King to know their destiny, but God has revealed it to Daniel, and Daniel to the King. And now we must find out what this dream was!

*You, the King, you saw what is to be. Behold! One great image! This Chief image! And its splendor, unsurpassed, rose before you and its appearance was terrifying! It is the image. Its head is that of good gold. Its chest and its arms is that of silver. Its belly and its thighs is that of bronze. Its legs are that of iron. Its feet are from that which is iron, and also from that which is clay. You were looking until a rock, which was cut out, which was not by hands. And it struck the image upon its feet which was the iron and the clay and it shattered the feet, so that they were shattered as one: the iron, the clay, the bronze, the silver, and the gold.*

# Chapter Two

*And they were all as chaff from the threshing floor of summer. And the wind carried them away and no place could be found for them. And the stone which struck the image, it became a Chief mountain and filled all the land. This is the dream."*

The King saw a single (one, a number) image that rose up before him until it finally stood upon the land. If we could picture a landscape of a rising sun where slowly we see the rim, the middle, then the whole sun we would have an idea here of what he saw. A head of gold appears, and as it comes up silver shoulders, then arms and its chest appear. This is followed by a bronze mid-section with bronze thighs. Iron legs below the thighs with iron and clay feet, finally, stands as "one great image" before the King.

It is an amazing spectacle and induces awe before it because of its sheer size and brilliance. But Daniel, in the preface to the dream, emphasizes that which is "afterward of days" and "afterwards" (the Septuagint has the phrase, "the latter days"). The King wants to know "what will be" of this statue, and it is this that has him concerned ("what is to be" and "afterward of the days" are equivalent expressions). Now we know why. The King saw a stone coming out of a mountain, but did not see any workers cutting this stone. It simply appears. That was a cut stone (like a slab) is probable here. It seems as if Daniel is making this feature known about this cut stone, but the King did not witness it being cut by any laborer. It just shows up and smashes the ruling image ("Chief" image) upon its brittle, mixed feet of clay and iron. This is what has the King up in arms. This, as noted in the text, is "afterwards". It marks the end, or the latter days of this one image. The single image is shattered, and since the rock hits its feet, the whole edifice at once comes crashing down so that it becomes like chaff in the wind. This is what has the King in such a panic. It's what happens to this image afterwards, in its latter days. The Chief image is replaced by the stone which in turn is made Chief when it becomes a mountain.

But that is not all. This mysterious building stone, this slab of cut stone that appears out of nowhere grows into a mountain that fills the whole land upon which the image was standing. That is, the shape of the cut-stone grows into a massive mountainous shape. The description of the appearance and greatness of the image is surpassed by the cut-stone. An image is one thing, but a mountain is quite another, and much, much larger! And, visually, a stone, although having a slab like appearance, is nothing to be marveled at other than the size it becomes (what it "becomes" is also emphasized in the text, what "will be afterwards"). There is no gold, no brilliance, no craft and artistry displayed in the frightening smashing of the rock. It's just a slab of rock, and there were no hands that were seen that cut this rock out.

Now, if we place ourselves in the King's frame of mind, as he lay upon his bed wondering what will become of his great Kingdom, and finally he sleeps thinking of this matter only to have this dream, we can see why he was so disturbed. The King himself is in the dream, looking at the rise of this glorious, terrifying image. Head raised, surveying this awe, he sees a stone appear, falling as it were out of the sky and landing on the feet of clay and iron. As a result, this entire image, made of the best of materials from the gold, silver, bronze, iron and an iron/clay base comes crumbling down. The visual imagery is noted in the way the image appears. First the gold is seen, then the silver, bronze and iron with the iron/clay feet. The stone strikes the iron/clay feet and, in reversal, the iron, bronze, silver and gold cave in. It would be like watching a controlled demolition of a building with the base exploding, and the rest of the building perfectly crumbling downward upon itself. It didn't topple. It collapsed.

The King is watching this collapse, with the head of gold being the last piece to fall downward. All upon which the head of gold rested now lays in smoldering dust. The debris, the smoke of the collapse, the wind that accompanies such an implosion eventually clears. The rock is left. And its growth becomes apparent. The whole land is under this rock-now-turned-mountain. Why would this disturb the King? If I were a King and was wondering the fate of my Kingdom and had this dream, I would be disturbed myself. A great image collapses before me! Is this me? Is this my Kingdom? What is this? And what is this other foreign rock out of nowhere that causes its demise? Is this an invading nation, another Kingdom? Who are they?

Because the imagery is somewhat vague as well (it is still a "mystery" before it is interpreted), the Chaldeans could have indeed "bought time" in order to "interpret" its meaning. In reality they could have placed any kind of "meaning" to it. Had the King told them the dream, and since there was no "voice" in the dream indicating anything, really, as to its meaning, then the Chaldeans were really free to make it mean whatever they wished. Nebuchadnezzar knew this. If there was a meaning to it, if the gods were really showing him what will be, then the only one who could decipher the dream would also be able to tell the dream. That is, the same god(s) that gave the dream would also be the same god(s) that have the meaning of the dream. There must be one whose god is with his flesh!

Daniel Unplugged

*"Now, we will declare before the King its pesher. You, the King, King of the Kings, who God of the heavens has given to you the Dominion, the power and the might, and the honor, and wherever the sons of the men dwell, the beasts of the field, the birds of the air, he has given into your hand, and has caused you to rule over all of them. You are it. You are the golden head."*

This is as clear as pesher can possibly get. The King himself is the head of gold. It is the God of the heavens that has given this Kingdom ("Dominion" throughout my translation) to him. In 1.1 we have already seen that the Dominion of Jehoiakim was "given" into the "hands" of Nebuchadnezzar. The King rules over other Kings as well (the Neo-Babylonian Dominion conquered other lands). There is a note of flattery here in that, so far, the interpretation is favorable. He is the head made of "good gold." We may also hear the faint text of Genesis 1,2 here in that Adam was given all the Dominion of creation, the beasts of the field and the birds of the air. For Daniel, however, his theology remains intact: it is the God of the heavens that "sets up Kings" and allots for their "times and seasons" to rule.

We may also note that the plural "we" is used. Obviously, Daniel's companions are with him, and although the dream was given to him, he shares this with his friends. Daniel's humility continues to shine throughout.

*"And in your place a dominion will rise behind the land out of you, of silver, and a third Dominion behind which is bronze, and it will have power over all the land. And a fourth Dominion will be strong like the iron – all in front of the Dominion which is the iron is smashed. And it*

Chapter Two

*shatters the whole like the iron which is crushing all these (before it). It will smash and it will crush. And that which you saw – the feet and the toes – from them which is clay, that is potter's clay, and from them iron, it will be a dividing Dominion. And from the firmness which is the iron it will be in it. All before that which you have seen, the iron will be mixed in the pottery of clay. And the toes of the feet were from iron and from clay. Of an end of the Dominion it will be strong and from it will be cracking. And that which you saw, the iron mixing in pottery clay, they mix in an offspring of a man, but they will not be clung together, this with this, even like the iron does not mix with the clay."*

It appears that the metals used in the image are going from a glorious head of gold to cracked and mixed feet of clay and iron. The beginning is "good", but the "end" is smashed. The foundation upon which this image stands is "brittle." With general architecture, the foundation stone is first, but here the head is considered first. However, it is based on a fragile foundation. The head is set on silver, and the silver is set on bronze. The bronze is set on two legs below the knees which are resting on two feet made of the iron and clay. Mixed iron and clay cannot hold the sheer weight of these other precious metals. This is a weak Kingdom. Its end will bring the entire edifice down.

That we are talking about "Dominions" that come from the King ("from you" or "out of you") which visualizes their rising up on the earth as the image comes into view (seeing the head first) should cause us to see this Dominion as a single ("one") empire based on succession "from" the King. That is, we are looking at the Dominion of King Nebuchadnezzar, the Babylonian Empire and 'what will become of it in afterwards days.' The Dominion after the King comes "from" him. Not much is said. The third Dominion is bronze and maintains the power over all the land upon which this image stands. It is the fourth Dominion that is concentrated upon with excruciating detail. This is the end Dominion, the final one of the single image of which Nebuchadnezzar is the head. He wanted to know the future about his Dominion, his empire.

The text emphasizes the fragile state of the feet of the legs (the whole image). The iron, at first, is a conquering Dominion. It smashes all which are before it. This does not mean that the iron smashes the bronze Dominion, the silver Dominion, or the gold one. That would contradict the obvious coming downfall of the single image in the end. The image does not smash itself! Rather, viewed as a single image, the legs march out and trample on "all that is before it" – other Dominions and peoples. There is a revival of sorts from the apparently lackluster Dominions of the second and third.

However, the fourth Dominion becomes brittle, fragmented, mixed. There is a puzzling phrase here that mentions the "seed (offspring) of man" being mixed. Daniel is simply explaining the "visions" of the dream that the King "saw", the "thought" of his heart while he lay upon his bed. The King, then, dwelled upon the details. He noticed these visions, and particularly, the "afterwards" part. This image is not standing on strong feet. It is mixed, and he knows that iron simply does not mix with clay (being the architect Nebuchadnezzar was). Something is not right here. And, while dwelling on this aspect of the image, a rock comes out of nowhere and hits not the gold, not the bronze or silver, not even the legs of iron, but the fragile, mixed feet. Mixed with an offspring of a man. Where did this clay come from? Why does the iron mix with something so weak and feeble? Who is this offspring? From the inscriptions, the Kings of Babel thought of themselves as from the gods. The germ of the gods was planted in the womb of their mothers. It may be that from "good gold" to "seed of man" at the lowest point where the image cracks is pointing out that they were not from gods. They were but mere seeds of men.

From excavations and histories of Babylonian times we can see numerous "images" that were erected and built to honor the gods and Kings. Great stock was put in the "seed", the next in line. Nebuchadnezzar's dream of this type of image displays what surrounded the city at that time. His focus on the details of the image is what troubles him precisely because they are not uniform. The feet crumble, and this should be the strongest part. The seed of a man, derived from the iron, is a weak link. Daniel is not adding a detail here unknown to the King. The iron is strong, but the seed of the iron is weak, like clay, and this lets us know, too, that we are dealing with a singular image of the King's Dominion. From numerous inscriptions the obsession with continuing the legacy of the Dynasty by the hands of the great gods was of all importance. Nebuchadnezzar here is being told his future. His Dynasty will not last. It will crumble. The gods are giving him a preview of the latter days of the Babylonian Empire.

Finally, we must also interpret this dream in light of the response of Daniel in his praise to his God. God "changes the times and the seasons." He "causes kings to rise" and Daniel sees the "rise" of Kings in this vision. God also causes their "passing away", which the wind here, "carries away" the chaff. Daniel's response, then, informs us that the King's dream is indeed troubling to him. And no wonder, for why would he be concerned with the fall of a Kingdom not his own?

Nebuchadnezzar knew enough about the dream and its image as to what it basically was saying: the image, this single edifice comes to nothing in the afterwards days. The next concern of these days is, what causes its destruction? Besides the brittleness of its feet, there is a rock that comes and brings down the entire image.

*"And in the days of those Kings the God of the heavens will cause to rise a Dominion for ages. It will not be destroyed. Its Dominion will not be left to people behind it. It will smash and put an end to all those Dominions, but it, it shall rise for ages. All before which you saw, that out of the mountain a stone was cut without hands, so smashed the iron, the bronze, the clay, the silver, and the gold, the Chief God has made known to the King what that which is to be after this. Now the dream is certain, and the pesher is trustworthy."*

The Kings mentioned here are the final ones which apparently are represented by the iron on one hand, and the seed/clay on the other. The final Kings of this Kingdom, the fourth Kingdom, will experience the crushing blow of the stone. And, again reflecting the wording of Daniel's responsive praise to the God of the heavens, God will cause to "rise" a Dominion that will not be left behind to another people (same word above in 2.21, "sets up" or "cause to rise"). There is no succession in this Dominion as there were with the image. It will rise for an indefinite period of time, into coming ages. Its steady rise from a foundation stone of sorts, a cut stone from the mountain (which is where foundation stones are taken) will not be destroyed. In 2.4 the King, for the first time, is addressed "King for ages". Daniel extols God as "for ages and to ages." The stone alone is established "for ages". Nebuchadnezzar will not last. The stone will.

Chapter Two

The wording previously was that the stone itself will become a mountain, the Chief mountain, whereas here the stone is taken from "the mountain" and God is called the Chief. The former is to be understood as the dream imagery itself. A stone is cut out without hands and becomes the Chief mountain. In the interpretation, the stone is cut out of the mountain, and God himself is the Chief (over the growing mountain and the mountain from which it is taken). The stone is taken from a mountain and becomes a mountain over which God is Chief (cutting, taking, causing to rise). What should concern us in the dream is whether there are two mountains, or one. The stone is "cut out" from a source, which is a mountain. This stone itself becomes a mountain (indicating growth) and "fills the whole land" upon which the image stands. There are, then, two mountains, one from which the stone is taken, and the other which the stone becomes, pushing away all the other mountains so that there is only one left on the horizon.

Further focus on the text yields the word, "people." This stone is a Dominion that will not be succeeded to any other people buts its own. Thus, this stone is a Dominion of "people" over which God is the Chief. It is another nation of people, and God is its Chief. It is cut out of an already existing mountain (people) and, therefore, considerably smaller than the mountain itself (obviously). The dream is focused on the stone, and not the mountain it is cut out from. A stone taken from an already existing mountain and this stone itself will become a Chief mountain rising upon the whole land to the ages (how long this takes we are simply not told). We are to conclude then, that a Dominion, a nation of people, will be the cause of the fall of the image. This people, although considerably smaller than the image itself (it hits the feet, not the body), and certainly smaller than the mountain from which is cut, will have God as its King and Chief, and one cannot topple the God of the heavens. This Dominion, therefore, is ages-enduring and cannot be destroyed. It belongs to the God of the heavens who Himself causes the rise and fall of all the other Dominions and their Kings. He changes the times and the seasons. He directs all Dominions and Kings. What He has given in the dream to the King (and to Daniel and his friends) is the assurance that God is the Chief of Chiefs and the King of Kings.

With the whole dream and interpretation made known, let us read again Daniel's responsive praise and adoration: "Let the Name of the God be blessed from ages and to ages for the wisdom and the power belong to Him. He changes the appointed times and the times in general, passing away Kings and he causes Kings to rise. He gives the wisdom to the wise and the knowledge to those knowing discernment. He reveals the deep, the hiding things. He knows what is in the darkness and with Him the light is let loose. To You, God of my fathers, I praise and adore, for you have given me the wisdom and the power so that now you have let me know that which we asked from you, for the King's word you have made known to us." Other Dominions and their Kings fail. They pass away. Babylon will have a succession of Kings, but in the end days will become chaff. However, God's Dominion, and His people's Dominion which is under his, will never be destroyed for God is their King "from ages and to the ages". The promises of God, the God of Daniel's fathers, the sons of Judah, sons of Israel, the sons of the Exile as the boys are called, will be kept. He will establish their Dominion after the smashing of Babylon and its successive Dominions. He will take a small stone cut from the people and establish a people of his own Dominion. A remnant. The final, last days of Babylon will be weak and brittle due to the relationship between a father and son Dominion, a father of iron and his seed, a son.

That Daniel has already mentioned Cyrus, "the King" at the end of chapter one, and then goes into the dream-vision of Nebuchadnezzar, which depicts the fall of his Empire, marks the 70 years of Exile. Arioch finds one who can interpret the dream, a "great man from the sons of the Exile." What Daniel sees is not that Cyrus is the stone. Cyrus is the one who brings back the "remnant" of the Exiled. The stone, a stone from a much larger mountain, is this remnant. From this remnant, God, their Chief, will cause a Dominion to rise into the ages. God's Dominion is kept distinct, however, from the Dominion he "sets up." Obviously, God's Dominion already rules and reigns over the world as the hymn of praise tells us. What is set up on the land, however, is a Dominion (nation) of people which receives its power from the Dominion of God. This is brought out by the end of chapter three and well into chapter four where we will discuss it further.

We must again always keep in mind that the author composed this book with materials that happened when they did, after all these events. The fact that Cyrus is already mentioned in Chapter 1 (1.21) tells us this. In other words, the final composition was collected together well after the King had his dream. Daniel lived at least until the third year of Cyrus and would have known of the return of his people to the land. However, he would have also known that the restoration of the sanctuary and temple came later. The King's dream depicts the stone as "becoming" a mountain, eventually over the span of the "ages". Thus, there is no problem with understanding the arrival of Cyrus as the beginning of the "stone" which represents the faithful returning to the land of "our fathers." God's "Dominion" would be established, albeit starting in the form of a foundation stone. Isaiah 28.16 proclaims that God will "lay a stone, a corner stone" as a "sure foundation". This will be accomplished when "the LORD Almighty will be a glorious crown...for the remnant of his people" (28.5). In Zechariah's visions, a "stone" is placed before the exiled-but-now-returned High Priest Joshua (3.9), and Jerusalem itself, after the Exile, is called, "a heavy stone" that cannot be lifted (12.3). These prophecies would not have been known by Daniel, of course, but they are in keeping with the imagery of a "stone" being established after the Exile. This was done by the decree of Cyrus.

We may also note that the section in Isaiah 45-48 announces the Fall of Babylon by the divine work of God through Cyrus (45.1). The description is one of sudden calamity (47.9). The Fall is when it is declared that, "The LORD has redeemed his servant Jacob" (48.20). But most notably, Babylon's destruction in the Prophet Jeremiah, who is mentioned in Daniel, uses the imagery we find here. God will destroy Babylon "for its guilt" (25.12) after 70 years. Nebuchadnezzar will rule for 70 years, and his Dominion will last throughout his descendants, ending with his "grandson" (27.7). The Medes will overtake it (50.9; 51.11, 28; under the rule of Cyrus, the Persian). No "stone" will be taken from Babylon, "a destroying mountain" (51.25,26). The remnant of Israel, however, is taken from Babylon, but they are not "of" Babylon. Babylon is "like a threshing floor" and is to be "trampled upon." They will be "broken and shattered" (50.23), piled up like heaps of grain (50.26). However, in the midst of

Jeremiah's lengthy prophecy against her, Israel will "be brought back…and I will forgive the remnant I have spared" (50.19, 20). Further, it is promised that after the seventy years, Jerusalem will "never again be uprooted or destroyed for ages" (31.40). That Daniel operates, then, within this time frame and accompanying imagery is fairly evident. A "stone" is "cut out" from Babylon, a destroying mountain, but not with "hands" – Israel is not Babylonian stock. Babylon is judged for her guilt because of how she treated the people of Israel. It is because she holds God's people that she will topple. Israel brings about their fall, and they will be restored and "never again be uprooted or destroyed for age."

As for the succession of the Dominions of Nebuchadnezzar, these speak of his sons, his heirs. Amil-Marduk, or Evil-Marduk as he is called in the Scriptures, particularly Jeremiah, (2nd Kings 25.27; Jeremiah 52.31), was the son of Nebuchadnezzar. Nergal-Sharezer (Neriglissar) reigned after this (he is mentioned in Jeremiah 39.3,13). He married Nebuchanezzar's daughter, Kassaya, and murdered Amil-Marduk. He was not of the offspring of the King, which may reflect that the silver comes after the gold, but bronze, a far less precious metal, succeeds. Nabonidus (the iron, a son in law to Nebuchadnezzar) was more fearsome than these and stabilized his Dominion for a number of years. His "offspring", however, to who the Dominion was entrusted as co-regent was weak. This is King Belshazzar (who will be discussed in more detail in chapter 5), who we now have conclusive evidence of his existence (interestingly enough, he is called "my offspring" in the discovered Nabonidus Cylinder written by that very King). It is this King, Nebuchadnezzar's "grandson", that Daniel utters the interpretation made by a "hand" that the Dominion was "divided" and has been "put to an end" (Daniel 5.26-30, as it was that very night by the Persian army). The brittle clay mixed with the iron, a divided Dominion, the clay who is "from the iron", the offspring of the man (Nabonidus), is the final collapse. The 70 years are completed. Cyrus issues the call for the "remnant" to be restored to the land of Israel. Thus, "in the days of these Kings", Nabonidus and Belshazzar, God causes his people to return to the land under the hand of Cyrus. The entire image is crushed and is no more.

*Thereupon the King, Nebuchadnezzar, fell upon his face and paid homage to Daniel – "Offerings and pleasing offerings be poured out to him," he said. And the King replied to Daniel and said, "Of truth, He who is your God is God of Gods, and Lord of Kings, and the one who reveals mysteries since you are able to reveal this mystery!" Then the King made Daniel great and gave him many great gifts and made him rule over all the province of Babel and Chief of the Prefects over all the Wise Ones of Babel. Daniel also asked from the King to appoint over the administration of the district of Babel Shadrach, Meshach and Abed-Nego, and Daniel himself in the gate of the King.*

Daniel, like Joseph, is elevated. And, so like Daniel, he takes his friends with him. Daniel is never one to take all the glory and credit. His humility constantly shines forth. One may write of their own humility (which is an action of the heart) without pride. One may say of themselves that they are humble and have actions to show or demonstrate that humility as an example. Daniel receives this honor as having come from what the Lord has done and not himself. This, too, illustrates that one is rewarded on earth from time to time in their obedience to God. One may also note the image of a Gentile King bowing down before a Jewish teenager! This image of bowing down and giving homage comes up in the next chapter.

It should not, either, strike us as odd that the King rewards Daniel. Why would he reward him if, in fact, Daniel just told him that his Kingdom was to collapse? In the next chapter this is answered by understanding the nature of ancient, near eastern omens and dreams. Fate is destined, but it can be altered if the future is shown beforehand as a warning of what may come.

## Chapter Three

*Nebuchadnezzar, the King, made an image which was of gold: its height, sixty rum. Its width, six rum. He caused it to rise in the Plain of Dura, in the District of Babel.*

If we are following the vocabulary of the text, this next episode is quite an indictment against the King. There is no "and" which usually comes at the head of a sentence. It abruptly starts with "Nebuchadnezzar, the King." Daniel and his friends have been exalted to high positions. The King has extolled the "god" of Daniel. This was no conversation, however, on his part. Daniel's "god of the heavens" is merely another powerful god among the Pantheon. That he makes an "image" here of "gold" and "causes it to rise" are exact links to the words of the dream and its interpretation. The image, in other words, would have looked like the image in the dream, but instead of various metals, it was all gold.

Secondly, if our interpretation is correct, and the image in the dream stood for the King's Empire with the succession of his descendants, Nebuchadnezzar makes this image of gold (which he was the head of gold in the dream) in direct response to the dream. Seeing that his Dominion was succeeded in lesser metals and finally in mixed-with-clay iron, and smashed, the King's image here is his response to what the god of heaven said. The god of heaven, Daniel's god, said that his Dominion will topple, but that the gold head was good. In order to assure his dominance, the whole Empire will be made good gold, securing his future rule "for the ages." We must understand here that the King is attempting to thwart the previous dream. The gods have given him a revelation into mysteries of what may happen, unless the

King does something about it. The dream is a portent; a possible future unless drastic action is taken. In obedience to Marduk/Bel, a great image is made in their honor – one of all gold. The King will not let their Empire be crumbled. In his religion, he has responded to the omen.

A "rum" is a cubit, or about a foot and a half. Thus, the image is ninety feet high and nine feet wide. Ninety feet is the distance between home plate and first base. It's massive. This is not strange, however, in that world. Statues exhibit power and might. They are meant to overwhelm the spectator. The plain of Dura is located within the city of Babel itself. Nebuchadnezzar's (whose name means, "Nabu, Protector of the Boundaries") dream would have been heard by the court, and its interpretation. Imagine, then, the embarrassment of hearing the destruction of your Empire! His response was swift. In light of the dream, the gods were foretelling him to make his Empire, his boundaries, secure. This is why he does what he does. However, he underestimates the god of Daniel, who "changes the times and the seasons." Nebuchadnezzar is attempting to do just that.

*And Nebuchadnezzar, the King, sent to gather the Administrators, the Prefects, the Governors, the Counselors, the Treasurers, the Lawyers, the Magistrates and to all Rulers in the District to come to a consecration of the image which he caused to rise. And so they gathered together, the Administrators, the Prefects, the Governors, the Counselors, the Treasurers, the Lawyers, the Magistrates and to all Rulers in the District to come to a consecration of the image which Nebuchadnezzar, the King, caused to rise. And they rose before the image which Nebuchadnezzar caused to rise. Then the Herald called with power commanding thus, "The people! The Tribes! The Languages! At the time when you hear the voice of the horn, the pipe, a lyre, the trigon, the harp, the wind pipe,*

Chapter Three

*and all kinds of music, fall and do homage before the image of gold which Nebuchadnezzar caused to rise. Whosoever does not fall down and do homage, in that moment he will be thrown in the midst of the furnace of the burning fire."*

That Nebuchadnezzar's image here is to be honored as representative of the gods, or god, his god, who has given him the Kingdom is shown by the call to all the representatives of the people of Babylon. They are to pay the same respect the King gave to Daniel's god when he "fell down and did homage" to Daniel. This act would have appeared to the people as an act of submission. Nebuchadnezzar, whose name is constantly repeated at this point, is reversing any such notion. It is not uncommon to read in the ancient world of the gods giving dreams concerning things to come, and that they could, if heeded, circumvent the prophecy. This call to the nations and the people hearkens back to the words of Daniel in his interpretation. The King had been given "all the peoples" as the "good gold". It is the good gold that must maintain this power to extend beyond the head and to the entire body of the image. It was not uncommon, either, to punish subversives with burning them alive in that time.

*All before this, in the appointed time when they heard like that which was commanded - a voice of the horn, the pipe, a lyre, the trigon, the harp, the wind pipe, and all kinds of music- all the people fell. All the people, the tribes, and the languages did homage to the image of gold which the King, Nebuchadnezzar, had caused to rise.*

We can note the pattern, which sounds repetitious to English ears, of 'X was said, then Y is done, X was said, then Y is done.' This follows in that the Dream of chapter two is followed by the image of gold story. The Dream of the head of gold was given (X), then Y follows – a story about an image of gold and falling down and paying homage. Daniel, who was appointed to the gate of the King, apparently was awarded a leave of absence for his interpretation of the dream. His other friends, however, remained in their new positions and would have been included in the call to worship the image of gold. The emphasis here is on all those who had administrative duties (which they did) and all the peoples that were conquered (which they were). There were to be no exceptions. This, then, reflects the fact that the King's acknowledgement of the "god" of Daniel was merely one among the Pantheon, but was certainly not "over" the King or the Kingdom as we are about to find out.

*In light of all this, at the appointed time, great men, Chaldeans, came near. And they devoured the pieces of the Jews.*

This is a strange idiom, usually not brought out in translation, but it is the rendering. The Chaldeans, the learned men of Babel, sought to devour their pieces, which is translated as, "sought to maliciously charge them." The image is that of an animal eating its prey.

*They replied and said to the King, Nebuchadnezzar, "King, live for the ages! You, the King, have set a command which all of mankind who hears a voice of the horn, the pipe, a lyre, the trigon, the harp, the wind pipe, and all kinds of music to fall and to give homage to the image of gold. Whosoever does not fall down is to be cast in to the furnace of the burning fire. There are great men, the Jews, which you have appointed over the District of Babel, Shadrach, Meshach, and Abed-Nego – these great men – do they not set above you, the King, a command? To your*

## Chapter Three

*gods they pay no reverence, and to the image of the gold, which you have caused to rise, they do no homage."*

The issue here is power. The King paid homage to the god of Daniel, but these three Jews pay no homage to the gods of the King. There is a command that is set above the King's command (lex rex), and this is tantamount to conspiracy against the King. The Chaldeans, seeking to preserve the meaning of the image, do not point this out because the lads were Jewish, but that they were not operating within the set command of the King. Obedience to God marks out those who are God's. This same word, "set", was found in chapter one where new names were "set" upon them, but Daniel "set" his heart upon the Lord. Once again, then, in light of what the Lord has revealed in the dream, Nebuchadnezzar's attempt of changing the times and seasons of his Kingdom as imaged in the golden statue cannot be given any endorsement from the Jews. God has spoken. The image of which the King is the head of gold will come tumbling down by the stone cut out without hands. God's word is above the King's. It cannot be changed or altered. That this is the meaning of their defiance is found in the reaction of the King.

*In this Nebuchadnezzar in rage and in fury said, "Bring Shadrach, Meshach, and Abed-Nego!" In this these great men came before the King. Nebuchadnezzar replied and said to them, "What is the purpose, Shadrach, Meschah, and Abed-Nego? To my gods you are not worshipping, and to the image of gold which I have caused to rise you do no homage.*

The relationship here between the many gods of the King and the image he set up should be noted. The King cannot comprehend a monotheistic theology. The idea that there is only one single Deity is absurd. Nabu-kedurri-ussur, "god, Nabu, protect the boundaries", is, after all, his name. Nabu was the son of the god, Marduk, the Chief god (also a son). There is no offense to Marduk when Nabu or Ishtar is worshipped, too. The way he figured it was that he paid homage to Daniel and their god, and was grateful for their god giving them the interpretation of the dream. So, why can't the same favor be returned? What would be the "purpose" of such an act of defiance against the King who has treated them (and their god) with such favor? Are they simply ungrateful? Are they traitors? Do they think that they have now arrived and are above the King's command? It is not difficult to sympathize with the King here! His rage was entirely justified given his theological convictions. Rage is generally the product of strongly offended and deeply set mores.

*"Now then. Behold! You are ready so that in the time when you hear a voice of the horn, the pipe, a lyre, the trigon, the harp, the wind pipe, and all kinds of music, you will fall down and do homage to the image I have made. And behold! If you do not fall down at that time I will cast you into the midst of the furnace of burning fire. And who is that god, he who will deliver you from my hand?"*

After calming down and asking them personally, seeing their faces, and they seeing his, the King gently implies that they are ready. "Enough with this nonsense! You will do as you are told!" The King takes their refusal to bow down to his image personally. This is appreciated more so when we understand that this image of gold was made in direct response to their interpretation of his dream. If we can the image of gold here as a response, a source of jubilee, for the fate of destruction has been avoided, then

Chapter Three

failing to observe the symbolic meaning appears to be a contradiction of the purpose of the interpretation.

The question that is asked, who is the god that will deliver you? is responded to in the next verse. However, in the Aramaic text, there is a play on words. Mishael (Meshach) is, in Hebrew, "who is god?" Secondly, who will deliver? Nebuzaradan (Nabu delivers), one of the names of Nebuchadnezzar's generals (Jeremiah 39.13), and perhaps a play off Azariah (Shadrach), whose Hebrew name meant, "God helps." What god in the Babylonian Pantheon would dare deliver them for such a blasphemous act against all the gods? Not even their own god, so Nebuchadnezzar infers, would favor them in their overt act of defiance. It would be unthinkable. Three against "all the people."?

*Shadrach, Meshach and Abed-Nego answered and said to the King, Nebuchadnezzar, "We do not need to answer you concerning this decree. Behold! It is what it is. Our God who we worship is able to deliver us from the furnace of burning fire and from your hand, the King, he will deliver us. And behold! Knowing not what it will be for you, the King, that to your gods we will not worship and to the image of the gold that you caused to rise we will not do homage."*

The absolute boldness here on the part of the three Jews is breathtaking. In the previous exchange in chapter two, the Chaldeans were attempting to "buy time." There was "no one able" to give the King's dream and interpretation. This caused him to fly into a rage. Here, there is a faith in God that is able not only to stump the King's command, and his punishment, but also issue a bit of a threat: "knowing not what will come to you, the King." The three are willing to suffer the penalty for their God will deliver them. Is the King willing to suffer the penalty for punishing his people for serving their God? That the three men knew that God would, in fact, deliver them is not revealed in the text. They may have (and this is implied) thought that their deaths were imminent. Nonetheless, their "deliverance" was assured. That is, what we find here is a hope of deliverance in the life to come. The faithful will be delivered and escape.

*Before this, Nebuchadnezzar was filled with rage, and the image of his face was changed against Shadrach, Meshach and Abed-Nego. He replied and said, "Make the furnace seven times more hot above that which it is seen to be heated!"*

This is because of their perceived defiance of the command. Their refusal, their complete lack of compromise or understanding enraged the King. The image of the face of the head of good gold as seen in the dream changed. Such defiance against the King and the gods of the King, the gods of the land of Babel, must be punished with extreme violence. It could not be tolerated. The King must act.

*So, to the mighty men, mighty in power who were in his power he commanded to bind Shadrach, Meshach and Abed-Nego, to cast them into the furnace of burning fire. And so these mighty men bound them with their coats, their tunics, and their caps and their clothing and they cast them in the midst of the furnace of burning fire. All before this, from which the command of the King being so urgent, that the furnace was extremely heated, the mighty men who took up Shadrach, Meshach and Abed-Nego were killed by the flame of the fire. And these three mighty men, Shadrach, Meshach and Abed-Nego, they fell down in the midst of the furnace of burning fire bound.*

## Chapter Three

The mighty men of the King are killed because the flames were so hot. The mighty men of faith were bound and thrown into the very midst of these hot flames. The play on the word "fell" is to be noted. They would not fall to the King's gods or his idol, so they "fell" (same word) into the flame instead. We may also note the word, "urgent," as well, for it was used in chapter two for the King's command to kill all the Wise Ones. However, in that episode, Daniel had some clout and there was a dream that bought him a night. Daniel is away in this setting and there is no dream to be interpreted, only a command to be obeyed. There could be no explanation given for the rebellion of the saints that would satisfy the King. Not even Daniel could offer an answer that could explain their insolence. The answer itself would be world shattering to the King: "we only have one God and we obey him over everything and everyone else, including you, the King. Your gods are not gods that we have any need to explain our actions. Do to us as you like. Our God will deliver us, but you and your image shall fall." The interpretation of the dream bolstered the faith of the three men. It is God who causes Kings to rise and to fall. It is God who will smash the image at the feet and set his kingdom above all the land. Having such hope in the ultimate deliverance of God, the men could do no other but accept their fate. There was no need to answer.

*Then Nebuchadnezzar, the King, was startled and rose in alarm replying and said to his Counselors, "Did we not cast three mighty men in the midst of the fire bound?" And they answered and said to the King, "The King, it is certain!" And he replied and said, "Behold! I, even I see four mighty men walking about unbound in the midst of the fire, and there is no damage on them. And his appearance, the fourth one's, is likened to a son of the gods!*

The story here is meant to defy every known thought or insight as to the physical properties of things themselves! The fire is so hot that even those who came near it were killed by it. These men were not only near, but in the midst of it! And, yet, they are not damaged at all. They are, in fact, walking around in the furnace. Their binding cords have been loosened (not burned). One whose mind is on the Scripture cannot help but to think of the burning bush of Moses. And in that story, one who appeared to Moses in a flame of fire was a "messenger of the LORD" (Exodus 3.2). This was a "great sight" for Moses (3.3), and the Lord called out to him, "in the midst of the burning bush" (3.4). Moses is asked to take off his shoes, and it is interesting to note that "their shoes" are not on the list of the items they wore when thrown into the fire. Yet, they are "walking" on the coals of the furnace with another being who appears to Nebuchadnezzar looking like a son of the gods (what else would he think?). It is noteworthy here to keep this image of a "son of the gods" when we come to chapter seven.

It is in this story that Moses hears the message of God, that He has come to deliver his people from the hand of Pharaoh and bring them into their own promised land. That we cannot but help to hearken back to this as the point here with these three men can be excused. Likewise, we are not told about this fourth being other than that he appeared visible the King. It may be, and the text seems to imply, that the others mentioned around the King did not see this figure.

*Then Nebuchadnezzar came near to the gate of the furnace of burning fire, replying and said, "Shadrach, Meshach, and Abed-Nego, servants of the Most High God, come forth! And they came forth, Shadrach, Meshach and Abed-Nego from the midst of the fire. And the*

Chapter Three

*Administrators, Governors, Prefects, and Counselors of the King gathered around and saw these mighty men, that the fire had no power over their bodies, and the hair of their heads were not singed, and their coats were not changed, and the smell of fire passed not among them. And Nebuchadnezzar replied and said, "Blessed be the God of Shadrach, Meshach and Abed-Nego who has sent his Messenger! Even he has delivered his servants who trusted him. And they changed the command of the King. And they gave their bodies so that they not worship and not give homage to any god except to their own god. Therefore, from me I set a decree for all peoples, nations, and languages, that anyone who speaks sinfully about the god of Shadrach, Meschah and Abed-Nego will be made limbs! Their houses will become rubble! For all before that, there is no god behind him who is able to deliver like this." Then the King caused prosperity to Shadrach, Meshach and Abed-Nego in the District of Babel.*

This chapter ends with a grand symphony of the previous words of chapter two, summing up as it were the two stories and strongly suggesting the tie between them. The image of gold is not removed, but the Jews are no longer required to bow down to them, nor are the people of Babel to speak falsely about their god. Their god has now become accepted within the Pantheon. The King himself acknowledges this, even though we must always keep in mind that he is still a polytheist (as the next chapter will further show). A great power resides with the Jews. Nothing like this has been seen before. This god has even sent one of his messengers (angels) to protect them. He did not save them from the furnace, but delivered them through the fire.

The amazing fact that they were entirely preserved is brought out in the details. Their coats were not burned nor even smelled like the fire. Their hair was not singed. Their bodies came forth as it were from certain death. It was their hope (trust) that saved them. They were willing to forego even death itself and suffer martyrdom if necessary. If death were to happen, God would raise them from the dead whole and intact. This is the point in this story and becomes the promised hope of Daniel 12.2. God will deliver his people and even though many of them will suffer and die for holding forth their testimony, they will come forth from the grave itself and "receive their inheritance" (Daniel 12.13). Even though I am jumping ahead to the last chapter, it is obvious the end of the Book is already hinted at here. Compromising the faith, speaking "evil" of God (false theology) is not to be tolerated – even when death is threatened. There is no need to give an answer other than the testimony of action: "we shall serve no other God, and we shall bow to no other deity. Our testimony itself is our answer." God will deliver his people according to his promise to Abraham, Moses, Isaac and Jacob, the "God of our fathers."

The King had no "power" over them. The King was given power by God to rule and reign over the earth. He has power over all things, including the elements. They "changed" the command of the King, and their coats did not "pass" nor were "changed", which in 2.21 God, who is blessed, changes the times and seasons, and causes to King's to rise and "pass". It is obvious that with these words in the text the author wants the readers to join in on the blessing to God who does these things. His Dominion rules all Dominions down to the elements of the hairs on the head. The Dominion which he will set up, the people of his Dominion, are to follow the orders of their God. This is how they are to prosper in the world, even though they are not of the world. The agency of God's people effects change in laws, policies, nations and Kings but only through faithful obedience to

God. At times the nations and peoples will threaten death, and even have the power from God, who set them up, to cause death. However, it is through this very avenue by which the God of heaven is bringing about his Dominion on the land (there is the heavenly Dominion and then there is the Dominion on the land, and the two are distinct even though derived from One Source). This teaches us, the People of the Most High, that the ultimate deliverance of God is transcendent and supernatural. Their bodies were preserved (which means he can preserve them from the elements – he has all power). Supernatural deliverance is required and is ultimately the remedy concerning the full inheritance of all that is promised.

It is worthy to note also the play on words with Abed Nego, "servant of Nego" who was, perhaps, referencing the god of Venus (some see "nego" as a corrupt form of "nebu"). "Abed" is the word for "servant" and now this "servant of Nego" is a "servant of God" (abed-elohenu).

## Chapter Four

The first three chapters mark more or less the first half of the reign of the King. How many years have transpired to this event in the King's life we are simply not told. There were, perhaps, many "stories" during Daniel's stay in Babel (and other places in that Empire) that were done. The author sees fit to mention only these few since they serve the greater purpose of Daniel's overall theme: God rules over all things. By understanding the vocabulary, certain key terms, that pop up throughout these stories we can see that all of them are being intertwined so as to weave a singular quilt. This next story concerning the King perhaps happens in the latter half of his reign (he ruled a staggering forty three years) for we find his grandson, Belshazzar, in the next chapter sitting on the throne.

*"Nebuchadnezzar, the King, to all the peoples, nations and languages which dwell upon all the land: May you grow in prosperity. The God Most High has performed signs and wonders for me. It is fair before me to declare his signs, what is the chief-est? His wonders, what is the strongest? His Dominion is a Dominion of age. His Rule is with a generation and a generation."*

Thus begins the King's own telling of what happened to him. He has seen signs and wonders from the God of the Jewish boys (now men). More than, perhaps, what we have recorded. This is the final entry of the King and marks his true conversion to the one God. Signs and wonders accompany the conversion of even the most hard. In light of the fact that in the dream in chapter two this God will "set up" a Dominion, it is not to be confused with his own Dominion. His Dominion is not "set up" and, in contrast to the "growth" of the King's and for the one to be "set up" by God, it is from the ages (past) and to the ages (future). Never is God's Dominion itself depicted to be set up through or by humans. Rather it is God who "sets up Kings and causes them to pass away." God's Dominion is neither associated with the Dominions of mankind unless he has so designated a particular people to be his. This Dominion, for example, the Dominion of Jehoiakim in Daniel 1.1 was "handed over" to King Nebuchadnezzar because they had broken his covenant with them. God rules. God rules over all the other Dominions, setting them up on the land, and toppling them down. The distinction in the dream of chapter two is that he is to "set up" a people (a nation, a Dominion) that will not pass away, regardless of whether or not it displeases him.

He would maintain within that Dominion a faithful regiment of people; a people to be described by the actions and faith of the four Jews in this Book, and through them execute a Dominion of people that will eventually displace all the mountains "on the land." His rule extends from a generation to a generation and will do so for the ages to come until it is the only mountain left on the land. God has all time (age) at his disposal. This will come out forcefully at the end of this chapter. It is the point of Daniel to impress upon his readers that God's Dominion of the Heavens has been, is, and will be the ultimate yard stick of all other Dominions. That he alone is ruling over all the nations to bring about this singular purpose throughout the ages past and the ages to come, from generation to generation. This should be the singular, crystal clear vision of God's Ancient Dominion.

*"I, Nebuchadnezzar, became at ease in my house, and flourished in my palace. A dream I saw and I became afraid. Images upon my bed and*

## Chapter Four

*visions of my head caused me trouble. So then I set a decree to gather before me all the Wise Ones of Babel who could make known the pesher of the dream. Thus they all gathered, the Magicians, the Conjurers, the Chaldeans and the Astrologers. I, even I, told the dream before them, but they could not make known its pesher. That is, until last before me came, Daniel (whose name is Belteshazzar, like the name of my god), that is he who has a spirit of holy gods in him. And I told before him the dream."*

It is not hard to miss the obvious parallel here with the dream in chapter two. They both relate to the King and his obsession of longevity. Here, however, the King tells the dream instead of concealing it. He makes no rash threats of death. Perhaps he learned something. Daniel is still called Belteshazzar, which basically has to do with the supreme deity, Bel (as in the city, Babel). We might also add that in the first dream Daniel is the last to be told and the last to be brought before the King. As in the first dream, the King utters the threat of death before he hears from the young Daniel. But here, being much older, the best is saved for "last". Daniel's prominence is in view. We may have in view here as well the principle that the last shall be first (exalted).

*"Belteshazzar, Chief of the Magicians, who I, even I know that a spirit of holy gods are in you, that no mystery presses you. Visions of a dream which I beheld, and its pesher, do tell! That is, my visions of my head upon my bed I saw what became – that is, a tree in the midst of the land and its great height. The tree grew greatly, and it grew strong, and its height reached to the heavens and its sight to the ends of the land. Its beautiful foliage. Its fruit abundant. Food for all within it. Under it the beasts of the field find shade. In its branches birds of the heavens dwell. And from it all the flesh is fed."*

The text still reflects that at the time of the request, Daniel is addressed as Belteshazzar. The King is still under the impression that though Daniel's god exists, he exists among the many others. Daniel is indeed gifted, and the long-winded introduction hearkens back to Daniel's introduction to the King's vision in chapter two. As this tree grew we also note that in chapter two the King's image rose and the stone "became" a great mountain. Growth assures future stability.

"*Seeing what is in the vision of my head upon my bed, and Behold! A Watcher, that is a Holy One from the heavens descended. He called with strength and said, 'Cut down the tree and cut off its branches. Strip off its foliage and scatter its fruit. Let the beasts under it flee and the birds from its branches. But, leave a stump of roots in the land and in a bond which are iron and bronze, in the grass which is of the field. And with dew of the heavens let it be wet, and with the beasts its portion in fodder of the land. Let its heart of the man be changed and the heart of a beast be given to it. And let seven times pass over it. Watchers have determined the word and a command of Holy Ones the request by reason that the living knows the Most High's mastery in Dominion of the man and to who that he pleases he gives it, and lowest of men he raises it.'"*

If we can picture the dream as it is so vividly displayed here, we can better grasp the vision. Babylon considered itself as founded upon the center of the land; the same image-dream of the King as seen in chapter two. The Watchers, or "holy ones" (angels) probably reflects more of the King's vocabulary than Daniel's. Nonetheless, they are simply angels for the same construction of words is found in chapters nine and ten concerning their activities having to do with "commands" and "decrees." Angels, in this Book, are seen as agents of the Most High that

Chapter Four

carry out his bidding. How the Spirit (intangible) causes the tangible to move. There is great mystery here, but we are given a peek into God's Dominion and its invisible, though very causative, ways.

We can see, more or less, the mirrors. God is "the King of Kings", and as the "Herald" in chapter three "declared mightily", so God has his own Heralds who "declare mightily." Daniel's theology as revealed to him is meant to further bolster the faith in the doctrine that God's Dominion, and his "administrators, governors, satraps" and the like, along with his "soothsayer" Daniel who speaks "the word of the King" is over and above all the Dominions of Man. It is the decrees of God that actually causes their being "set up" and their being "ruined up." It is apparent by this time that Daniel's hymn of praise in chapter 2 is the dominant theme of this book. The rise of Nebuchadnezzar and the terrible events and atrocities of war is ultimately the Most High's doing, who "gave" King Jehoiakim into his hand (chapter one). Here, God "gives" Dominion (Kingdom) to whoever he pleases. Nebuchadnezzar would not be King if God had not given it to him. And, do we not find this same theological outlook with Jesus of Nazareth: "Then saith Pilate unto him, Speakest thou not unto me? knowest thou not that I have power to crucify thee, and have power to release thee? Jesus answered, Thou couldest have no power at all against me, except it were given thee from above" (John 19.10,11).

Such conviction must be based upon the firm fact of the reality of God's Dominion, which is neither "set up" nor "raised". It is. It is "over" the Dominions of all mankind, and Nebuchadnezzar, one of the greatest kings of all time must come to know this fact.

The tree, like the head of gold, singularly represents Nebuchadnezzar (not his Dominion, for it is not "cut down").

Ecclesiastes 3.18 is remarkable here: "I said in my heart for reason of sons of the man, God, to cleanse and to see that they are beasts, they to themselves." In other words, in his heart he considered that God's dealings with mankind is but to expose them as beasts, mere creatures. We find this same thing here. Nebuchadnezzar has a heart, but let his heart be changed to a beast ("he changes times and seasons") for seven-times. This is no difficult thing. The decree has been uttered; the request is carried out. The word, "request" implies a requester, and that would be Daniel praying for the King. He asks, and he receives (we find the same situation in Daniel nine, with the same word-idea). The King, coming after the horrible "sentence" he "decreed" concerning the three Jews in chapter three, is asked in prayer to be humbled. That he has no power over God's people. And here, as in Daniel nine, we find that the people of God, the "wo/men" of earth participate in God's Dominion along with the angels, the watchers, and God's Court (who is issuing these "decrees" from his heavenly court room/palace). When God's people are caused to suffer at the hands of Nebuchadnezzar, God responds. The decree has come down. Nebuchadnezzar must pay.

The imagery of "iron and bronze" again reflects the same image-dream in chapter two. The head of gold is not crushed until all the others in its Dominion fall, and here the King is left with iron and bronze as a stump and root. We are not told how long this "time" of "seven" is. Many have assumed it to mean seven years, based on the parallel story in Joseph and Pharaoh's dream. However, here it is simply "seven times." "Time" as an Aramaic word, has been used already. Daniel asks, "for time" in chapter two. God changes the "times and seasons." There was the end of the "time" after the three years of Daniel's training in chapter one. The word "years" is simply not mentioned, nor are we at liberty to supply it. Also, in keeping with the fact that a Babylonian year was marked by two seasons, Winter and Summer, the dream implies Summer, when "dew" is on the grass and the animals are eating fodder on the ground. Thus "seven times" may mark either a little over half a year, or maybe seven weeks. The King is brought under a spell or a very bad bout of temporary insanity. We are not at all to think that for seven years his throne was abdicated! Rather it is spared by an "iron and bronze" stump and roots as we know from the image-dream of chapter two.

*"This is the dream I saw, the King Nebuchadnezzar. Now you, Belteshazzar, the pesher do tell! All before that are Wise Ones of my Dominion are not able to make known the pesher. But you, you are able for a spirit of holy gods is in you." Then Daniel, whose name is Belteshazzar, for one moment his thoughts troubled him! The King replied and said, "Belteshazzar, do not let the dream and the pesher trouble you." Belteshazzar answered and said, "My Lord, the dream concerns those who hate you! And its pesher concerns those who are your enemies! The tree which you saw, which grew and was made strong and its height reached to the heavens and was visible to all the land. And its beautiful foliage, and its much fruit, that is food for all are in it, the beasts of the field dwell under it, and the birds of the heavens dwell in it branches. You, the King, are it. You who have grown and have been made strong. And your greatness has grown to reach the heavens and your Dominion to the end of the land. Now that which the King saw, a Watcher, that is, a Holy One descending out of the heavens and said, 'Cut down the tree and destroy it! But, the stump of the root leave in the land with a bond of iron and brass, among the grass of the field and let it be wet with the dew of the heavens. And with the beasts of the field its lot until that which is seven times passes over it."*

Daniel, for the first time, is troubled. The same word is used for the trouble the King had, too. What was the meaning of this dream? The tree is cut down, stripped, but the stump if left to take in the dew of the heavens. It is shackled, banded with iron and bronze. Its portion is with the beasts of the field. Here the word "destroyed" is used, replacing the description mentioned earlier. After the tree is cut down and stripped it is, basically, destroyed. Yet, a stump of roots left. The dew of the heavens holds out the possibility of life springing forth again (growing). The image is that the Tree is under the heavens, and grows upwards towards the heavens. The Watcher, however, descends out of the heavens (is higher). The Watcher commands the dew of the heavens to wet the stump for the seven passing times. These times are said to "pass over" the stump (not the tree, the tree is destroyed) and again remind us that the sun and the moon "pass over" the land. This is hardly descriptive of seven years. "times" here simply remains indefinite other than the number "seven" – which is probably meant to convey completion of the passes of the decree. It is a sentence, a prison sentence if one likes, denoted by the use of shackles (bonds, fetters, bands – the word is also translated elsewhere as, "prison"). Nebuchadnezzar is bound for "seven times" which will pass over him. He is not being completely destroyed, however. A stump is left.

Another concern is Daniel's response when he understands the dream. Is this a wish that it was the King's enemies that the dream was about? Daniel knows that the Dominion will topple. The dream is about the fall of the King. Is he expressing as a preface his service to the King because the dream is about him? This would seem to go against the general idea already in the Book. Rather, is it that God's messenger is an enemy of the King, and hates him? After all, the Watcher acts as no friend to the King! He is

## Chapter Four

an enemy that is uttering his destruction. Other lands and nations may be enemies of the King, but to have God as your enemy is an entirely different matter! God is upset with the King and has uttered a decree to cut him down until proper worship is voiced by the King. If such does not happen, the King is as good as dead.

*"This is the pesher, the King, and the decree of the Most High which has overcome you, my Lord, the King. As to you, they are driving from man, and with the beast of the field will be your dwelling place. And the grass, like oxen, to you they will make eat. And dew of the heavens, to you, they make wet. And seven times will pass over you until which you know that mastery of the Most High in a Dominion of man, and that he gives it to whomsoever he pleases. And of that which they said, to leave the stump of the roots which is of the tree, your secured Dominion to you, from whence you will know the masteries of the heavens. Therefore, the King, let my counsel be pleasing to you. Redeem your sin in righteousness; your iniquity in favor of poor ones. Behold! Duration will be towards your prosperity!"*

The powers of the heavens will drive Nebuchadnezzar away from his court and palace. He will be as one exiled and live in the wilderness, so to speak. We are not to imagine that the King literally transforms into a beast. Rather, "like a beast" (a bout of insanity) he will roam for a period of "seven". The King is being greatly humbled by the hand of God. God will demonstrate his mastery over his Dominion, as he has done over any Dominion of man. This is all in keeping with the first hymn of praise in chapter two. God gave King Jehoiakim over the Nebuchadnezzar. He gave to Nebuchadnezzar his Dominion. Now, he is giving him a time of humility. However, God will not entirely destroy the King for his sins. A stump is left (a remnant). It will grow again, being secured by iron and bronze.

Some translations have "break off your sin" whereas the Aramaic favors, as other translations have, "redeem your sin." Repentance is marked by leaving behind the old ways and going about new ways that express the point of changing sinners to saints: acts of righteousness to the poor and needy, the lowest concern of the King. "The King's heart is in the hand of the LORD, and turneth it whithersoever he willeth, like a river" (Proverbs 21.1). "By mercy and truth iniquity is purged: and by the fear of the LORD men depart from evil" (Proverbs 16.6). "When the LORD is pleased with a man's conduct, He may turn even his enemies into allies" (Proverbs 16.7). Here the enemies of Nebuchadnezzar will become his allies when he repents and his conduct is changed. God changes the heart. If Nebuchadnezzar should know these things, how much more those who claim to follow the God of Daniel!

*The whole (dream) overcame Nebuchadnezzar, the King nearly twelve months later, upon the King's palace in Babel while he was walking. The King replied and said, "Is this not the Chiefest Babel which I, even I built for a house of Dominion, in strength of my power, and for glory of my honor?"*

The narrative gives some time of reflection on part of the King and Daniel's counsel. Almost a year passes and we find the King hardly considering it. Rather, walking along his palace roof, reminiscent of another King who did the same (2nd Samuel 11.1-ff), the King is basking in his own accomplishments and glory. He did this, and he built that. Nations have been conquered and wars have been won. The palace and the majesty of Ancient Babylon, a wonder of the world, was an amazing feat. But the King takes the accomplishment as his own doing. It is to be noted that the usual

Chapter Four

phrasing, "and he replied and said" is found in dialogues. The King is, in this narrative, replying to the interpretation and counsel of Daniel. "Before destruction one's heart is haughty, but humility goes before honor" (Proverbs 18.12). "Pride goes before destruction, a haughty spirit before a fall" (Proverbs 16.18). This dialogue of the King is the reply of his wicked heart. He will not heed. He is too great to consider Daniel's counsel.

*While this utterance was in the mouth of the King, a voice from the heavens fell, "They are saying to you: 'Nebuchadnezzar, the King, the Dominion has passed from you!' And from man, in regard to you, they will drive away. And with oxen of the field your dwelling, the grass of oxen to you they will make you eat and seven times will pass over you until you know the Most High's mastery among man's Dominion, and that he gives it to whoever he pleases."*

A singular voice (of the Lord) falls from heaven concerning the Watchers who are busting at the gate to deliver the sentence. It was held back, but now no longer. We catch a glimpse of the heavenly Dominion of the Most High and His Palace Administrators, Satraps, Governors and Heralds. This is the Council of the Most High. He makes the final decision. Why wait nearly a year? "Deliver it now!" they say.

Daniel, as the author, in the first chapter simply reflects "upon his heart" that he should not be defiled. In chapter two the Lord gives him the interpretation of the dream. In chapter three one like a son of the gods appears with the three sons of Judah. And now, here we have Watchers with decrees and sentences, uttering words from the Most High and carrying out his will over the Dominion of man. They are speaking, acting as agents and intermediaries between "the heavens" and "the land". This is a progressive way in literature of building up to what will become a full tour de force of heavenly activity in the latter chapters. Everything under the sun, which God made, works to his good in spite of the prideful, sinful, iniquitous heart of man. When the purpose of the Most High needs to turn even the heart of a King, he does so. His plan will not, cannot be stopped. The exile of the King is his will to produce repentance. Likewise, so Daniel's readers would have "got" (and later will "get"), their Exile serves the purpose of the Most High. From nations, to Dominions, to individual people (like Daniel) and the King, God's purpose stands and comes to its end.

*In that moment the word came to its end upon Nebuchadnezzar, that is, they drove him from man. The grass he ate like oxen and from dew of the heavens his body was wetted until his hair grew like birds of preys' hair, even his fingernails grew like birds nails.*

Nebuchadnezzar acted in such a way and became such a way as to be compared ("like") oxen and birds. It must be noted that it is the stump of the roots banded by iron and bronze that is "his body" and not the tree. The tree was cut down, stripped, and destroyed in the vision. Only the stump remained (with its roots). Therefore, his body, like the stump, is made wet by the dew of the heavens. He was the tree. He is now the stump with roots (descendants). His Dominion has not ended and even a cut down tree grows again unless its roots are destroyed.

It has been a popular image to depict the King here as being transformed into some sort of werewolf creature, but this is simply not the picture detailed here in the text. His hair grows long, of course, and we may couple this with the duration of the "seven times" (hardly seven years). The same can be said of his fingernails. It doesn't take that long to grow these things.

That Nebuchadnezzar is being visited upon because of his hurling the Jews into the fiery furnace is noted in that their hair was not at all affected, nor was their bodies. Here, however, his hair and his body are affected. Trees were stripped for many reasons, one of which was fuel for fire. Nebuchadnezzar had the furnace heated "seven times hotter" – and so here he is driven into the country fields away from man for "seven times." You reap what you sow. But, the Lord is merciful. The King deserves what his "enemies" the Watchers wanted: swift destruction. What he got in return was a changed disposition in life. There is no hint in the text of that which would grammatically note a conditionality between God and Nebuchadnezzar. There is no "if" here. God determined to change his heart. Rather, this and that will happen until, not if, the King acknowledges God Most High as total sovereign and only sovereign. Imagine it like the game of "uncle." God does not force himself to be sure. However, he knows how to get a man to say, "Uncle! You win!" Through this, also, God, who is the Changer of hearts, times, and seasons, necessarily must change the heart.

*"Now at the end of the days I, Nebuchadnezzar, my eyes looked to the heavens and my understanding was restored over me and I blessed the Most High and to him who lives to the age I praised and I glorified him whose Dominion is a Dominion of age, whose Rule is generation to generation. And all who inhabit the land are not taken into account. And he wills it, doing among the force of the heavens and those who dwell on the land. There is none to strike with his hand and say to him, 'What have you done?'" At that set time my understanding was restored over me, also were honor and my Dominion, my majesty and my splendor.*

Daniel Unplugged

*And to me my Counselors and Nobles sought. As concerning my Dominion it was re-established and surpassing greatness was again given to me. Now I, Nebuchadnezzar, praising and exalting and glorifying to the King of the Heavens, all of whose works are true, and his paths, judgment. To those walking about in pride he is able to bring low."*

It is difficult not to see true conversion on part of the King here. His confession, unlike his previous ones, where Daniel's god is merely a very powerful one among the Pantheon. Here there is no mention of the genitival "of the gods". He is the King of the heavens. And, we might add, the term "blessed" is used for the first time by the King. Daniel used it previously in the hymn of praise in chapter two. Thus, there is a steady progression, even noted in the beginning of this chapter, how Daniel's god was one among many, and Daniel was his agent – a spirit of the gods. That changes here.

The fact of the matter is, as far as we have on record, we do not know much about King Nebuchadnezzar. There is some record of his building campaigns and his absolute devotion to Marduk, Nebu, and the rest. But these texts are within the first twelve to fifteen years of his stellar career. These sources come from what are called the Nebuchadnezzar Chronicles, Cylinders, and Inscriptions. The British Museum (BM) also HOUSES tablets referring to his 37th year. There are other mentions in the Scriptures (Ezekiel, for example, a contemporary of Daniel, 2 Kings, Chronicles, Ezra-Nehemia, Esther, and Jeremiah). From what we know he had one daughter, Kassaya (who married Neriglissar, the third King of Babylon). He may have had others. He also had several sons, six in all it appears. Nabu-suma-ukin (Awel-Marduk, or Evil Merodach in the Bible, a "man of Marduk") was his eldest and succeeded Nebuchadnezzar after he died in 562 B.C.E. The King was around seventy years old when he died.

# Chapter Four

We do not know when this chapter occurs in the King's life. Since we do know that he lived to be of long age, it is safe to assume that this happened somewhere in the second half of his rule. That he conquered Tyre is known, and that he invaded Egypt late in his life (568 B.C.E.) is attested, and many think Daniel 4 is situated before this time. As for Daniel, who undoubtedly witnessed the political shakeup over the next several years, he is simply silent. Daniel would have known of the Jews in the city, and would have known of Amel-Marduk's release of Jehoiachin (Jeremiah 52).

There is, interestingly enough, an old Babylonian poem which might refer to his brief period of indifference. The text is translated often as implying the idea that Nebuchadnezzar's rule was made greater than it had been. This is not necessarily the case, however. It may be that with his brief downfall, he was "revived" and "restored" with his previous "surpassing greatness". The image that he dreamed of in chapter two contains the description, "the image is great, and surpassing brilliance". As we have said, the similarities between there and here is that Nebuchadnezzar, the "head of gold", has been cut down as a tree. He has lost his "surpassing brilliance" as ruler for a period of "seven times". Being restored again, that is being given the addition of life as King, a King of previously described "surpassing brilliance", is implied. Thus, we should not expect to find in the Babylonian history the idea that he expanded his Dominion, grew in greater power, militarily speaking.

Some, based on the idea that Nebuchadnezzar went insane for seven years, have tried to pen down this story and date it. It is impossible to do. The King did not "lose his mind" for seven years, and the numerous ways that time is indicated in this chapter more or less tells us this. "Near the end of twelve months" is mentioned. That's a specific year. "At the end of the days" is the exact expression in chapter one after Daniel completed his three years training. That was a specifically spelled out time period: three years. "Seven times" is unspecified. However, based on the dream, it wasn't any longer than a spring or summer season (Nebuchadnezzar was not wandering in the dead of winter). Some have supposed that his son, Evil-Merodach took his stead and was killed in two years. His son, Labasi-Marduk, who is not even mentioned in one ancient list of Kings, didn't last long at all (probably within a year). Then, Neriglissar ruled for four years until he was killed. Thus, some have supposed that Nebuchadnezzar was insane during this span of political assassinations (and that this is the reason for their rise). Daniel would have witnessed all of this, but strangely, and I think conclusively, does not mention it because it is not what happened. The political coups between Evil-Merodach, Neriglissar, Labasi-Marduk, who was murdered to bring in the last King, Nabonidus and his son, Belshazzar did happen, but not during Nebuchadnezzar's lifetime. He was dead. Supposing the King went mad for seven years and roamed the countryside like a werewolf or something is the stuff of myths, not Daniel, who reports nothing of the kind.

I may note that in the Dead Sea Scrolls, the seven years of Nabonidus is mentioned, apparently either confusing Nebuchadnezzar, or attributing something else to Nabonidus' time of rule. Another idea is that Nabonidus, and not Nebuchadnezzar, is the subject of Daniel. The Prayer of Nabonidus (whose son is Belshazzar, which we will note in the next chapter) discovered among the Dead Sea Scrolls, states that Nabonidus suffered affliction for "seven years". Several proposed redactional theories have been offered. None are conclusive, or command assent (regardless of "consent").

The "seven times" is summed up, finally, with "at the appointed time my understanding was restored over me" – meaning that this was when the seventh time passed over him, restoring him. It is important to note that the King is restored before he praises and exalts God Most High. At the seventh "passing" he is restored and then praises God. Seven things are given to the King: 1. His understanding. 2. His honor. 3. His Dominion. 4. His majesty. 5. His splendor. 6. His Counselors and Nobles. 7. His greatness. This is further confirmed in that the Watcher marked six things to be done to the tree (not the stump of the roots): 1. Cut it down. 2. Cut of its branches. 3. Shake off its leaves. 4. Scatter its fruits. 5. Let the beasts flee it. 6. Let the birds leave it. These are the things to happen during the seven times to "pass over" him, leaving him as a stump of roots. As such, "at the appointed time (singular) my understanding was restored over me and I praised God Most High." That is, "at the end of the days" of the six passings, the seventh passing was restoration of his mind with understanding: God is sovereign over all. That hardly took a year! Thus, God "determined" six passings of judgment, and a seventh passing "over" his understanding, restoring his clarity. One could see it as six punches, with the seventh being, "had enough, yet?" Although many Commentaries assumedly state seven years here, some others, and myself, are convinced that the above exegesis flows directly from the text itself. Nebuchadnezzar, according to this historical document, which records his own words, was a new man who lived a long age. However, the dream of chapter two still remained. After the gold head comes the silver, bronze and iron mixed with clay. Daniel jumps right into the iron mixed with clay Dominion, the fourth Dominion of the dream, in the next chapter.

# Chapter Five

The last word in the Aramaic text is "bring low" (a verb). The next word is, "Belshazzar" introducing him for the first time during his last day and night. Chapters seven and eight are situated in his first and third years of rule, respectively. As an author, I cannot but help to think that this starting with the King's last day of his rule is followed by visions of Daniel in his first and third year as ruler is to make a point. It is a literary technique various authors have used. In other words, at this point, Daniel has been chronological, but in chapter seven and eight that ends, and then resumes in chapter nine-twelve.

We have, now, information concerning King Belshazzar that prior to the mid-half of the nineteenth century we did not. Indeed, Conservative Christian scholars have noted that Daniel was the only ancient reference to this King by name. Herodotus calls him by his Greek name, Labynetus, as well as his father by the same. On record, Nabonidus is the "last King" of the Babylonian Empire. However, we now know that he had a son. His name was Belshazzar and he shared his Dominion directly under him. Nabonidus, from all accounts, spent the greatest part of his career in Tema far outside Babylonia. He was a warrior-king and stabilized to some degree the Dominion of Nebuchadnezzar who died in 562 B.C.E., yet, on the other hand, was attracting antagonism from the priests of Marduk (Nabonidus favored the moon-god, Sin).

King Nebuchadnezzar, son of Nabopolassar, whose seed was planted in his mother's womb by Marduk himself, the Great God (so the King proclaimed), had many sons and a few daughters (three we know of, Kassaya, Ba'u-asitu, and Innin-etirat, and possibly Nitocris). He had four sons (we know of Amel-Marduk, Marduksumusur, Marduknadinahi, and Musezib-Marduk ) and probably two marriages (Amytis and Nitocris). Kassaya, it has long been assumed (without full proof) married Neriglissar (Nergalsareser, probably the same as Jeremiah 39.3). Or she may have been another one of Nebuchadnezzar's daughters. Nonetheless, Amel-Marduk (562-560 B.C.E. mentioned in Jeremiah also), his direct son (and eldest, though Kassaya appears to be his firstborn) ruled after his father's death. He was murdered through intrigue and Neriglissar (560-556 B.C.E.) came to power. He had a son named Labasi-Marduk and lasted for a year or so or maybe less (we are not for certain). This brings us to Nabonidus (555-539 B.C.E.) and one named Belshazzar (co-ruled 551-539 B.C.E. ?).

At this point what historians offer are called, "reconstructions" based on "filling in the gaps" of what we do not know. This is done by utilizing methods of "inductions" (inductive reasoning) inferred from the archeological records. What is also noted is a deep discussion on the differences between "probability" and "possibility." Various "theories" are proposed on these methods, with some that have greater consent (consensus) than others. As I made know in the beginning, I start with the biblical record.

The popular proposed "theory" is that Nabonidus married Nitocris, a daughter of the King (Nebuchanezzar) and had a son named, Belshazzar. We have an unidentified "Queen" in chapter five as well and much speculation as to who she is has been published. We simply do not know. It is safe to say that she was not Belshazzar's wife and probably (!), then, the wife of Nabonidus (if we follow Herodotus, she was the wife of Nabonidus, and speculate that she was a daughter of Nebuchadnezzar since he married a woman named Nitocris. Some have proposed that she is the Widow of Nebuchadnezzar and married Nabonidus).

Belshazzar, who most certainly existed, was the son of Nabonidus, and thus, if married to a daughter of Nebuchadnezzar was a "grandson" to that King. Possible. Several "reconstructions" have been theorized and each of them have "plausibility" to them, which is really the only "test". The word, "son" for example, as found in this chapter, need not mean "direct son". Daniel is called a "son of Judah" (he wasn't a direct son of Judah, the man), and he is also called the "son of Israel" (he wasn't, not directly). He is also called, a "son of the Exiled". Numerous examples can be cited.

Another factor, sometimes not paid attention to, is that Jeremiah said, "Now I have given all these lands into the hand of Nebuchadnezzar, the king of Babylon, my servant, and I have given him also the beasts of the field to serve him. All the nations shall serve him and his son and a son of his son, until a time of his own land comes." (Jeremiah 27.6,7). Thus, the son of King Nebuchadnezzar was Amel-Marduk (mentioned in Jeremiah 51). Neriglissar married Kassaya, Nebuchadnezzar's daughter and they had a son named Labasi-Marduk who ruled more or less a year. Thus, "his son (Amel-Marduk) and a (grand)son (Labasi-Marduk) of his son (Neriglissar, a son-in-law)." Reasonable. Also, 2 Chronicles 36.20 reads, "and they became to him (Nebuchadnezzar) and his sons (plural) servants." This passage, which mentions Jeremiah's word, undoubtedly sees "his sons" (plural) as "his son, and his son's son" as the same, whether a son, a "grand"sons, or sons "in-law" (or even one who is simply on the throne at the time as heir and not related biologically at all).

The point in all of this is that a plausible reconstruction can be made without the fullness of proof (lacking, or simply not discovered yet). Belshazzar was once thought of to be a completely made up character. That has been smashed. There was a Belshazzar, there was a Queen, and there was a man named Daniel (who was called Belteshazzar – whose similarity of name with the King in chapter five shouldn't be missed). The text of Jeremiah is not saying that only three Kings will rule Babylonia. Three Kings will rule (related) "until (whenever) a time of his (Nebuchadnezzar's) own land comes" (which allows for unrelated Kings and allows for an indefinite time up to seventy years mentioned in Jeremiah). Another way of seeing this is that Nebuchadnezzar's son will rule, and his grandson (Labasi-Marduk from his daughter married to Neriglissar).

Thus, it is of no surprise to this reader that Daniel, basing his reading on Jeremiah (which we know he read according to chapter nine) simply skips the shake-up of Amel-Marduk (mentioned in Jeremiah), Neriglissar (probably the same mentioned in Jeremiah 39.3) and right to the "second in command" to King Nabonidus, Belshazzar (since Daniel is offered "third in command" by Belshazzar). The Canon of Ptolemy skips Labasi-Marduk's reign. We must not let the fact that we do not have "all the information" at our fingertips (no scholar of this period does) dissuade us, but from what we do have several reconstructions (theoretical in nature) can be made. Of course, the only problem we would have to defend is that Daniel was what Jesus called him: a Prophet. Defending that takes us away from the empirical data and into the epistemological arena.

The Book of Daniel was obviously not written with the concern of modern historians as he was with what chapter one shouts at us: "the first year of King Nebuchadnezzar (1.1) .... the first year of Cyrus the King (1.21)." Seventy years. Chapter five brings us to the year 539/538 B.C.E., the first year of Cyrus on the very eve of the Fall of Babylon (the first year of his rule over Babylonia, not his first year as Ruler of the Medes and Persians). This first year of Cyrus marked the end of Jeremiah the Prophet's word that the Exile would last seventy years, and this is Daniel's focus. He doesn't name the Queen, nor mention Nabonidus (by name), nor Amel-Marduk, Neriglissar or Labasi-Marduk, or the sons of Nebuchadnezzar, nor his daughters. And why should we press him to do so when it is simply not the point of his Book? The author has committed no error. He cannot be charged with "historical blunders" since we do not have all the details at our disposal (and even what we have conflicts with what else we have!). If I mention my son, Hunter, and that's all you hear, would you "infer" that I have only one son? This may be the case, even probable. However, it would be false. I have two sons, and two daughters. You don't know everything.

Thus, my own "hypothesis" is that Jeremiah foresaw the rule of a son, a "son-in-law" (which is a son), and a grandson. He also adds that Babylon will rule for seventy years – until a time for his land comes. This allows us time for Nabonidus, who was also a son-in-law who married Nitocris, a daughter of King Nebuchadnezzar. Nabonidus, who is called Labynetus in Herodotus, had a son, which would be the grandson of Nebuchadnezzar – thus, a "father" to Belshazzar. One of the missed considerations of Daniel is not who he mentions, but what he fails to mention – or leave simply undisclosed because it was, at the time of its composition, known. That is, those who would have read this Book in the post-Exilic times, the many who did come back to Judah from Babel, would have known who the King (Nabonidus) was, his wife (Nitocris), and their son (Belshazzar), and that he was, for all intents and purposes, "the King" over the District of Babel, over the Chaldeans. Of course this supposition is based on the assumption that Daniel was a Prophet, who saw dreams and visions and could interpret them (which is ruled out automatically).

It is October 12th, 538 B.C.E. Seventy years of the Babylonians have passed and the "word of the LORD to the Prophet Jeremiah" (Daniel 9.2) has now come to its fulfillment:

*Belshazzar, the King, made a great feast for a thousand of his Noblemen. And before the thousand he was drinking the wine. Belshazzar said, in flavor of the wine, for the utensils of the gold and the silver, which Nebuchadnezzar (a father of him) had brought from the temple in Jerusalem, to be brought. So they drank with him — His Noblemen, his paramours and his concubines.*

Belshazzar is throwing a holiday party. We have read these words, more or less, in the first chapter. That was the beginning of Israel's Exile. This is the end of it. Babylon held "feast" and "wine" (the Aramaic for "feast" here is "bread" — bread and wine) for seventy years and this is their last one.

I have translated the fact that Nebuchadnezzar is "a" father (rather than, "the" father, which would have more force if direct father-son were meant). Nebuchadnezzar is actually, so it can be supposed, his Grandfather (for which there is no Hebrew expression other than "my father's father" or simply, "a father"). The article ("the") is not used throughout this chapter for the King's father, and there are plenty of examples that can be shown on this point to those who absolutely insist that Daniel is in error here regarding Nebuchadnezzar as his direct father. We have a similar expression in 2.23 where Daniel praises the "God of my fathers" (plural) without the article. How many "fathers" did Daniel have?!

Belshazzar is pictured here as one who is drunk with wine. It is, then, a madness of power that he should call for the items

Chapter Five

of the gold and the silver of Jerusalem's temple. This is simply a reminder to the reader that his end is up. It is never to be lost that these are holy, consecrated items of Solomon's Temple in Jerusalem. Now they are being used by foreigners and party-girls (wives is not necessary here and is not the meaning, and "concubines" here are more or less party-girls, female dancers and singers – entertainment). We have no record of Belshazzar being married, and the text of Daniel does not indicate this either with absolute clarity. This is a young King probably in his late twenties.

*Thus, utensils of the gold which were brought out of the temple of the House of God in Jerusalem were brought out. And they drank with the King – his Noblemen, his paramours, and his concubines*

The repetition here underscores the blasphemy. Further, the added "House of God" highlights the point of the author. A Jewish reader here, imagining a drunken feast with the noise of music, laughter, lust and concupiscence, would have been greatly offended and outraged, and yet at the same time saddened. For, as chapter one has stated, "the Lord gave these into the hands of the King." Strange fire broke out and killed priests for mishandling the items of God in the days of Samuel the Prophet. Destruction is ready to break out here.

*They drank the wine and praised gods of the gold, and the silver, and the bronze, and the iron, wood, and the stone.*

As I interpreted the image of the dream of Nebuchadnezzar in terms of his sons' ascendency – one after the other – and as we have seen that the King, depicted as a stump of roots banded by iron and bronze, here we have the article ("the") with each of the sections of the dream-image. In chapter two the article also accompanies these nouns. Since this is the last day of Nebuchadnezzar's Dominion, it only makes sense that the image of the King's dream is deliberately highlighted here (the list here immediately conjures up the image ordering). "Wood" has no article, but "the stone" does, and this, too is a reminder of "a stone" in the dream. Nebuchadnezzar's dream, which he tried to prevent in chapter three by building an entire image of gold, revealed the utter devastation that was to come in the "latter days" of his Dominion at the crushing of "the stone" and its "god". And now it has come. The seventy years of his end, decreed by the word of the Lord to the Prophet Daniel has arrived. The "time of his land" is here. The "wood" here, may be in reference to the "tree" image in chapter four. It is only used here (5.4, 23). Adding in "wood" and "the stone" here strikes me as purposeful.

*In it, the moment, fingers of a hand of a man came forth and wrote in front of the lamp stand upon the plaster of a wall of the palace of the King. And the King beheld the hand's palm that was writing.*

Following the image of the dream in chapter two, here we see the Divine Hand, whereas in the dream a stone is cut out of a mountain without human hands – the Divine Hand cut it out. As in the dream, the Divine Hand has now arrived. The "hand" that delivered Jehoiakim into the "hand" of Nebuchadnezzar (1.1.2) is now delivering the Dominion into another "hand."

*Then the King's splendor changed and his thoughts alarmed him; the joints of his loins were loosed and his knees which knocked against each other.*

Chapter Five

The "legs of iron", the fourth Dominion of the dream-image in chapter two are now "knocking together", teetering on a fall. We have read the words of the King's "face" changing in chapter three (God changes the times and seasons, same word throughout these chapters). We have seen where Nebuchadnezzar was "alarmed" and "troubled" by his dreams. The added dimension here of King Belshazzar's legs knocking together out of total panic (and remember, he is a bit tipsy with the wine) is sort of comical. The party has ended. The debauchery has ceased. The hallucination of the King, intoxicated as he was, is real.

*So the King mightily cried out to bring in the Conjurors, the Chaldeans, and the Soothsayers, the King replying and said to the Wise Ones of Babel, "Any man who proclaims this writing and reveals its pesher will be clothed with the Purple, and the chain of the gold on his neck. And bear the Third in the Dominion title."*

The Third in rule (5.16, 29) is used with the article and so I translate it here as well. It is obvious that the Third in command implies a Second and a First, and this has led many to suppose that Nabonidus is inferred – who is simply not present at the banquet (he was defeated just two nights before in Sippur, and fled). Did King Belshazzar have this kind of legal authority? It matters not. The fact is that he declared it (under the influence of the wine, and in a state of irrational panic – it is a snap judgment made in a state of emergency since the gods have appeared and have written a possibly omnibus message). Belshazzar cannot interpret the script (he cannot make sense of it).

From what we know of Nabonidus, he was not present at this feast. He returned earlier that last year in April, but left again for war (he does confront the armies of Persia in Opir and Sippur and is defeated). Cyrus, however, has reissued his campaign from the east once he made it across the rivers (namely the many rivers adjoined to the Tigris to the Red Sea). There was a skirmish (the battle in Opis) and the Babylonian army was forced back into the fortified city (and Cyrus "slaughtered many" according to the Nabonidus Chronicle), well stock-piled at this time. Belshazzar trusts in the massive fortifications of the city of Babel (and its gods, for his name means, "Bel protect the crown") and allowed himself to buy some considerable time. What he did not know was the political intrigue behind the scenes, possibly involving the very "Chaldeans" (priests of Marduk) he has summoned (who do not appear as panicked, and who we know welcomed the Medes and Persians).

Literarily speaking, this is a repeat of chapters two and four. But, we should not assume that these are the same Magicians that appeared before Nebuchadnezzar. Decades have passed since then. This is a new group. Belshazzar's co-regency with his father, Nabonidus, probably came in the later years of his absence in Tema. We know that Nabonidus ruled from 555-539 B.C.E. and at some point his son shared the chair of the Purple, sitting in "the palace", bringing out the booty of Nebuchadnezzar. He was acting as "the King" for all intents and purposes, drunk with power, and hardly concerned (until the hand appeared) about the ruler who was a few miles away coming up with a plan to get into the city (Cyrus). His army had been there for a few months.

That Belshazzar did rule for at least three years is told to us in 7.1, and 8.1. That he conducted a good deal of business affairs and the like we know from the cuneiform texts. There was a chain of command, so to speak, that when the President is confined, the Vice-President becomes acting Commander and Chief. War was in the air. The Persians aligned themselves over the Medes (who continued as a nation and a people under one head, Cyrus, and who is also called the King of Elam in one text). The religious ceremonies concerning the gods were not being celebrated. The Dominion was teetering, and the King is getting drunk.

*Then came in all the King's Wise Ones, but they were not able to proclaim the writing, nor could they make known the pesher to the King. Thus the King, Belshazzar, was greatly alarmed, and his splendor changed even more. Even the Noblemen were perplexed.*

The Chaldeans, who made up the Wise Ones, or were the chief scholars, are not said to be perplexed. The Noblemen, however, were. The Wise Ones could not decipher the strange script on the wall. But the text does not say that they were at all worried about it. The King was, and his Noblemen were as well. The Chaldeans and the lot were not at the party. They were "called" in.

*The Queen, because of the words of the King and his Noblemen came in to the house of the banquet, replied to the King and said, "The King! Live to the ages! Let not your thoughts be alarmed. Nor your splendor, let it not be changed. There is a great man in your Dominion who has a spirit of the holy gods in him. And in the days of a father of yours, light and understanding, and wisdom – wisdom of the gods – was found in him. And the King, Nebuchadnezzar, a father of yours, caused him to rise, Chief of the Magicians, Conjurors, Chaldeans, Soothsayers – a father of yours, the King! All before this excellent spirit, that is, keen knowledge, and insightful interpreting of dreams, and declarations of riddles, and loosening of knots was found in him, in Daniel, who the King set his name, 'Belteshazzar'. At this time let Daniel be called and he will declare the pesher!"*

If we went by the history books, this is Nitocris, so named by Herodotus. That she was known to Daniel should be plain simply because he does not have any need to name her. She was not present at the banquet, perhaps too refined for such extravagances at such a time of looming threats. That she is near the party is certain, hearing the words (the music stopped), perhaps keeping an eye on her son. She knows the stories and repeats them in a summary way here utilizing the vocabulary of the previous dreams, the story of the fiery furnace and the last dream of the King.

If Nebuchadnezzar died in 562/561 B.C.E. and Nabonidus came to power in 555/554 B.C.E., it is quite perceivable that Belshazzar simply never heard this in detail, or of this Daniel person (although he does know Belteshazzar). The text of Daniel 1.21 does not say that Daniel remained in the palace as Chief Magician "until the time of Cyrus the Persian." It simply says "and Daniel was." That he was not appointed as an official is also made plain from chapter two. He requested to be "at the gate" (2.49). He is the last person to be brought in during the now lengthy reign of King Nebuchadnezzar (chapter four), and is absent in chapter three. With the shakeup of the various Dominions after him, Daniel is simply phased out and a new group(s) of astrologers, Chaldeans, Magicians and the like come in (each King has their own peoples to staff their court). And, because Daniel sought no sort of promotion for himself (2.48, 49), he preferred to be on his own, so to speak. He is not summoned to the requests any more for visions and dreams from the King(s), until now, being remembered by one Nitocris.

There are two other points here. The Dominion is called, "your Dominion" (King Belshazzar's), noting that the author sees each subsequent King of the Babylonian succession as Dominions in and of themselves. I bring this out because of the dream-image in chapter two mentions these successions as Dominions, thus there is no issue with seeing a succession within a Dominion as a Dominion itself represented by each King. Second is the constant mention of Nitocris' pointing out, "your father". There seems to be great emphasis on this point. Doesn't Belshazzar know that Nebuchadnezzar is his maternal Grandfather? It is pointed out, too, in the beginning (5.2). Emphasis is laid on the fact that Belshazzar is an "offspring of man" – he is related to the Great King. The dream-image of chapter two highlights the fall of Babylon in the Fourth Dominion as a mixture of iron (Nabonidus) and an "offspring of a man". The Kingdom then, a Queen without her King, and a son-King (second in command) with the Medes and the Persians outside the District, is a divided, teetering Kingdom! Daniel has brought in all the elements of the previous chapters so far, but he is not done yet.

*Thus, Daniel was brought before the King. He replying, the King, and said to Daniel, "You? You are Daniel, who is from sons of the Exile of Judah, who the King, my father, brought from Judah?"*

This is the last time we read of Daniel referred to as Belteshazzar (except for 10.1, but it is noted that he *was* called Belteshazzar there). Why does the King act surprised here? We know that Daniel "continued about the King's business" (8.27, which was written in the "third year of Belshazzar, the King", 8.1). Yet, he was known as Belteshazzar, not Daniel. His identity of origin was not known to Belshazzar which further underscores the point that Daniel, the Jew, simply faded himself out of the Magician business and simply conducted himself with the King's affairs as a clerk. In short, following the letter of Jeremiah, he lived out his life in Babylon in a normal fashion (Jeremiah 29.4-

ff). We are not to imagine, and the texts do not tell us this, that Daniel continued on with the same prestige as he did with Nebuchadnezzar. Daniel never made a name for himself but was called in times of need. The Queen remembered who he was, being older than her son, Belshazzar, and familiar with her father, Nebuchadnezzar (who from all likelihood was dead before Belshazzar was born). "There is one Daniel, who you know by the name, Belteshazzar." Thus, upon seeing Daniel, the King breaks into a description that reveals his astonishment. "You're Daniel?" He adds what the Queen does not say, "a son of the Exile, the Jews?" Belteshazzar was certainly an able administrator, aged by this time (late seventies in age, maybe eighty). He kept to himself and made no fuss about his past, boasted no pride in his previous called upon abilities and was not called upon during the years of Amel-Marduk through Nabonidus (twenty some years). This accounts for his omission of "historical" events. He is called upon one last time, however, reminding the reader of the Exile of the Jews – seventy years. He went by his Babylonian name.

*"I heard about you! That a spirit of the gods is in you. And light and insight, and surpassing wisdom is to be found in you. And at this time the Wise Ones, the Conjurors have been brought before me so that they proclaim this writing and make known its pesher. But, they were not able to proclaim a pesher for the King. Now I, I hear about you, that you are able to interpret pesherim, and to loosen knots. Now! Behold! You are able to read the writing and its pesher you can make known to me! The Purple you will put on, and the chain of the gold upon your neck. The Third in the Dominion you will bear title."*

We should not be alarmed, again, and seemingly with the Queen's approval, that such a great feat of magic is to be rewarded for obviously if the gods speak through such a one, if such a person has a spirit of the gods incarnate, one would want that person exalted!

*Afterwards, Daniel answered and said before the King, "Let your gifts remain with you, and your rewards give to another. Nevertheless, the writing I will read to the King and the pesher I will make known to him."*

"Afterwards" indicates that Daniel has seen the writing (which is by the King in front of the lamp stand of the palace). He knows what it means before he utters his words (God instantly gave him the gift of interpretation). "Keep your gifts, and your enthronement, I won't need them!" It may be, as well, that the Chaldeans were not too keen on deciphering the writing either – since they were not in alliance with this King or his father, Nabonidus. Why would such a reward be wanted when it is hoped that some sort of transfer of power takes place? Daniel knows a transfer of power is coming: keep your Purple and your gold chain – give it to another (it will be given to another anyway!). Knowing the meaning of the cryptic words, Daniel begins to recite the history of Nebuchadnezzar (chapters one through four), skips the preceding Kings and move right into the Dominion of Belshazzar, the Queen and her Absent King. The book has been building up to this time. The whole image-dream of King Nebuchadnezzar is getting ready to be smashed in a single blow because of a rock to be taken from a mountain and become a people, a Dominion that will never again be uprooted.

*"You, the King, The God The Most High, the Dominion, the greatness, the honor and the majesty, he gave to Nebuchadnezzar – your father."*

We may note that "live forever" or "live to ages" (as said by the Queen) is absent here. Nebuchadnezzar established Babylon as it was and made it Babylon the Great. His sons merely inherited it. What was once a head of gold is now iron mixed with brittle, fragile clay.

*"And from the greatness which he gave to him, all the peoples, the nations, and the languages came trembling and fearing him. He who he was pleased he slayed, who he was pleased he kept alive. He who he was pleased to exalt he exalted, and who he was pleased to bow low, he bowed them."*

This is an absolutely amazing attribution Daniel ascribes to Nebuchadnezzar. The very attribute of God described in Daniel's praise in chapter two is found here given to the King. What is added is another attribute found in Deuteronomy 32.39; 2 Samuel 2.6; 2 Kings 5.7; that God puts to death and makes alive. It is quite obvious that God's "eternal" Dominion runs the affairs of the Kings and the he shares his power with those Dominions. This accords well with Jeremiah and Ezekiel as well.

*"But when his heart was lifted up and his spirit grew strong to be presumptuous, he was brought down from the throne of his Dominion and his splendor was made to pass from him. And from the sons of man he was driven, and his heart was likened to the beasts, and with the wild donkeys his dwelling. He was made to eat the grass of oxen, and dew of the heavens wetted his body til he knew God Most High's mastery in the Dominion of the man, and whosoever he pleases, he sets up over him. And you, his son, Belshazzar, do not bring your heart low before all of this which you know."*

## Chapter Five

We can now see the proper link between chapter four and this one. Daniel, omitting the "seven times", knows that Belshazzar would have known the brief illness of the King and the reasons for it. It was perhaps the reason why Amel-Marduk was nice to King Jehoiakim the year he ascended to the throne of his father (2 Kings 25:27). Belshazzar would have heard these stories to whatever extent that he learned them. Whether or not he heard the correct version of them is another matter, and it is apparent that he did not know that Belteshazzar was the Jewish Magician of fame many decades before his time – or just didn't put two and two together. Also, Nitocris informs Belshazzar only of the fact that Daniel was a great Conjurer of the gods. Daniel relates the story of Nebuchadnezzar's brief period of mental imbalance, a story Belshazzar knew, but apparently in the version he heard, "Belteshazzar" was left out.

*"And against the Lord of the heavens you have lifted yourself up, even with the utensils from his house they have brought before you, and you and the Noblemen, and your paramours, and concubines drank the wine with them and the gods of the silver and the gold, and the brass and the iron, the wood, and the stone that do not see, hear or know you have praised, but to the God, which your breath is in his hand, and in all your ways you have not glorified. Thus from before him he sent the palm which is of the hand and the writing to be written."*

Much can be said concerning the word, "hand" up to this point. The Lord gave Judah into the hand of the King. Nebuchadnezzar was given into his hand all that he possessed. The three sons of Judah were delivered from the hand of Nebuchadnezzar. Finally, in chapter 4, "none can stay his (God's) hand." "The hand" has shown up here, the Divine Hand, the Hand that is not a human hand, the Hand that will cut a stone from the mountain and cause it to rise.

*"And this is the writing which was inscribed: MNA MNATQL and PRSYN. This is the pesher of the word: MNA – The God has numbered your Dominion and has ended it. TKL – you have been weighed in the balances and you have been found deficient. PRS – divided is your Dominion and it has been given to a Mede, who is also a Persian." Thus as Belshazzar had said, they put upon Daniel the Purple and the chain which is of the gold upon his neck and they proclaimed over him mastery of the Third in the Dominion. In that very night Belshazzar was slain, the King of the Chaldeans. And Dar-ya -vesh the Mede received the Dominion while a son of a year sixty and two.*

The writing is Aramaic but appeared as consonants without vowels. If seen as one word, mn'mn'tkluparyn, one can understand how the Chaldeans simply could not interpret it. It could mean a variety of words and meanings. The word "riddle" is used in this context and one can imagine a word-jumble here, a cryptogram of sorts that needed deciphering. There have been a variety of ways even the most learned of Commentaries have suggested.

That there is an obvious play on words (metathesis) is noted in the interpretation itself, using verbal forms (mn' is a noun, menah is a verb meaning "divided" in terms of counting things, thus, "numbered"). However, mn' (mene) is also a weight of fifty shekels of silver (hence, the "balance" and "deficient" words are monetary metaphors – see Ezekiel 45.12 for 'mina'). This is a weight of silver measured twice (mene, mene).

Tekel is equivalent to the Hebrew shekel, which was a sixtieth part of a mina. The verb, tekal, means "weighed". Thus to weigh a mere shekel and have the balance less than a shekel is to denote poverty. A tekel is a far cry from a mina.

Peres has few things going on. First, it is a unit of weight of a half mina. Second, it means "divided" (like menah, but not in the sense of counting money). Some lexicons have "torn away" – ripping apart. We hearken back to chapter two, "the Dominion shall be divided" (2.41) concerning the fourth one of the image-dream, "mixed in part (minah) with strength and in part (minah) broken". If the three letter consonant is pointed another way it means Persians (parsyn, paras, which means "pure"). Here, "your Dominion is divided" which may mean that it was between Belshazzar and Nabonidus, a divided Dominion between clay (Belshazzar, who is the seed of Nabonidus) and iron (Nabonidus). Some have seen in these monetary designations the weighing of the Kings of Babylon. Thus, Mene is Amel-Marduk. The second Mene is Neriglissar, and the third is Labasi-Marduk, whose rule was only during a year (worth less than a shekel). Nabonidus and Belshazzar are worth half a mina each, considerably less than Nebuchadnezzar (the head of gold which is worth more than all of his sons). If that is the case, then chapter two is again brought to bear. Either way, chapter two envisions the collapse of the Babylonian Dynasty, being "divided" in its "last days", given to another, and received by him. There is no objection to Daniel being crowned as third highest by the Chaldeans if they knew of the plot of the Medes and Persians who were creeping into the city. His promotion would be meaningless, and wouldn't last long, so they thought.

Belshazzar is said to be slain. By what or who we are simply not told. His "breath" was in the "hand of the God" who "slays and keeps alive." Since there is no mention of anyone killing him (which is quite odd), it may be inferred (I think should be inferred) that since his breath was in God's hands (as we were just told), God simply took it from him, killing him on the spot through fear and panic upon the Medes and Persians entering the city without a fight (his knees were already knocking and his face was flush from fear). The text before us mentions no warfare whatsoever and this is what is presented to us in Herodotus as well, who even mentions that they were dancing and singing when the Medes and Persians took the city! Nabonidus was captured after he returned to Babylon (the city was already taken) and allowed to live out his life (from what we know, or speculate). The Aramaic here does not necessitate that a soldier killed him. He was slain by God.

Another matter of concern is that "the Dominion" (Babylon's) is passed on to another. In this case, the Medes and the Persians (which I will discuss further at the heading of chapter six). "The Dominion" is given (singular subject, "it is given") to the Medes and Persians (which make up the singular Dominion). The one who received this Dominion is Dar-yaves (Darius) the Mede. However, the singular Dominion is given to a Mede and a Persian. There is nothing that hints in the cryptogram of a Mede. "upharsin" (translated, "and a Persian") is not pointed or exactly spelled the same in the interpretation. There it is "peres" with the singular "paras" standing for "Persian". "The Mede" in the final verse is with the article ("the") whereas the first occurrence is not. It is quite allowable, then, to see this person, Dar-yavesh, as the Mede and a Persian. Since "he received" (compare with "will be given") the Dominion it follows that "your Dominion has been given to a Mede, even a Persian – Dar-yavesh." The Mede is none other than Koresh (Cyrus) the Persian (1.21). "PRS – your Dominion is divided and has been given to a Mede and a Persian" – even though "Mede" hardly comes from "peres" in

Chapter Five

the cryptogram – it is added. The Persian (PRS) is a Mede, and a Persian (that is, why doesn't the writing on the wall have 'parsyn-mdn' instead of just 'prsyn'?). There is no verb that could be played off "Madi" (Aramaic) like the ones played off mene, tekel and peres. The noun Madi (Media in Greek) simply means "middle land" (mada in Persian). Hence, "your kingdom has been given to a Mede, who is a Persian" is ambiguous. But, when Darius is seen and known by name, he is not called a Persian, but "the Mede" – the one mentioned, who is also a Persian. Belshazzar's Kingdom, the Kingdom of the Babylonians, was a single dominion conquered by one Ruler, not two, and one Dominion, made up of two lands, but ruled by one Ruler: Cyrus. Thus, the cryptogram only mentions the Persian. Why, then, if the prophecy announced the kingdom given to a Persian, would it turn right around and say that it was given to a Mede named, Darius? Because they are both the same.

There may be another play on words here, too. 'Dari' is the word for "gold", and gold coins were called, "darayaka" (Persian word, used towards the end of the sixth century B.C.E.). In 1 Chronicles 29.7 we find "10,000 darekemon (darie) of gold" for the service work of the House of God. The same measure of gold is found in Ezra 2.29; 8.27. Thus, the Dominion of Babylon is weighed in silver (sigloi – Greek), but it is found wanting and given to another who is "pure" (Persian) "gold" (Dari-yavesh). A new "head of gold" has come. Still others have found that "dara" is the Old Persian word for "king" and that Dar-yavesh is simply a royal title, not a name (as some define his name as meaning, "holding", taken from the verbal stem 'daraya' with the usual Persian suffix added to "vau" which means "good" – "holding the good"). What is of further interest is that Marduk, according to Nabonidus (Sippar Cylinder) told him that the Medes would be "no more". He then mentions Cyrus who conquered the Medes (yet did not dissolve their Dominion as "the Medes"). However, Cyrus was, in fact, a Mede himself on his mother's side (Mandane, his mother's name who was a Mede)! He is also called in one inscription, "King of the Medes." Herodotus equally plays with the name Darius and states that in Greek (the language of Herodotus), Darius means, "deed doer" (which is highly unlikely. Herodotus uses the Greek word, "erxain"). If "avu" – "I conserve, preserve" - is meant (daravuash) then 'conserver, holder of gold' may mean 'darayavesh' where the final "sh" is a pronominal suffix.

I bring this up because of the gallons of ink that have been used in trying to identify this Darius the Mede. There is no record of Cyrus or any other Persian being called Darius except Darius I, who was the third King of the Persians (and was not a Mede). Some have imagined that the author of Daniel (someone in the second century B.C.E.) simply got the wrong "Darius" here in our chapter. However, from what we know, Cyrus, the King, (1.21) is the anticipated, and prophesied King, the "anointed one" (Isaiah 44.28; 45.1, 13). Yet, Isaiah also mentions that God will "stir up a Mede" against Babylon (Isaiah 13.17). Jeremiah also mentions that the "Kings of Media" will come against Babylon (51.11, 28). With the conclusion of 2 Chronicles, it is Cyrus King of Persia who "fulfills the word of the Lord" (36.20, 22, 23). Ezra 1.1-ff opens with the same exaltation of the King who decrees the return of the Exile, a theme we have seen running throughout Daniel. Neither Isaiah nor Jeremiah refers to the Persians by name. I submit that Daniel is simply using a royal title, Darius ("king"), or a play on a gold monetary value (Dari), or as "the holder of the good" to show the fulfillment of the Prophets: Cyrus will come and defeat Babylon, the King of the Medes and Persians (they were a single Dominion which is now the virtual

Chapter Five

consent of historians). The Mede was stirred up, Cyrus, King of both Persians and Medes. Further, Cyrus is linked to the "rising of the sun" (Isaiah 41.25; 45.6) and his name means, "sun" (Khur in Old Persian). He was the Mede who would "trample on [Babylon] as a potter treading clay" (Isaiah 41.25). The dream image of chapter two has legs and feet of iron and clay. Of course, the sun is colored yellow, or gold.

If we look at the issue from a different angle, It becomes very hard to believe that the author brings a character into the story at just this point who no one has ever heard of before. He mentions Belshazzar and takes for granted that the readers know him as such. He does not mention the Queen's name again indicating that she was simply known. He is familiar with Jeremiah, who mentions the "sons" of Nebuchadnezzar, and even Amel-Marduk (and possibly Neriglissar). Yet, we are asked to believe that he brings in someone entirely unknown, a Darius the Mede? Every Jew knew that Cyrus (who is known also to the author) was the key focal King who decreed the return of the Jewish Exiles. Daniel has already anticipated such a return (1.21) and in the dream-image of the King. The Seventy Years of Jeremiah is an overarching theme, and yet he brings in an unknown, made up character named "Darius the Mede"? This consideration alone has led me to conclude (with other scholars) that Dar-yavesh is simply a play on words and functions as a "dual fulfillment" of the Prophets: the Medes will come and sack Babylon, and Cyrus will come and sack Babylon (who is a Mede and a Persian). They did under one King, Cyrus, who was the Median King, of the seed of the Medes (on his mother's side), and the King of the Persians. The fact that a later King(s) would be named Darius (who minted gold coins, dariekoi) suggests that the name was already in use. Some have argued that the name of the dariekoi was not derived from his name, but from the word 'dari' (yellow, gold). Since his name has that root in it, it is highly likely that Darius I minted gold coins because of such association (gold coins were already being minted by the Lydians before Darius I). If his name means "conserver of the gold", why not mint his own coins after his name's sake? Cyrus is "Koresh" (KRSH) in Hebrew. Khor ("sun") vash ("like") would then mean, according to many, "like the sun." Dareyavash, then, may mean "like gold." "Gold" in the Babylonian cuneiform is "churussi" (CHRS) from which "CRSH" (Coresh) comes, possibly.

There is one other issue here in the text. Dar-yavesh (Darayavahaus in the cuneiform texts) was "sixty-two" years old, which was the exact age, more or less a year, of Cyrus when Babylon fell. Some have supposed this fact and yet accuse the author of simply applying the right age to the wrong King! That there was a Darius I of the Persian Empire we know. But his reign (521-486 B.C.E.) mentioned in the Scripture is far off the timeline of Daniel (obviously). It does show, however, that "Darius" (which may mean "golden one", "preserver of gold") was a known name and was certainly a Persian name. Hence, in my understanding, the Golden one follows the fall of the silver mina, the shekel (tekal), and the half mina (peres). He was sixty two. He was a Mede and received the Kingdom of Babylon: Cyrus the Persian.

Concerning the phrase, "like a son of sixty-two years" we may have a rough guess, "about sixty-two years old". The word, "kebar" is two words, a preposition and the word "son" (bar). Daniel uses it in 7.13 ("one like a son of man") and 10.18 ("like the appearance of a man", though 'bar' is not used). Thus, "one like a son of sixty and two years" = somewhere around his early sixties. This accords with Cyrus to a tee and the dates we do know of him. No other candidate would work (though many have been suggested). Mentioning age, which we find nowhere else in Daniel, is an identification mark because he does not use the name, Koresh, but Dar-yavesh (both having "sh" as pronominal suffixes attached – a Hebrew phoneme – Koresh in Persian is simply Kur-ush. Khorvash, like Dari-ush. -vash – Cyrus was also called, according to Ctesias, Argadates before he was named Khurush which is probably not true, but nonetheless shows how multiple names are thrown around). 'kebar' is used with noting the 'old age' of persons in Scripture, and hence the Septuagint uses the word, 'geras' (old age – we use this word in 'geriatric', the medical field concerning elderly people). We will consider other issues as they come to our attention.

In short, the writing on the wall is a cryptic play on words that summarizes Babylon's end and their being handed over to a Persian (and a Mede). The silver coins have been weighed and a mina, two minas, a shekel and two half minas do not equal a daric of gold. The sun has risen and Koresh has come. With a bit of wisdom and riddle, Daniel calls him "Daryavesh the Madi" knowing full well his readers would have seen the point and knew who he was talking about. Assuming that Daniel is who the text says he was, he was fully competent in the international affairs of the King's business – he knew treaties, monetary values, and the languages (chapter one). That he is simply playing a word game here should, then, be no surprise (one of his own "crytpograms"). The context has already established word-play. And, for a while, he calls him Daryavesh (he has already called him Cyrus – 1.21). However, in 6.28 he identifies him, and in 10.1 we are in his third year of occupation over Babel. He is only called Daryavesh in his "first year" (6.1-ff; 9.1; 11.1). This from Daniel who called Babylon, "Shinar" in 1.2.

## Chapter Six

*It was good before Darius and he eventually established over the Dominion one-hundred and twenty Administrators to be in all the Dominion. And above from them were three Overseers of which Daniel was one of them. It was to these who the Administrators gave to them the commands and the King was not harmed.*

The picture here strongly suggests that the transference of the Dominion to the Mede and Persian Dominion was good, or pleasing. From the historical accounts, this appears to be the case. After the offense of Nabonidus towards the gods and his son in control of Babel, the people were relieved. There was no internal struggle to overthrow the New Dominion. Thus, in typical Persian administration, Satraps are set up over the Districts. The event that follows is in the earliest part of the first year of Darius/Cyrus reign, before he gave the decree to restore the people to Judah (and others, too), and, I believe, plays a role particularly for Daniel and his people. We may note, in keeping with the interpretation that Darius is Cyrus, that this King has sovereign power to "establish" Administrators (which were also more or less "kings/governors" to a degree as it concerned power), and over them, "Overseers". The King was over them all. Some have argued that this Darius is actually the General of the Medes, or a King of the Medes. Several theories have been floated from Cyaxares II, Astyages, Guburu, Cambyses II who was son of Cyrus, and so on). If we understand that "daryavesh" is Daniel's own cryptic riddle, the problem for "looking for him" in history vanishes. After all, he was called Belteshazzar, and now he gets to call the King a name of his own choosing. What is fascinating about this is that after Cyrus, and his son, Cambyses II, a Darius I came to power in the Persian Dynasty.

Administrators/Satraps (achashdarpan – Aramaic; xsacapa-van – Persian; dahyava – Persian; satrapeia – Greek) is the usual translation given here that the Septuagint uses "satrapes" for the Aramaic term in Daniel. There is considerable debate over whether or not Satrap is meant here; whether or not what many assume here as "Satraps" or simply very powerful governors of the various Districts, lands, provinces, cities and peoples. That they were to protect the King from damage, or harm that is for sure. It was an intricate web of political rulers to the King, to protect his Dominion, and to solidify it against foreign invaders. They would collect taxes and wages as well for the support of the centralized government (the eyes and ears of the King so to speak). Daniel, with his knowledge and experience, was valuable in terms of the information he knew and the expertise he displayed. He was Senior, wise, humble, and full of knowledge and wisdom (being at this time around eighty years of age, yet quite fit – remember, Nebuchadnezzar was around this age or so when he died).

We have encountered this word (achashdarpan) before in 3.2, 27 (Ezra 8.36; comp. Esther 1.1) with Nebuchadenzzar's court. It appears as a title from a compound of words and means something along the lines of a guardian of the court. They reported to the King the affairs of the Dominion. The appointments took place within the following month or two of his enthronement and many of them, like Daniel, were from the previous administration of Babylon. Thus, they were all gathered together in the court before they were sent out into their respective Districts.

## Chapter Six

*Thereupon this Daniel was distinguished above the Overseers of the Administrators all before who an excellent spirit in him was. And the King planned to cause him to rise over all the Dominion.*

The plan was a thought of the King voiced to his Administrators and no doubt reflected the age of Daniel and his experience. Daniel would have been given power to that of a co-regent. The King sought for their opinion concerning this matter. It is of note, too, in keeping with my thesis that the image-dream of chapter two foresaw "the people" who God would "cause to rise…and rise forever" (same word, qum, 2.44). Here, Daniel, a "son of Israel" is caused to "rise" over the Dominion. However, how God's people rule, and how the kings of the earth rule are not the same in terms of their nature. That this marks the beginning of the rule of the people of God after the image-dominions have been smashed appears to me to be quite plain.

*Thereupon the Overseers and the Administrators were seeking an issue to find concerning Daniel about the Dominion, that is, any corrupting issue. They were not able to find any before him, who is trustworthy, nor any negligence nor corrupting thing were found over him. Thereupon those stronger men saying that, "we cannot find concerning this Daniel any issue except to find against a law of his God."*

The similarity here with 3.8 (see comment) is to be noticed (also, the phrase later used in 6.24, "chewed to pieces" which is translated as, "accused") that not all of the Administrators were involved in this plot. Some render "stronger men" as "certain men" (specific ones), which does reflect the meaning; "great men" distinguished from the rest. All of them gathered to see if they could find a charge they could bring against Daniel (which was more or less vetting Daniel since he was being possibly nominated to a higher office). When it was seen that there was no record of wrongdoing, certain men got together to find a way to entangle Daniel. If he is to be nominated to an even higher office, he has to be made to look bad for the job. That they knew of "the law of Daniel's God" means that Daniel knew of the Law as well, for he would have been raised in accordance with the stipulation of parents to train up their children in the law (Deuteronomy 6.7-ff).

It is easily recognized that the story here is parallel with the story of the three friends of Daniel in chapter three. They are absent here, yet we know that Daniel (Belteshazzar) remained in Babel (1.21). The only thing they could "dig up" so to speak would be his religious convictions which ran counter to the culture. The Persian Kings were no doubt just as religious as their Babylonian predecessors, and maintained the Pantheon of gods which included Marduk and Nabu (Cyrus credits Marduk for his reception of Babel). They were also of the religion of Zoroastrianism (Cyrus was Magian) which allowed them to absorb with tolerance other religious faiths. The text makes it clear that Daniel is not in any wrong whatsoever, not even in his religious practice. He states this in 6.22 – he has done the King no "harm" (6.3).

Thus, we are to think of this conspiracy against Daniel as one that is entirely fabricated, attempting to place him in an act of rebellion to the Crown. Since these were men appointed by Cyrus they were trusted as well (their validation would have been checked). In the case of the three Jews in chapter three, there was a case of possible disobedience to the command. Here, however, it does not appear to be the case.

## Chapter Six

*Thereupon these Overseers and Administrators thronged together over the King and thus saying to him, "Daruis, The King! Live to the ages! All have counseled together, the Overseers of the Dominion, the Prefects, the Administrators, the Counselors, and the Governors to establish a statute for the King, to make strong a decree that any who petitions a petition from any god or man for the next thirty days except from you, the King, he will be thrown into a pit of the lions! At this time, let the King establish the decree and sign the writing which none can change according to Mede and Persian law."*

What happened is that the Council all got together to vet Daniel. There was no wrong to be found with him. Frustrated, a few of them got together to hatch a plan that would entangle the old man; get rid of him forever (foul Jew that he is). Calling again the Council (which would have included Daniel) they draw up a decree in honor of the King: no petitions could be made to anyone's god or to anyone in authority unless first made to the King for the next thirty days. The penalty is death by the King's lions. Upon this these few men enter before the King with their petition to sign!

It may seem to be an odd request. However, the King has just been installed over Babylon. This is probably a Commemoration edict. It was not a permanent law ("thirty days") of the first month to celebrate his enthronement. It is not a ban on worship or praise to the gods. The word, "and man" is added noting that the authority of the new King is to be honored for thirty days. No "petition" is to be sought apart from the King's blessing. Thus, from all appearances the edict is couched in terms that would be flattering and honoring to the King, causing no unrest among the inhabitants.

The term for "petition" is found in Daniel 4.36 where Nebuchadnezzar is restored and his Counselors and "strong men petitioned him" again. Also, Daniel "petitioned" Nebuchadnezzar (2.16) and God (2.23). It is a form of prayer in terms of asking for a specific request from God or man. Here the temporary "ban" (so to speak) is not against worship and praise (the priests of Marduk would have loudly rebelled!), but against asking for specific needs to be granted by someone in authority (whether God or man) other than the King. This was not a ban specifically against Daniel for it also would apply to any person that "petitioned" their god(s) or any man in authority (authority to grant what was being asked for). Thus, the decree was a foible of honor to the King – that he and he alone for thirty days be shown respect by his newly acquired people. As such, and apparently thinking Daniel was one of the "all" who agreed to such a decree, the King assents.

A word must be said about the pit of lions. Lions, we know, were kept by the Babylonians for a variety of reasons. As such, they had to be penned up somewhere. We have some references to such a thing in the cuneiform texts, but not so much as we find here. Throwing a criminal in the fire was nothing new, but throwing them to the lions does not appear to be a common form of punishment. The term "pit" is a hollowed-out area either from the earth or a cavern. It was not a coral or a cage, nor a stable. The punishment is severe, perhaps extreme, but in light of the petition to the King and his honor, who would refuse? What kind of person could not simply cease from requesting from those in authority or their gods unless they first go to the King? Only a seditious person, a person so bent on dishonor to the King and the Medes and Persians! In this light the requests would be brought to the King for his approval, so as to let him "get to know" his people. The King is not being asked to be worshipped as a god. As already mentioned, Daniel "petitioned" Nebuchadnezzar (2.16). The lions would have belonged to the previous King Belshazzar and the "pit" was already there near the King's palace. Either face the Lion King (Ahasuerus) of Persia and show respect, or face the King's lions! Thus, association with the new King and the lions (instead of beheading, stoning, the furnace) seemed appropriate. The decree is meant for the local District and could not possibly apply to the whole territory of the Medes and Persians, and it was temporary. How bad could it be? No one would dare risk such a thing.

*All before this, the King, Darius, signed the writing and decree. And Daniel, as such knew that which was signed, the writing, went to his house opening windows concerning it in his upper room facing Jerusalem. And three set times in the day he knelt upon his knees and he bowed and gave thanks before his God as always he did before this time.*

Darius is being deceived by these few men in that he does not know that it was written to "get" Daniel. Had he known this he would have been furious. He is being manipulated by a conspiracy! Daniel knew what the edict meant and had no intentions of violating it (we know this from 6.22). The two words here for the forms of prayers ("bowed and gave thanks") are not "petitions." Daniel knelt, then bowed while on his knees, and gave thanks. Darius I issues an "edict" that required the bowing before God in prayer for "the King and his sons" (Ezra 6.10 – Aramaic). If anyone violated it his house would be burned (Ezra 6.11-12). The second word simply means "praise" in the form we find it here (Aramaic), but means "confess" in Daniel 9.4 (Hebrew). Daniel is simply praising/confessing while kneeling and bowing before his God. He is violating no decree, and if there was such a demand as strong as a petition required, he would have simply let the King know such.

Daniel prays in the morning (Laud), Evening (Vespers) and before bed (Compline). This is found in the Psalms as well (Psalm 55.17). "Come, let us bow down and kneel, bend the knee before the LORD our maker" (Psalm 95.6). That Daniel has seventy-years in mind in the first year of Cyrus is found in Jeremiah 50.3-ff). After Babylon falls to a nation from the north (Medes and Persians), "the people of Israel and the people of Judah together will go in tears to seek the LORD their God. They will ask the way to Zion and turn their faces towards it." Babylon was to be made a complete desert wasteland according to the word of the Lord. The threats against it uttered by Jeremiah (and Isaiah) are that of annihilation. However, we may find intercession here. Daniel had already interceded for the wicked Counselors that were threatened with death by Nebuchadnezzar. Since God gave him the interpretation of the King's dream, their lives were spared. Seventy years "for Babylon" has passed, and Israel has been in Babylon for several decades as well. A new King has come and Jerusalem once again comes into the picture (as it has done throughout these stories). That Daniel does, in fact, petition the King to let his people return to Judah may be implied in this story as we shall see.

*Thereupon these great men thronged together and they found Daniel seeking and showing favor before his God.*

Here we find another word already used in 4.24, "to show favor". Daniel's "petition" is showing favor to his God. The word "petition" is used here and is the one specifically mentioned in the edict. However, these men who were huddled outside of his house wrongly interpreted this. He is not requesting from God anything, and that is the nature of the Edict. The Edict, as stated, was not a total ban on prayer for thirty days, as this would have angered every soul in the Dominion. Daniel is simply worshipping his God and there was no crime against that. These men, however, have what they want: they have "found" corruption by seeing him bowed down as he was. From this they issue the false charge to the King which, as we shall see, is entirely fabricated. To make a petition to the Lord, Daniel would have bowed down and asked for such. Thus, we are not told that they heard Daniel, but merely that they found Daniel in the form of one petitioning his god. They assumed that he was breaking the command.

*Thereupon they came near and saying before the King concerning the Edict of the King, "Did you not sign an Edict that any man who petitions from any god or man for thirty days except from you, the King, is to be thrown into a pit of the lions?" The King answered and said, "The word is truthful. According to Mede and Persian law it cannot pass away." Thereupon they replied and saying before the King that, "Daniel, who from sons of the Exile of Judah, sets over you, the King, a command! And over the Edict which you signed! Three times in the day he petitions his petition!" Thus, when the King heard the word he was greatly wroth over himself, for concerning Daniel he set his heart to deliver him. And up to the sun going down he was struggling to rescue him.*

These conspirators are operating within the Edict in that they are going before the King with the petition against Daniel. They first get the King to commit to his own signature. "That's what I said." Then they present the case. Clever. The wording reminds us of chapter three where a command is set over Nebuchadnezzar. A King cannot go back on his own word uttered so recently as this one. He would look like a fool and trust in his rule would be diminished. He must show power. However, Cyrus has undoubtedly spoken to Daniel and heard of his abilities and knows his tenure. He knows, also, that according to the vetting of his nomination to a higher office there was no corruption or records of any scandal. We would also be at liberty to say that the King knew of the miraculous powers Daniel's god displayed through him. Cyrus has set his heart on Daniel, which the same expression we find in 1.8 concerning Daniel himself. Cyrus is caught between a rock and a hard place. The sun (which is the meaning of his name) has gone down.

The "command" which they charge Daniel with "setting over" the King is what the Administrators are to "report to the King" (6.3). Thus, from the text, we can see that they were issuing a charge that would have "brought harm" to the King and his political power. Daniel was not just some exiled Jew. He was being considered for top office and surely such a scandal, if word ever got out, that the King showed him favor over and against his own Edict would spell disaster in the press! Loyalty to the Dominion, loyalty to the King's word must be maintained in order to keep peace. Like it or not, the King had to abide by his ruling. That he did not like it at all is made known. Was there some way? Some way to "get around" what the many "witnesses" here "saw" and claim they "heard"? This would pit the King against the very ones he just appointed! If he showed favor to Daniel, he is screwed. If he shows favor to the Administrators (the few gathered here, the conspirators), Daniel is screwed. These thoughts must have kept him up all night! The one has to pay the price rather than the many. May God have mercy.

## Chapter Six

*Thereupon these great men thronged together over the King saying to the King, "Let the King know that according to Mede and Persian law that no Edict or Statue which the King has established can be changed." The King spoke and they brought in Daniel and threw him towards the pit of the lions. The King replied and said to Daniel, "Your God of which you are a revering one to him, the continual one (Bithediyra'), deliver you."*

After some time in the day, til sunset, these men left the King alone. However, at sunset they return. This is what is at stake and the King knows it: he cannot utter a law, sign an Edict, or establish a statute only to reverse it the very next day! Caught up in the celebration of his new Dominion, the King has signed an Edict that, regardless of how frivolous it was, is "law" – even for thirty days. If a King says, "no new taxes" and then says, "we are going to impose new taxes" he has just marked the end of his trustworthiness.

There is no trial here. Daniel is not allowed to "give an answer" in defense. He is not asked for one (unlike chapter three). There is a strong suggestion in the text that the King has allowed the court to rule in the favor of the accusers, for he cannot withstand a scandal at this point without looking incompetent. Rather, knowing Daniel, he hopes that his god will deliver him, Bithediyra' (which may be a name he calls Daniel). Daniel is called, "the continual one" –steadfast and sure, devoted and absolute. A great man.

More on the lion's pit. He is "cast" or "thrown" towards it, and the King is present. He speaks to him after he is placed in the pit (not lowered, but thrown, as in chapter three where the three Jews are thrown into the fire). This pit apparently would have had some door or cover and is probably a cavern with two or three floors hewn out (the word here for "pit" means "hewn out"). The lions were not kept in terms of a zoo. They were not probably kept for long, either (being used for training warriors to fight). We may imagine that as far as nutrition went, they were not fed a regular, healthy diet. These are not domesticated cats used to some routine. There was an entrance to this cavern or pit which a net could be placed over to capture them. One could hear them, but not see them. It is sundown. It is pitch black in the hole.

*One stone was brought and set above the mouth of the pit. And the King sealed it with his signet ring and a signet ring of his Noblemen so that the matter was not changed with Daniel. Then the King returned to his palace.*

The picture one can imagine here is that the guards hurled Daniel into this cavern/pit of sorts. They find a rock to mark the sentence of the King. He has his ring and a ring of his Nobles and marks it (dripping wax on it, then sealing it). The King is alone here. He has done all that he can within his power in order to maintain his stature in this quagmire of political intrigue. "May your God deliver you, Daniel. That is my hope and prayer." If Daniel is mauled as he descends the steps to the bottom floor of the darkness, the King cannot tolerate hearing the screams of a man being mauled, and so he departs to his palace. But, he is himself torn apart at the thought. As far as he figures it, Daniel's god will deliver him, and if that is the case, the charge against him will be dropped for the gods have not stirred up the lions to eat him. This, then, would allow full prosecution against the so called "great men" he appointed as the manipulators of the King. Death would be the only proper punishment; eye for an eye, sentence for a sentence. The King would be entirely cleared.

"Stone" is mentioned here, and in 2.34, 45, and in 5.4, 23. The stone that is promised to rise and grow (God's "people") after the 70 years, that shows up in 5.4, 23, and that here is brought and placed over Daniel at the end of Babylon's rule may signify that although God's people "rule" through obedience to their God and his laws, this often turns out as persecution. God's people rule through tribulation.

*And he passed the night fasting. Usual accompaniments upon retiring for sleep were not brought up before him. And his sleep fled on account of it.*

From all before, all that we know, Daniel was beloved by many. He was an old man and his reputation was excellent. The King is clearly torn here for he, too, had gained such a respect for Daniel that he planned on giving him a very high office over the District of Babylon. It is to be remembered here that no one outside the Council knows what has transpired in these few days. The Edict was freshly drafted and adopted. The charge against Daniel was immediately brought before the King. There was no public information being given here other than the Edict. Daniel is not arrested, but simply brought in and sentenced. Word would, however, spread concerning his death. The charge would be sedition. The King was faced with having several witnesses who he appointed as being liars, or Daniel was the one who simply disobeyed the King, which he could not have, either. It was difficult to understand how this man, Daniel, would have done such a thing – had he done it. Yet, he cannot quite believe that the two Overseers and a few Administrators he freshly appointed could hatch such a conspiracy. It would be a direct violation of the King's "plan" to have Daniel appointed!

Such a scandal could not rock the new Dominion. Either Daniel was guilty and deserving, or the Administrators and two Overseers were bearing false witness – to which upon discovery they would be held accountable. They were, as far as their credentials were concerned, deserving of their offices. However, their characters being revealed in this episode would only be rightfully punished – either way, the King could not trust such men, if Daniel was in direct violation, or if these men were simply false witnesses. Only the morning will tell.

*Then the King arose in the early morning at its light. And he hastily rushed to the pit of the lions he went! When he came near it, to the pit, to Daniel, in a sad voice he cried, he replied and he said to Daniel, "Daniel! Servant of the Living God – your God! Who you are revering to him, the continual one (Bithediyra')! Was he able to deliver you from the lions?" Then Daniel with the King spoke, "The King! Live to the ages! My God sent his angel and he shut the mouth of the lions and they did not destroy me! All before that which is before him he found pure to me! And also before you, the King, I did no crime!*

The King rose as the sun rose and rushes out alone to see if he is alright. Daniel ("God is my Judge") is delivered! He is pure, and he does not hesitate to state his case: "I committed no crime against your Edict". This means one thing, and one thing only: the King had been manipulated! The King had been tricked! Lied to! His own personal choice for Daniel to be elevated to a higher office was attempted by these men to be thwarted! Traitors! Cowards! Scoundrels! The worst of the worst! The god of Daniel has rescued him from an impossible situation. Daniel must be who he says he is!

## Chapter Six

*Then the King was exceedingly happy over him. Then he ordered that Daniel be taken up out of the pit. And Daniel was taken up out of the pit. And there not any injury found on him because he trusted in his God.*

The guards have showed up and the King ordered them to go in and take Daniel out of the pit, which they did. This lets us know that he was in a cavern that descended into the ground with steps leading to the floor. The King did not need to remove the rock which was set above the entrance (mouth). If the descent was fashioned in the likeness of a ladder fastened to the wall, the lions would not have been able to get out on their own. Thus, Daniel was "thrown in" but "helped out" by the guards. The lions themselves could be retrieved by hooks and nooses when needed.

*And the King commanded and they were brought, these great men who chewed his pieces – of Daniel. To the pit of the lions they were thrown! They, their sons and their wives! They did not come to the lowest part of the pit that the lions powered into them. And all their bones were broke into pieces.*

This adds a little more detail to this pit. If a ladder reached down to a descending stair case, which further reached the floor, the lions could get to the stair case, and even to the ladder (they couldn't climb the ladder, however). It must have been a horrible thing to witness and hear the cries of these families. The treachery, however, was on their own heads. Simply taking the lives of the men would have caused an issue of revenge – sparing a Jew over a Chaldean! Thus, the whole lot is thrown in. With Nebuchadnezzar, he did not exact revenge on those who "chewed the pieces" of the three Jews (3.8). Their charge was actually a crime: they were not going to bow to an image, period! Daniel, however, has committed no crime – his prayers to his God in no way violated the Edict – they were false accusers. Daniel could have easily complied with such an Edict for thirty days and yet remain devout and observant in his regimented prayer life, which he was prepared to do.

This brings us to the issue that the King here, Cyrus/Darius, the first year of the Medes and Persians, and the end of the seventy years decreed for Babylon, meant that Jeremiah's prophecy must come to pass. The people of Judah must be restored to their land. The stone in the dream image must come since the image of Babylon has been shattered to pieces (as depicted here with the Chaldeans bones being shattered). I cannot help to wonder that the "one stone" set over the mouth of the pit of the lions is not in some subtle way hinting at the dream of Nebuchadnezzar. This is the Dominion which was prophesied. God would set up another Dominion of his people and it would never again be uprooted. The decree of the King cannot be changed (unless God changes it).

*Thereupon Darius, the King, wrote to all the people, the nations, and to the languages: which dwell upon the land: "Greatly prosper! From before me a decree is set that in all the Realms of my Dominion they are to tremble and fear before the God of Daniel, for he is the Living God. And he endures to the ages, and his Dominion is never destroyed, and his Dominion never ends! He delivers and rescues and makes signs and wonders in the heavens and the land and has delivered Daniel from the hand of the lions!" And this Daniel prospered in the Dominion of Darius (that is, in the Dominion of Cyrus the Persian).*

I believe that shortly after this event, Cyrus issued the decree we find in Ezra 1.1-ff (and elsewhere). It is the capstone of the

## Chapter Six

set of material that makes up Daniel 1-6 and ends with the very wording of the dream-image of chapter two. The stone taken from the mountain, as we discussed there, is the remnant of Israel that comes out of Babylon. Now that the Babylonian Dominion has ended, Cyrus proclaims that Daniel's God is a living God (we may not see here, however, conversion).

The phrase, "his Dominion will never be destroyed" is virtually word for word in 2.44. His "Dominion never ends" is also found there. Cyrus/Darius (the vav explicative is used in my translation, indicating that Darius and Cyrus are the same), then, his "first year" marks the transition from the seventy years of Babylon and the decades of Judah's Exile. Daniel is delivered from the lions hand and so are his people. There is a resurrection motif here as there was in chapter three, too. God has shown power over the animals (chapter six), over the nations (chapter five), over the mind of a King (chapter four), over the elements of fire and the body (chapter three), and over the destiny of Babylon (chapter two). His Dominion is an everlasting Dominion and he sits on his throne judging the nations, orchestrating his Dominion over every facet of life to bring about "whatsoever he pleases." And with the end of this story, God has now brought Cyrus/Darius just as predicted, and has convinced him of the necessity of returning these people to their homeland through Daniel. Daniel and his three brothers are Kings and Rulers who reign with God in his Dominion as they maintain their faith in what is unseen; what is hoped for and believed. Their faith in what is truly certain, what Nebuchadnezzar came to confess, and what Cyrus has now witnessed for himself, is that God's Dominion is not of this world – it does not change nor pass away. It is not subject to the conspiracies of men, the threats of Kings, or the punishments of Rulers. It has a Command from above; an

Edict of its own, a Decree from on high. God rules among the nations and there is no other like him.

We already have been given a peek into this invisible Dominion. God communicates with his people. He does so through revelation and understanding that is not at all rooted in what it seen. It is a cognitive faith; a faith that can rightly be called, "knowledge" in the truest sense of that word. But, its facts are not gained through the empirical, but the non-empirical. Occasionally, God shows up in a mighty way, and angels, watchers, attend to his every order. We are getting ready to peer even further into this invisible Dominion of God. Although there are similarities with the created order, there are radical differences. It is a strange world, almost forbidding.

Daniel progressively unfolds his visions in the next chapters. What began as the dream of a King concerning his Dominion unfolded into a display of power over fire so that not even their bodies were burned, not their hair singed. There are "watchers" and "angels". God orders decrees, sentences and punishments. These angels carry them out. Such is the invisible Dominion! Who could possibly resist whatever this God desires to be accomplished? It appears that all power belongs to him, and he gives this power even to his own (2.23). God makes alive and he slays. He changes the times and seasons. He alters Dominions, setting them up, and pulling them down. This Dominion does not change.

There is a hope here: God's Dominion will set up another Dominion, a Dominion that starts off as a rock and becomes a displacing mountain until it is the only mountain left on the land. This Dominion is a people – people like Daniel, Ahazariah, Hananiah, and Mishael. They themselves are a Dominion of people, small in number and the Dominion to be established in them on the land will never be uprooted, never destroyed precisely

Chapter Six

because they are participants in the invisible Dominion, a Dominion that transcends the elements and renders them of no effect. Their Dominion is not of this world, either. It comes from above and is derived from his very own Dominion; a Dominion within a Dominion. As Daniel has demonstrated, faith is alive apart from the rituals of the temple he so desires, from the city of Jerusalem he so wants to see restored. The power is found "upon the heart" (1.8) and comes through the heart; a heart changed. Where one has a changed heart, one has direct access to God, his throne, his temple, and his Dominion. As we shall see, the next section of the Book launches out into visions and dreams. The first set are recorded in the years of King Belshazzar, which means that Daniel saw these visions before he was faced with the Conspirators and the lions. With such grand vision, we know why he uttered no word as he was brought in and thrown into the pit. Like a lamb to the slaughter, he uttered not one word and willingly went to his death knowing that God will deliver him either through death (resurrection) and over death (shutting the mouths of the lions). Either way, Daniel had absolutely no fear. He would be redeemed and proven innocent and acquitted before his Judge. He has seen the books opened. He has recorded his visions for us to read and believe them as fact, even though we may not have the same experience he had in receiving them. Revelation is revelation, whether written down or directly received. Faith is all that is required.

## Chapter Seven

God is our refuge and stronghold, a help in trouble, very near. Therefore we are not afraid though the earth reels, though mountains topple into the sea -- its waters rage and foam; in its swell mountains quake. Selah. There is a river whose streams gladden God's city, the holy dwelling-place of the Most High. God is in its midst, it will not be toppled; by daybreak God will come to its aid. Nations rage, kingdoms topple; at the sound of His thunder the earth dissolves. The LORD of hosts is with us; the God of Jacob is our haven. Selah. Come and see what the LORD has done, how He has wrought desolation on the earth. He puts a stop to wars throughout the earth, breaking the bow, snapping the spear, consigning wagons to the flames. "Desist! Realize that I am God! I dominate the nations; I dominate the earth." The LORD of hosts is with us; the God of Jacob is our haven. Selah (**Psalm 46**).

*In year one of Belshazzar, King of Babel, Daniel saw a dream and visions in his head upon his bed. Afterwards he wrote the dream; a head of words was said.*

The time that marked Belshazzar's first year of reign, or rather the co-regency he was given by his father, Nabonidus, is difficult to pinpoint. From 8.1 it is clear that he ruled in this fashion for three years during Nabonidus' absence in Tema (which is fairly well documented). If we place the last night of his rule in October of 538 B.C.E., then we can safely place these visions somewhere before such time. His rule appears to have been during the ten-year absence of his father and if that is the case, we are looking at 548/547 B.C.E. without being precise. What is interesting here is that after the victory over Belshazzar at the end of chapter five, we find the author editing his work to place these visions (of chapters seven and eight) before that fall. That Babylon is to fall is certain. The King's dream in chapter two makes that plain and chapter five verifies its collapse. However, in the same fashion as Nebuchadnezzar, Daniel has a dream "on his bed in his head". Upon awakening it appears that he dictated to himself what he saw and heard (or quite possibly to another scribe under him – that someone other than Daniel took his writings and added their own editorializations appears certain), giving the description of the visions and the words that were spoken in his head. The dream is singular, but the visions are plural. It was a dream of visions and spoken words by the interpreting angel later to follow.

*Daniel replied and he said, "I was seeing in a vision during the night and Behold! Four winds of the heavens breaking forth to the chief sea. And four chief beasts came up from the sea; one differing from the other. The first is like a lion, and to it wings of a bird of prey. I was seeing until its wings were plucked off. And it was lifted from the land and upon feet like a man it was made to rise. And a heart of a man was given to it."*

If the vision of this first animal is strange, then you are seeing correctly. This is a weird vision. The four winds of the heavens (north, east, south and west) are swooning down upon the visionary "sea" (the sea) and churning up the water. Out of the sea comes four animals that are different from each other. The first

## Chapter Seven

is a griffin of sorts, a flying lion (a well-recognized image found throughout the Ancient Near East in various parts). Someone plucks off the wings and it crashes to the land (it flies from the sea and crashes). However, it is lifted up (by someone) and made to stand on its feet (not that it has feet like a man, but that it is standing on its feet like a man – on its two legs). Now it is just a lion without its wings. However, being helped up, it is "given" some life – a heart of a man, which will keep it alive for some time (although not able to fly anymore). There is, in other words, some life that is propped up, but not all that it had originally. A lion operates according to its design. Man's heart, however, is deceitful above all things. That fact that a lion is given a heart of man is not a good image; it's given the heart of a sinner.

*"And Behold! Another beast, a second one, likened to a bear. And it was made to rise on one side. And three ribs were in its mouth between its teeth. And thus, they are saying to it, 'Rise! Eat more flesh!'"*

Like the lion, the bear is caused to rise (by someone) on the land. Thus, Daniel saw this beast come up out of the sea and it collapses on the land, but it is caused (by someone) to rise on its side (imagine a bear lying flat on its back, then being rolled to its side). It is then commanded to get up (which we assume that it does) and continue finishing up the flesh it was eating before it collapsed (which we are right to assume that it will eat – bears don't eat lying down on their backs). The reader would know that animals have far more than three rib bones, therein the fact that he is told to eat more means to get his fill, for three is hardly enough to fill anyone! So far, these animals need a lot of help. Both of them are made weak to some extent, and the bear may even be near death before it is commanded to get up ("rise").

Thus, like the lion, life is given to it so that it continues to do what a bear does: eat flesh (so that it lives). These are the first "words" Daniel hears being uttered in the dream. We are to assume, then, that these words are from the powers of the heavenly host.

The Septuagint uses arktos (bear) from which we get the Arctic region (Ursa Major, the Great Bear). In the Classical Greek period there was the cult of Artemis at Brauron which held a bear festival in worship to the Goddess. Young girls would dress as bears and dance to the sound of flutes. The bear in Scriptures is a ravenous beast. Both the bear and the lion are left uninterpreted.

*"After this I continued seeing and Behold! Another like a leopard. To it were four wings of a bird upon its back and four heads to the beast! And a realm was given to it."*

The leopard is another commonly used symbol around the Ancient world, but particularly in Egypt. The priests wore leopard skins and many reliefs picture the leopard standing with nobility. Unlike the lion, the leopard comes out of the sea, but it is not in flight. A realm is "given" to it and it does not seem to suffer the injuries of the first two beasts. However, the wings are not the wings of a bird of prey like the lion's, but of a simple bird or fowl (different word from the lion's wings). In other words, four wings of a fowl cannot possibly generate flight for a four headed leopard! The leopard, in other words, is not soaring, but is grounded. It cannot fly, and so its wings remain. Nonetheless, in order to let it remain active as the others, it is "given" a realm.

These three animals were common enough in the Scriptures. The prophets use them as nations or peoples that would attack

Israel. "Therefore a lion from the forest shall strike them down; a wolf from the desert shall devastate them. A leopard is watching their cities; everyone who goes out of them shall be torn in pieces, because their transgressions are many, their apostasies are great" (Jeremiah 5.6). "As if a man fled from a lion, and a bear met him, or went into the house and leaned his hand against the wall, and a serpent bit him" (Amos 5.19). These are carnivorous animals and their symbol means nothing more than that. Daniel does not elaborate on them any further. That each of them is made weak is to be noted, however. The lion's wings are clipped and needed a new heart to live. The bear is flopped on the ground until it is moved on its side and commanded to rise and eat. The leopard is a lopsided, four headed, four-winged beast with wings hardly adequate to make flight, and so it is given a realm to maintain (since it cannot get one on its own). There are forces at work on these animals that help them along, and "they" even command the bear to rise and eat.

Another factor is that there is no indication that these are animals replacing one another in successive order. Daniel is not seeing, nor hinting at any type of succession here. They arrive on the land from the sea from which they were churned out of. The "great sea" is not identified either (it is the visionary sea, the sea from which all things burst forth). Daniel sees these three animals all together on the land. One of them has been clipped, another is made to rise and eat, and the third cannot fly but is given a realm nonetheless. "Realm" associates us with a Dominion (as does "the land" upon which they are on). All three of them are active at the same time, given life so to speak and maintained by forces not their own. Both the lion and the bear are "caused to rise", whereas the third is not (because it cannot fly and does not fly), and so it is "given" a domain (caused to rule). These are the features that are to be kept in mind and what are brought out of the text.

*"After this I continued seeing in a vision of the night, and Behold! A fourth beast! Terrifyingly fearful! And exceedingly strong! And to it were great teeth of iron eating and shattering. And the remnant its feet were trampling. And it was made different from all the beasts which are in front of it. It had ten horns."*

This beast does not appear to be weak at all. It was changed ("made different") from all the others to be sure, but we do not see any indication of the weaknesses in the others. There are no wings, no multiple heads, but there are ten horns. Like the bear, it is eating its prey while trampling on "the rest", or "the remnant" on the land. The other beasts are in front of it (strongly suggesting that they are contemporary with it in the vision). The vision is a monstrous depiction of savagery. Unlike the other visions, this one frightens Daniel. He goes on in this vision to write down further details:

*"I was especially directing attention on the horns and Behold! Another horn, a small one, came up between them. And three from the first set of horns were rooted up from before it! And Behold! Eyes, like eyes of the man were in this horn, and a mouth speaking great things."*

This more or less finishes the initial description of what he saw. Attention is directed to the horns. There are ten of them (he counted them). As he was looking at them, he noticed another horn popping up in between these horns, an eleventh horn. As this horn comes up, three of the ten horns are plucked out, also strongly suggesting that the three horns that are removed are contemporaneous with the little horn. This leaves us with an eight-horned beast (10-3=7+1=8) and not a ten horned beast. It is a very strange image. A beast with four legs (presumably) tramples on the land, eating with iron teeth. It had ten horns, but three of them are removed leaving a total of eight. This little horn has eyes in it, and has a mouth that utters great things (he must have heard what was said, but does not record it). Like the lion who has a heart of man, this horn has eyes and a mouth like man, which again points to the pride of man. The eyes of man are never full, and his mouth utters violence because his heart is corrupt. These are human Dominions.

*"I continued seeing until kingly thrones were hurled, and (I saw) a seated Ancient One. Concerning his garment: like white snow. And the hair of his head: pure wool. His royal throne is a flame of fire, its wheels, burning fire. A river of fire flowed coming out in front of him. Thousands of thousands ministered to him. Ten thousands of ten thousands arose before him for a judgment while He sat. And books were opened.*

There is no shortage of Scriptures that speak of the throne room of God in this manner. "My wrath will break forth like fire and burn, with none to quench it, Because of your wicked acts" (Jeremiah 21.12; see also Isaiah 3.13-14 more specifically; and numerous Psalms; Ezekiel 1.1-ff). When God sits (quite at rest) upon his throne, acts of judgment commence and thrones are cast down. He raises up Kings and he causes them to pass away. There is no description of his face. He is bright and shining and fire consumes his Chair (rendered in the way of the fiery furnace in chapter three). We are not told of who these thousands are. They are without any specific number. Are these the souls of those who have fallen asleep, yet stand before him day and night? Are these all to be considered "angels"? We are not told, but the best understanding is that they are an admixture of both. There is the company of "thousands of thousands" and there is the company of "ten thousands of ten thousands" suggesting a difference between the two groups. The scene is of a courtroom, a gathering of mighty powers. The Judge is seated on the throne, and the writings are opened. A case is being prosecuted, and the Dais attends to the Ancient One's verdict concerning this blasphemous, little horn.

Before, we have seen the angels in chapters three, four and six. We saw a hand in chapter five. Throughout all of this the God Most High, the God of the heavens, the Living God, the God whose Dominion is from generation to generation, who sets up and throws down Dominions, who does as he pleases and consults no man, whose Dominion is eternal and has no beginning nor end, and will never be destroyed, who changes the times and the seasons and who will "set up" a Dominion (a rock) that will become a mountain that moves out all other mountains (a people), is now, for the first time, "seen" in the Most High Heavens on his throne from where all he purposes on the land originates! The throne is where all the "plans" and "masteries" over "man" are hatched and by the myriads at his beckon call carried out and implemented on the land. The rest of the Book of Daniel is a small portion of what is written in the books before him. Thrones will be thrown down. Thrones will be raised up. Generations will come, and generations will go, but he who sits enthroned remains forever. This is a recorded vision of a man of God, written down as he saw it – it is real, true, trustworthy and how it is in the Reality (unseen) behind the appearances of things seen (history).

## Chapter Seven

*"I continued seeing after, from the voice of the great words which the horn was speaking, I continued seeing until the horn which belongs to the beast was slain, and its body was destroyed, and it was given to a burning of fire. And the remains of the beasts, their realms were eventually taken away, that is, a lengthening of life was given to them until an appointed time and a length of time."*

The sense we get here is that Daniel's "seeing" the horn speaking great things was suddenly interrupted by the great throne scene. The horn is speaking great things and as he is doing so, the throne vision breaks in and Daniel sees that God is hardly disturbed by these great sayings, but is, rather, preparing to bring the hammer down on him. A horn rooted on a beast which is stirred up by the powers of the heavens is mouthing great things – as if he is in control or something – and then Daniel sees the utterly, inexplicably, massive throng of the God of the four winds of the heavens. Who is in control, here? A freakish horn, or the Ancient of Days?

Thus, after this vision (during his dream) Daniel resumes commenting on the horn who is speaking great things. "After" he sees God, the voice of the horn is still speaking and he continued to see until this horn is slain (remember, it had ten horns, but three were uprooted and are no longer on the beast). Then, the little horn in his time is brought to an end by being given to a burning fire (presumably, the judgment of the Ancient of Days, whose throne is full of fire, a stream of burning fire, from which fire consumes the throne).

However, what about the remaining beasts and the three horns, who were in front of (the LXX uses "encircled" around the fourth beast in 7.7, 19) the eight horned beast? What happens to them? Here we are assured that they are contemporaneous with the fourth beast as with each other. These beasts do not represent successive Dominions, but contemporaneous Dominions. These others, "their remains", are simply allowed to remain. They are "given" a prolongation of life. This matches the imagery of the dream in that the lion is "given" a heart of a man (life), even though his wings have been clipped. The bear is raised up and commanded to eat (life). The leopard is "given" a "realm" (same word here). Eventually, at some indefinite "appointed time" and "season" or "length of time" their "realms" come to an end. We are given no specifics. This is the last thing said about them in this dream (one more bit of information is given about the horn in the interpretation that follows).

To better understand the language here, we need only confer with what the Prophet has written so far in the first six chapters. All of the language here is found there so that there is no mistake as to what he wants the reader to understand (if the reader has been paying attention). First, Nebuchadnezzar's "realm" was "taken away" (5.20). His Dominion "passed away" from him (4.31 – using the same word under a different verb form). God causes Dominions to "pass away" (2.21) and changes the "times and seasons" – 2.21, which I have here translated as "appointed time and length of time." Daniel's advice is that Nebuchadnezzar repents so that his Dominion is "lengthened" (4.27). In short, His "realm" was "taken away" and yet, he is "given" it back (4.25). Thus, the beasts (the remainder), and we may include the three horns plucked off the fourth beast if applicable, are the "remainders", and they are allowed ("given") their realms for however long their specified time is determined after the destruction of the little horned beast. Therefore, with the wording here and visually with the dream itself, these three beasts are contemporaneous with the fourth beast, and even outlive the little horn. It would be a great injustice to the dream and the text to suggest that these are successive beasts, or represent successive empires.

I must note the rather unusual construction we find in the Greek text (LXX). It reads, "and the ones around the beast, he (God) took away their power, but until he did that, they were given a time of life until a time and season". The word "encircled" is also used in 7.7 and 19 (a different form) for the trampling of the fourth beast's feet those "around" it (it is used also in 5.6). This may reflect the translators' idea of the other beasts being "encircled" around the fourth beast, or around the "sea" from which they all came (contemporaneous), not to mention the possibility of the other three horns that were plucked off (Daniel does not say that the little horned killed them). Thus, we are not told that the fourth beast was entirely destroyed when the little horn was killed and destroyed. Clearly, however, whatever "remained" of them continued on for a time and season after the little horn was destroyed.

*"I continued seeing in visions of the night and Behold! With clouds of the heavens one like a son of a man came, he was. Even to the Ancient of the days he reached and before him they brought him near. And to him a Realm, and honor, and a Dominion and all the peoples, the nations and the languages to him pay reverence. His Realm is a Realm of age which shall never pass away, and his Dominion shall never be destroyed."*

This ends, technically, the "visions" that Daniel saw in his "dream" at night. These visions (plural) were of the great sea being churned up, and each of the four beasts coming out of it. Another vision was the interjected vision of God's throne room. Another was the fourth eight horned beast of which its little horn was killed and burned, whereas the remains of the animals lived on. Finally, he sees another vision of one "like a son of a man" who "comes" (erchomai in the Septuagint), being led into the presence of the Ancient of days by the myriads. The Septuagint has the verb pareimi for his arrival before the Judge, which is the verbal form of the word parousia (Greek). The Septuagint actually uses a string of verbs here, "he was present and the one having been presented (paristemi) was present (pareimi) to him." These words, erchomai and parousia are found throughout the New Testament in reference to Jesus, particularly in Matthew and in John's Revelation (John's imagery in chapter one explicitly refers to the vision here).

Thus, the coming of the one like a son of a man is to the Ancient of Days, and being led into his presence, he is made to be present. The Ancient of Days then awards him with a realm, honor, and Dominion. As a result, the peoples, the nations and the languages pay reverence to him. The titles and string of honors here is nothing new the readers at this point. They are the exact same as ascribed to King Nebuchadnezzar and to King Cyrus/Darius. We are to imagine, then, that this "son of man" person is "given" what God has been giving to the Kings (realms, Dominions on the land, empires, 2.37). The difference is that they eventually "pass away" or their Dominions are "destroyed." This one will not pass away nor ever be destroyed. Daniel means for us to compare and contrast these Dominions in his book with the Dominion that is given to this enigmatic person who has been led into the throne room of the Ancient of Days and "appears as one present" before him. What he is handed, or given, is a Dominion that is to be understood in terms of an earthly Dominion (as it has been in Daniel); it is to be contrasted with the Dominion of God which is eternal and is his alone in the heavens. God's

Dominion rules over all the Dominions of the land because he gives them their Dominions and takes them away. This son of man personae is given a Dominion in the same manner, but his Dominion over all the land will not be taken away or destroyed (unlike the rest of the Dominions of the sons of men). Also of note is that the nations "will serve" him, a verb used in Daniel only for God (3.12, 14, 17, 18, 28; 6.17, 20).

What is also to be noted here that the phrase, "never be destroyed" hearkens back to the dream-image of Nebuchadnezzar in chapter two, and the declaration of King Cyrus in chapter six. God's Dominion is a Dominion that cannot be destroyed, and it is not a Dominion that is "set up" but one that simply "is." It is eternal. It is already fully and entirely in operation over the mastery of men. Daniel has made this clear. However, a "rock" was to come, and The God of the Dominion of the heavens was to "set up" a Dominion "which will never be destroyed, not left to another." These two Dominions, one that is eternal and the other that is "set up" are now linked with this "one like a son of man." He is made a King. God Himself is already a King of the Kings (as Daniel has already said previously). However, it appears that here he is enthroning a King "like a son of a man". He is setting this King with the same attributions that he already possesses throughout the book.

When, who, how are not specified. It is not even attached necessarily to the fall of the little horned beast. Rather, it is another "night vision" within the dream of several "visions" (plural). It pops up, so to speak, out of nowhere and it is entirely unexpected (unprecedented in Daniel up to this point). The parousia of this son of man, his arrival to the Ancient of Days and being given his own Dominion over all the others is, at this point, a mystery.

What should be seen, however, is that there is a progression of events. Four beasts arise altogether, and one of them is very powerful among the others, exemplified eventually in an eighth king, a little horn. This king is killed, and the other dominions remain until a time and season. It is within this time and season, at some point a son of man approaches the Ancient of Days and receives a kingdom of his own, and nations and peoples will serve him. There is a hint that this son of man personae is likened to the Ancient of Days himself. He "stands" before him, and is given the "service of the nations" – "service" which, as noted, is used exclusively for God in Daniel. The service that is to be given to God is given to the one like a son of man, which may indicate a divine nature of this figure, acting "as" the Ancient of Days representative, standing in his place, and receiving worship from the nations due to the Ancient of Days. The variation of the TH text (150 AD) and the Old Greek (OG), or LXX (Septuagint) suggests many ideas that have been greatly explored by scholars. Of course, I am maintaining the integrity of the Masoretic Text (MT).

*"My spirit was troubled, I, Daniel...in the middle of the sheath...that is, the visions of my head alarmed me."*

Strange way to put it. Daniel's body is metaphorically a "sheath" in which his "spirit" is troubled and alarmed by what he saw (2.1,2; 4.2 where the same is said of Nebuchadnezzar). For Hebrew anthropology, man is a body with a head that has thoughts within his spirit. His spirit resides "in" his body (like a sword in a sheath). Daniel's "gut" hurts. His head hurts. These visions are emotionally draining on him. He has no real clue as to what the meaning is to what he has seen, and neither does the

Chapter Seven

reader (at this point). And, as we have seen in the previous dreams (chapter two and four), he seeks an interpretation. It may be that this is how he received the interpretation of the King's dreams. He saw the image of the King (the statue) and it was "revealed" to him what it meant (an angel must have told him in a dream). That is why Daniel could repeat the details to the King. In the other dream (chapter four), Nebuchadnezzar tells him the images. Daniel is puzzled for a moment, and then interprets it. Here, he is puzzled, alarmed and troubled, and so he asks an angel, "what does this all mean?"

*"I came near to one from those who were standing and petitioned the truth from him about all of this. And he spoke to me and a pusher of the words he caused me to know. 'These, the great beasts, these four are four Kings who will be caused to rise from the land and the Holy Ones of the Most High will receive the Dominion. And they will possess the Dominion until the age even to an age.'"*

Here we are explicitly told that the four beasts represent four Kings who are "caused to rise" on the land (which the visions show). This would be the first set of the visions. Then he sees a vision of the Ancient of days, followed by another vision of the remaining beasts and the destruction of the little horn. Another vision is given where he saw the one "like a son of a man" who is given "a Dominion". In the interpretation, however, this vision is left partially unexplained. However, "the saints" are introduced, receiving a Dominion of their own. They will possess this Dominion for an age and beyond (some see this as expressing the notion of "forever and ever"). If we left the vision alone and as it now stands, we are given no idea of what "horns", "three ribs", "four wings" and such are to represent, if anything significant at all. These are four Kings (later called, "Dominions"), and the Holy Ones will receive the Dominion (Darius, "received the Dominion" in 6.1 – same word). Thus, taking the Dominion conveys an earthly Dominion (as it did for Nebuchadnezzar and Darius). God "gives" these Dominions "as he pleases" ("know that the Most High rules in the Dominion of men, and gives it to whomsoever he will" – 4.29). He gave a Dominion to Nebuchadnezzar, and to King Darius. Here four Kings are given Dominions and finally, the Holy Ones ("the saints" – plural) of the Most High will be given "the Dominion" and they will possess it forever. God "gave" the Dominion of King Jehoiakim over to the "hand" of Nebuchadnezzar (1.1). Basically, the angel gave the long and short interpretation! If the four beasts represent four Kings, then we know that one of them will be "slain" and "burned" by the consuming fire of God's throne. The remains are allowed to live for a time and season. This is not enough for Daniel, however, and he presses on. However, to repeat, God's Dominion is over all these Dominions, and he gives these Dominions on the earth as he sees fit. God is not giving his own Dominion to them! These are Dominions, or Nation-States that we know as political powers over peoples, by peoples. Thus, what the son of man is given, like Darius, is a Dominion of people who are under his rule, and this Dominion is to be received by them. It is a Dominion like the others and is set among the others. The difference between them is that this Dominion of people is forever and will never pass away. It will outlast all other Dominions.

Another point to raise, and one often missed, is that these are four Dominions that will (in the future) arise. The Babylonian kingdom is finished, and the Persian/Median kingdom was, by the time of Belshazzar's reign, well established. Daniel is being told that these are four Dominions that will arise in the future.

The phrasing, "and I came near to one of them standing" uses the same words in 7.10, 13, where the "myriads stood" before the Ancient of Days, and the son of man "drew near" and was made to "stand". In the same descriptive fashion, then, Daniel "draws near" to one of the myriads who "stood" before the Ancient of Days.

*"Thereupon I was concerned about the truth about the fourth beast which was changed from all of them, extremely fearful, its teeth of iron, its nails of bronze, devouring, breaking, and the remnant its feet were trampling. And the ten horns that are in its head – and another which came up. And the three which fell before it – that is, the horn that had eyes to it and the mouth speaking great things, and his chief appearance from his companions."*

Daniel has added a few features here that were not written down at first. Here he mentions the nails of bronze and the fact that these three other horns are the little horn's "companions." They are contemporary to whatever extent, but certainly not distant in terms of relation. It is also interesting that he does not focus on the "one like a son of man" which is amiss here in the interpretation. This personae is not interpreted. Some have imagined that the "saints of the Most High" represents the "one like a son of man", but this is not borne out in the text in terms of a necessary connection. The fact that the saints receive a Dominion and reign, and that the son of man is given a Dominion as well and reigns may suggest a relationship, but does not necessitate one in terms that one "stands for" the other so that they are the "same."

*"I continued looking, and the horn made war with the Holy Ones and was able over them until the Ancient of the days came. And the Judge gave to the Holy Ones of the Most High. And the appointed time was reached, and the Holy Ones possessed the Dominion."*

Just when we thought the visions were over, Daniel adds a few more details. However, is this something he is seeing after he saw the vision of the fourth beast and the Ancient of the days, or is this an additional seeing at the time he is asking the angel to make him understand? In other words, Daniel sees the visions of the four beasts, and then sees the Ancient of the days and the arrival of the one like a son of a man receiving the Dominion. After which he asks for an explanation, and during this he sees yet another vision concerning the fourth beast which ties it together with the judgment of the Ancient of the days. "The remnant" (always with the article, "the") that is being "trampled upon" are "the Holy Ones of the Most High." This trampling is taking place under the reign of the Eighth Horn (a King) on this fourth beast. During this time of prevailing an "appointed time" was set and reached. At that time, the Ancient of the days gives a Dominion to the Holy Ones – an earthly Dominion. The other three beasts are allowed to live for "an appointed time (same word) and time" afterwards.

We must also point out that the saints are involved in a war with this horn/beast, and they are trampled and given over to him. This cannot be said (and is not said) concerning the one like a son of man. Is he trampled on? Does this beast make war with him in term of trampling on him? This aspect further scores the notion that the one like a son of man is not the same as the saints of the Most High. The saints and the son are two separate entities. The angel continues from there:

## Chapter Seven

*"Thus he said, 'The fourth beast will be a fourth Dominion in the land which is different from all the Dominions. And it will eat all the land and will trample it and shatter it.'"*

More information is given. The beasts are now called "Dominions". The fourth one does not eat these Dominions. These Dominions, then, are certainly contemporaneous. The horn of the fourth beast is slain, but the other three Dominions are allowed to live for a lengthened time afterwards. This fourth Dominion is larger than the others, and has more "land" than they do. However, more to the point and glaring: these are four Dominions that will be caused to rise from the land. Daniel is writing in the "first year of Belshazzar" – the final years of Babylon. He could not possibly, then, be referring to one of these Dominions as Babylon that "will rise from the earth" when, in fact, he saw this vision when Babylon was a few years from being eradicated! This is rather obvious, then. In other words, Babylon is not one of the beasts that Daniel saw, and neither would be Persia/Media.

*"'And the tens horns from it, the Dominion, are ten Kings who will rise, and another will rise after them. And he will be changed from the former ones, and will bring low three Kings.'"*

The ten horns of the fourth beast are ten Kings, but three of them will be brought low (Nebuchadnezzar was "brought low" in chapter four – God "changes Kings" and "causes them to rise and to pass away"). Thus, God will grant this fourth beast its Dominion, and it is granted that this eleventh horn shall become the eighth by removing three (note, these three are contemporaneous with each other). This eighth horn is a King who will remove three Kings (his "fellows" or "companions") of this Dominion. Quite specific. Quite specific, indeed.

*"And he will speak words concerning the Most High, and he will wear out the Holy Ones of the Most High and attempt to change appointed times and law. And they will be given into his hand a time, and times, and half a time. But the Judge will sit and his Dominion will be made to pass away, utterly destroyed to the end. And the Dominion, and the Realm, and the greatness of the Dominion under all the heavens he gave to a people of Holy Ones of the Most High. His Dominion is a Dominion of age, and all the Realms will serve him. And they will obey him.' -Thus is the end of the word. I, Daniel, my thoughts were greatly alarmed. And my brightness changed over me. And the word I kept in my heart."*

This "little horn" becomes the main focus of the vision, this and the victory of the saints, who are now the "people". If we remember, the "rock" that will become a "mountain" (and eventually the only mountain), is a "Dominion" that "will not be left to another people." It starts as a rock, and in these visions it is granted the status of being a "Dominion" like other earthly ones. The "rock" is the starting point of this Dominion. However, during the time of this "little horn" the "people" will become its own Dominion – there has been, then, "growth".

Nonetheless, there is coming a trampling of the saints, decreed by the Judge. They are "given" over to the trampling of the fourth beast for an appointed time ("time, times, half a time"), which is left entirely unspecified (Nebuchadnezzar was passed over seven "times"). Judgment in God's Dominion, the Eternal Dominion, will be decided in favor of the saints and their Dominion on earth. The "end" here is when the little horn is "destroyed", whereas the remains of the beasts (Dominions) are allowed to live on for their own "appointed time" and "long time." There is no focus at all on these other Dominions. They are not the focus because they are not the ones that are to "trample" the "remnant" people of God. Out of this trampling, however, a Dominion of the saints will emerge triumphant.

Many have come to the conclusion that Nebuchadnezzar's dream and the visions of Daniel's beasts here are one and the same. However, upon comparing them together, the differences are far more than are the similarities, if any. Upon comparison, rather, it is easily seen that they are not the same at all. The King's dream concerned his own Dominion and the continuance of it through his heirs to the throne. Daniel's visions of four Dominions, four Dominions that are contemporary with one another and not "successive" in any way as indicated in the dream of the King, envisions a "trampling of the saints" and a showing up of the Ancient of the days. The King's vision confirms the fall of the Babylonian Empire and the establishment of a "rock" taken from a mountain, which eventually, over the span of time (ages), grows into a mountain.

I interpreted the rock as the return from exile, yet under the auspices of Persia. Israel did not have any independency. Daniel's visions here have nothing to do with a return from exile (which has been a dominate theme throughout). Rather, the Holy Ones (the saints) are "trampled" – this assumes that they have returned from their exile and have been returned for quite some time since they are pictured in the dream as living during the "rise" of four Dominions! If the saints are being "trampled" after their exile (certainly not before, and certainly not during), then the rise of four contemporary Dominions must be explained. It is not explained here, for no specific Dominion has been named. However, as Daniel progresses on, that is about to change.

We may note before leaving this set of visions, that the vision of the son of man being given a Dominion, being such a key figure, is left without any further reference. The parallel of the "receiving" of the Dominion by the "saints" has caused some to think that they "stand for" the son of man. This is not convincing, however. The saints are trampled on and handed over a time, times and half a time by the little horned beast. This is not said of the son of man. In literary criticism what is often left out is meant to make a point. The fact that the author focuses in on the little horn and its identity – over and against focusing in on the son of man – is telling. There is a connection between the saints being trampled and the little horn being destroyed when the Ancient of Days renders his judgment in favor of the saints. We must ask the question of the visions which Daniel does not ask: Does the separate vision of the son of man and his being given a Dominion coincide with the victory of the saints? Since the interpretation is apparently left out concerning the identity of this son of man, and since there is no aspect of his being trampled on for a time by this little horn, specifically, then making "the saints" stand for, symbolically, the son of man appears difficult. If the identity of the little horn were known, then we may gather to make a guess as to when this son of man appears.

What may emerge, then, is that Daniel sees the visions of four contemporary beasts – Dominions. The other three are left alone in terms of their importance because the fourth monster tramples and makes war with the saints under the rule of the little horn (a King). Judgment is rendered to the saints after a time, times, and half a time and they are rewarded with a Dominion of their own. But, that is not the end of the night visions. Daniel also saw one like a son of man being given a Dominion as he arrives before the Ancient of Days – is ushered into his presence and made to be present. Who this person is, is left out. When this event happens is not stated. By leaving it out of the concern of the Prophet, and focusing in on the fierce war with the saints by this little horn, notes that the son of man vision is separate from the events of this war. Textually speaking, it appears that it may be included with those events, but not necessarily. This is a point to keep in mind as we continue.

There is one final aspect that some scholars of Daniel have noted, and that is that the 'saints of the Most High' are being "given" a Dominion by the Ancient of Days, who is the Most High. However, if the Most High is represented by the son of man, who is exalted above the nations (Most High), an interesting understanding arises. In Genesis 14.18-ff we first encounter the term "Most High" (elyon) associated with God, "possessor of heaven and earth." The next is Numbers 24.16, where the Prophet Balaam "sees visions" of the Most High, and what he saw is that "a man" (LXX) or "a star" and "sceptor" that will come "out of Jacob" and "Israel"; a ruler of the Most High. Israel, too, is called "most high" (Deuteronomy 26.19; 28.1). It is the Most High who "gave" the nations their lots (32.8). Elyon is used only four times in Daniel (7.18, 22, 25, 27). The "saints of the Most High" are "given" a dominion that has been "given" to the Son of Man. God, the Most High, is not giving the dominion to Himself! He already is the possessor of the heavens and the earth and the giver of what is his. Thus, the "Most High" in these passages is the Son of Man, the highest exalted Man, the star of Jacob, the sceptor of Israel; the highest title that can be given to a man by the Ancient of Days, who is the Most High God. "And he (the Most High) will give to you (singular) most high above the all the nations which he has made for praise and for name and for beauty and for you (singular) being Holy People (saints)" (Deuteronomy 26.19). The Son of Man is given this, and in turn the Saints of the Most High are to "receive" the kingdom he has been given by the Ancient of Days, the Most High.

In this way, the visions of the Son of Man being given a kingdom blend. The Son of Man is the representative Man of the Most High, sharing in the glory, power and might of the Ancient of Days. The Most High gives to the Son of Man the same status as stated in Deuteronomy 26.19 for Israel. One of their sons will be exalted elyon. As such, the Son can then "give" to the "saints" who are to "receive" what he already previously received: a Dominion over the nations. There is an order, then. The son of man must first appear before the throne of the Ancient of Days to receive all power and a dominion above all (elyon), and a name above all names. With Daniel, this happens at some point after the Ancient of Days destroys the little horn (the coming in judgment of the Ancient of Day in 7.22 against the little horn), and within, or after the "time and season" of the "remainders" of the beasts' authority passes away. With the Representative of God, and Man before God, being given a Dominion and the fact that his Dominion will be successful (unlike Israel, who did not obtain such status), then he is the one as man to give to man what God has intended for man: Dominion over the earth in righteousness (holiness, saintly-ness), destroying the enemies of God once and for all.

The Son of Man, then, restores to man by possessing with righteousness a Dominion over the heavens and the earth as a man that is not susceptible to death or a contingently based "if", which is contingent on whether the son of man was successful or failed. Every man, and the nation of Israel itself, failed, starting with Adam because of sin. But, this Son of Man will not fail. He will "reach" and "draw near" to the throne of the Ancient of Days and receive a Dominon forever. With this in hand, he can rightfully give to the saints, the holy ones, those who love and serve the Ancient of Days and the Son of Man in righteousness, that which he has been given. The saints are then in possession for the first time a grant of guarantee of Dominion that will eventually bring about "the heavens and the earth" as their possession, having under them the same that the Son of Man has under his feet. Daniel announces, then, "the time" ( ho kairos - Greek) when this will happen.

The blending together, then, the words of the Son of Man being given a Dominion, of "coming" before the Ancient of Days precedes when "the time came" for the Saints to receive the kingdom (his kingdom). In Daniel 7.13 the Son of Man "came" (atha in Aramaic) before the Ancient of Days. The LXX uses "pareimi" for this verb, as we noted. The TH text (Theodotian), which is based more on the MT, uses the Greek verb, phthrano (to come) here and in 7.22. The Aramaic of Daniel uses matah in both places noting the blending, but also the differences. The time came for the Son of Man to receive a Dominion, to be followed at some point afterward for the time when the Saints receives the Dominion. This is spelled out, as mentioned above, in 7.27 where the Dominion is given to the people (many, plural in meaning), followed by "his (singular) Dominion is everlasting, and to him (singular) will they serve (plural), and heed (plural)." The Son of Man is revered, not the people. The Son of Man is the one who has been given all dominion, who in turn gives this to his people. The Son of Man is the representative of the Ancient of Days, sharing in his glory, and in turn the people who hear the Son of Man are his representatives on earth while the Son of Man is in heaven before the throne. The fact that the Son of Man has been given "the kingdom and the dominion and the greatness of the kingdoms under the whole heaven", which in turn, "shall be given to the people of the saints of the Most High" demonstrates that all that God, the Most High, Possessor of Heaven and Earth and all that was created, possesses, and has been given to the Son of Man, will be given to the Saints. The inheritance of the Saints is that which is "under the whole heaven". All of it in "subjection" to him, will be in "subjection" to them.

# Chapter Eight

*In the third year of King Belshazzar's Dominion, a vision appeared to me – I, Daniel – after the one that appeared to me in the beginning.*

Belshazzar's reign was soon to end. The Babylonian Dominion in this vision and in the previous one is not Daniel's concern. As stated in the previous vision, he saw four Dominions that will rise together on the land, and none of them are the Babylonians (which would simply make no sense to say he saw the Babylonian Dominion as a beast that "will rise on the land" in the final years of Belshazzar!). As we get closer to the demise of the Babylonian Dominion, in the third year of Belshazzar, Daniel records another vision to be added to the previous one. This one expands on what he saw before, and what left him "alarmed." "What do these four beasts mean? When are they coming? What does it mean that the saints are to be trampled? This one that comes like a son of a man, who is that? Jeremiah said that after the seventy years of Babylon, Judah would return to her land and be prosperous. What is this trampling of the fourth beast? Are we to be trampled again?" Questions, questions. If we place ourselves in Belshazzar's third year and were expecting the fulfillment of Jeremiah to become a reality within a few years more (the subject of chapter nine), it can be understood that Daniel was alarmed by what he saw. It made no sense. Jeremiah said restoration, wealth, prosperity, new covenant and the nations would worship the Branch! What is this business of being trampled again by a future fourth Dominion? When is this going to happen?

We should also note that the text has now switched back to Hebrew. From 2.4 through the whole of seven the text has been in Aramaic. Daniel is leaving the Aramaic speaking world and now back in his own element as he anticipates the fulfillment of the Hebrew Prophets. There were two visions given to him as Belshazzar's reign was coming its end. Babylon, as we shall see, like the previous vision, is nowhere to be found.

*Now the vision I see – at the time I saw I was in the palace of Shushan which was in Elam, the District – now I see in the vision that I was beside the Ulai River.*

A bit of geography is needed here. Shushan (Susa, today called, Shush in Iran) was an important and strategic city of the Persian Empire. It is located east of Babel in the Province of Elam (Median territory). It was the capital of Elam, captured by Cyrus around 540/539 B.C.E. – during the time when Babylon fell. What is fascinating is that Nabonidus resided in Susa. According to the inscriptions, he left there and returned to Babel in its last year (April, 538 B.C.E.), and left that city months before it fell under his son, Belshazzar (October). Prior to this he had not been in Babel for a number of years (thus, the years of Belshazzar's "reign"). Susa fell to the Greeks under Alexander, and then the massive Seleucid Empire (which began in 312 B.C.E.). It became, eventually, the capital of the Persian Empire (whether under Cyrus, or his son Cambyses II, or Darius I). Daniel sees himself there at the brink of a major change of Empires (Isaiah 21.2-ff mentions a coalition of the Elamites and Media in the overthrow of Babylon).

It is quite interesting that Cyrus plots his course to Babel from this city. The Ulai stream (Eulaeus, modern Dez) flows from the Zagros Mountains into Elam (Khuzestan). It is connected with the ancient Choaspes, from which, reportedly, Cyrus stockpiled water for the venture west to Babylon. In Daniel's affairs with the Dominion of Babylon, he would have known and frequented this place, interacting with the locals and customs. It is a tradition that he was buried in this area (he never ventured back to Judah as far as we know).

*And I lift up my eyes and Behold! One ram standing towards the river's face. And to it were two horns. And the horns were high; even one higher than the second. And the highest one comes up behind the former. I saw the ram pushing towards the sea, and to the north, and to the Negev and no beast could stand before it. And there is none snatching from its hand. And it does what it pleases, and it became great.*

There is one ram with two horns, one horn growing taller than the other. From Susa, it heads east ("towards the sea" would be the Mediterranean), north and south (The Negev is south of Palestine, occasionally Egypt itself). From Susa, then, Babel is east, Media is north, and Egypt is south. If we are to use what we know so far about "beasts", this single beast (Dominion) has two Kings or Dominions that heads towards Babel, Media and Egypt. No beast (Dominion) stands before it (unlike the three beasts that stood "before" the fourth in chapter seven). This is a further confirmation that the four animals he saw previously were contemporaneous, since three "stood before" the fourth. Daniel has seen a lion, a bear, a leopard and a monster. Now he adds another, a ram with two horns. The phrase, "does what it (he) pleases and became great" was descriptive of Nebuchadnezzar, and becomes descriptive throughout the rest of the Book for Kings. God "does as he pleases in the heavens and gives

Dominion to man as he sees fit." Daniel is to always be read in light of what has preceded in its pages.

*And while I was observing, Behold! A male goat, a hairy one came from the west over the face of the whole land, and it does not touch the land. And the male goat, a horn of vision between its eyes.*

While he sees this ram covering over the areas of Babylonia, Media and the Negev, south of Judah, another beast enters the vision, a male goat with a horn of vision (some translations have "a conspicuous horn"). Again, we can deduce from the previous vision that this is yet another Dominion with a prominent King. And so, we have a lion, a bear, a leopard and a monster added to a ram and a goat from the west (where the term "west" is used instead of "towards the sea"). This goat is not from the sea, but from the far west. It does not touch "the land", which could indicate "the Land of Israel" as it is often called. The ram heads towards the Mediterranean Sea which borders the Land, and specifically south (the Negev) of the Land. We have to keep in mind that Daniel does not have a satellite image of the globe here (like we do).

*And he comes to the ram, owner of the horns which I saw standing before the face of the river. And he runs to him in the fury of its power. And I saw him reaching near the ram and was embittered to him. And he strikes the ram and shatters the two horns. And there was no power in the ram to stand before his face. And it threw it to the land and trampled it. And there was none to snatch the ram from his hand.*

The descriptive conclusion of the goat striking the ram is same when the ram was in power. Why the ram had power, like

## Chapter Eight

Nebuchadenezzar, none could stand for God had given him all things – for a time. Here the ram enjoys its power for a time. None can stand against it. However, a goat comes along and strikes the ram, throwing it down and trampling on it. The goat has now been given Dominion and power and none can snatch from his hand (except the Lord, of course). Thus, what we see here is one Dominion going to war against another and subduing it. We do not see any of this in the previous vision of the four beasts. The bear certainly eats his fill, and the third beast is given a realm. The three stand, however, before the fourth beast, who also tramples the whole land. Nonetheless, they remain while the eighth horn of the monster-animal comes to an end. Here, the picture is one of annihilation. The ram rules the realm for however long, and then the goat comes and replaces him entirely. The four beasts of the former vision are not these beasts here.

*And the male goat, the hairy one, became exceedingly great. But at its mightiness the great horn was broken. Four came up in its place – a vision- to the four winds of the heavens. And one from the others, from them one horn came out, a little one, and grew exceedingly great toward the Negev, and to the sunrise and to the Glorious.*

The descriptions remain the same as they have been throughout the Book. However, a sharp turn focuses on the "little horn" that comes "out of the four" and the "four winds of the heavens". This language unmistakably calls us back to chapter seven and the "four beasts" that came up out of the churning sea "to the four winds of the heavens" (7.2). Out of these four beasts, a "little horn" comes up and treads the whole land. There can be no doubt that these two visions are connected, and that the "little horn" here is one and the same "little horn" there. This also means that the four horns that come after the horn of the shaggy goat are the four Dominions (beasts) in chapter seven.

This "little horn" becomes a massive Dominion and heads to the same Negev region, to the east (sunrise) and the region of the glorious ones (some translations have "beautiful land" – "land" is not in the text, but this does not discount the translation. The word is a noun, not an adjective. It also has the article, "the", and may, as above, have reference to "the land" crossed over by the shaggy goat, that is, Israel. Israel is called, "the desired land, the beautiful inheritance" (Jeremiah 3.19). We will have to see if the interpretation bears out.

*And it grew towards the host of the heavens. And it causes a fall to the land from the host and from the stars. And it tramples them. And from him he took the continual and cast out the arrangement of his sanctuary. And a host was given in addition to the continual because of transgression. And he threw truth to the land. And he did. And he prospered.*

This is highly enigmatic to say the least. The horn grows in its power and attacks the Captain of the host (army – a common phrase in the Hebrew). It stirs up a fall in the land (assumedly Judah) concerning some of the army and even the stars (the saints?) and it tramples both. The "continual" is generally understood as the "continual offering(s)" of the daily arrangement in the Temple in Judah (all throughout the Book of Numbers this word is used). The sanctuary is not destroyed, but the daily arrangements within are cast out. The phrase "because of transgression" is a bit of an issue. Is this because of the horn's transgression, or the host? Throwing "truth" the land is akin to chapter seven where the little horn attempts to change the times and law. There, he "tramples the Holy Ones" because they have "been given" over to him by God. We find the same here making us certain that the little horn in both visions are one and the same King, the eighth horn of the fourth beast.

As I have stated, the trampling of the Holy Ones assumes that they have returned to the land and have been restored. Here the vision expands this to include the fact that the Temple itself with its continual offerings has been restored as well. The Holy Ones even have their own army over which there is, like in the times before the Exile, a "Captain of the host". In Joshua 5.14, 15 and angelic being is called, "the Captain of the host". The High Priest and priests in general are also called a "Captain" or "Prince."

Lamentations 2.2 states, "He hath not pitied any of the pleasant places of Jacob, He hath broken down in His wrath The fortresses of the daughter of Judah, He hath caused to come to the earth, He polluted the kingdom and its princes" (with other examples of this kind of language) suggests that the "transgression" of the prince, the priest, or the High Priest is at fault. Judah is thrown to the land and her princes. In other words, they are being "given over" yet again to this King (horn) because of transgression. It is as if the Exile is taking place all over again and Nebuchadnezzar is back in town!

*And then I heard one of the Holy Ones speaking, and one of the Holy Ones said to a certain one, "Until when is the vision, the continual offerings, and the transgression, a desolating one set? And holy things and host a trampling place?" And he said to me, "Til evening. Morning. Two thousand and three hundred. Then the holy things will be put right."*

Even though the interpretation has not yet been given, it is becoming clear simply based on the previous vision that Judah is to undergo yet another desolation of sorts due to "the transgression." This is what "the vision" is about. It is an "appointed time" (7.22) – a "time, times, and half a time" (7.25), or here, "twenty three hundred days – mornings and evenings." That is, the "vision" concerns several things to happen within this span of time. The vision concerns the "coming up" of the little horn. Within this time the continual offerings will be "taken away". The host of the Prince will be "at war" (7.21) with this horn. They will be trampled, the holy place will be rearranged until "it is set right" again. Two thousand and three hundred days, if theoretically multiplied by an assumed three hundred and sixty days (a year) equals to a little over six years. It is a nice round number, but gives the general idea.

At some point in time Judah is to be thrown into a war of desolation and profanation of the holy place. There will be even a falling of the host and some of the stars. This will last for a decreed time (for several years). Not good news. Two beast will arise and the second one, the goat, will sprout four more Dominions, which were pictured in chapter seven. Four beasts that come from the four winds of the heavens. Out of these four, a little horn will come and wreak havoc on the saints and their land, and their sanctuary and religious arrangements. This is will last for several years. The sanctuary will be "set right" again.

The word for "set right" is an important term. "Cleansed" in some translations do not capture, I believe, the meaning. The word is often translated in many other places as "justified" or "made righteous." Those who teach the doctrine of "justification" use this very term. However, here, the sanctuary is desecrated. The "arrangement" of the items in the sanctuary is "cast

## Chapter Eight

out". The "foundation" is disturbed. This, again, implies that the Temple is rebuilt. Daniel is seeing this in the "third year of Belshazzar." The Exile is still in force. There is no Temple, no land, and no priesthood. Yet here, there is, and it will be thrown down again. The only "reason" given is "the transgression." Is this saying that when Israel returns, she will once again have to undergo a major catastrophe because of sin and rebellion to God? If I were Daniel I would be appalled. However, the Temple is to be "set aright" again. The period of these events is an "appointed time." It has a beginning and an "end" (as we shall see). I will continue, as I have been doing, to comment and refer back to these visions as the images of Daniel become more and more pronounced. In chapter seven we saw four beasts and a little horn. Here we see two more beasts that precede these four, but the little horn not only "makes war" with the saints, but now is shown to trample the temple as well. Hopefully there is a jubilant outcome! And, there is. The Ancient of the days will take his seat and judge the eight horned beast, particularly the eighth horn that causes this destruction.

*And it was while I saw the vision, I, Daniel, that I sought an understanding, and Behold! One standing before me like an appearance of a distinguished man. And I heard a voice of a man in between Ulai. And he called and said, "Gabriel, make this one understand the appearance!"*

The term I have used in my translation throughout, "strong man" or "mighty man" is found in the Aramaic as it is here. It is the same family of words as "distinguished man", and in the name, Gaberi-El ("Strong man of God"). Thus, as in the court of Nebuchadnezzar and Cyrus, they had "strong men" of their "army" (host), and Daniel himself is a "strong man" or "mighty man." The angel, Gabriel (this is the first time an angel is called by name), appears before Daniel. Most likely he was the one in the fiery furnace, and in the lions' den and the one who was the "watcher" of the King's dream. Perhaps. Nonetheless, these angels look like people. They are the "host" of heaven. They are mirrored in the "host" of Dominions, too. As God in his eternal Dominion has his army, so also Dominions on earth have theirs. However, not only are angels a part of this, but actual human beings who understand and worship the true God are included in this "host". The mirror between the actual material creation (Genesis 1) and the invisible creation (the heavens and their host) all falls under the Dominion of God, and is the Dominion of God. He rules the heavens and the earth.

Typical of Daniel, he seeks further understanding of what he has just seen. In the vision he is still on the banks of the river Ulai, where the ram will storm out against Babylon in just a few short years. This, in turn, will bring about the end of the seventy years of Babylon's power and the rise of Cyrus and the Medes. It is Cyrus who is the named "anointed one" of Isaiah 44.28. It is he that gives the Edict for Israel to return to her own land. Daniel is seeing something here about a ram with two horns and a goat with one horn, out of which four horns come, and one of them is a treacherous disaster. The Temple has been rebuilt. What is the meaning of this?

*So he came beside my standing place, and while he came over I was terrified, and I fell upon my face. And he said to me, "Understand, son of man, concerning time of end, the vision." And while he was speaking to me I fell asleep with my face to the land. And he struck me and set me up upon my standing place. And he said, "Behold! I am going to declare to you that which is in latter part of the indignation, for it concerns an appointed time of end."*

Daniel is beside himself in terror. He is a mere mortal, a son of man. The vision is an entire span of events with a beginning, middle and an "end". The angel is going to declare to him the latter parts of the vision (which, again, means that there is beginning and a middle part). First, however, he tells him the beginning parts.

*"The ram which you saw, owner of the horns, are Kings of Media and Persia. And the shaggy-male goat is a King of Yavan, and the great horn between his eyes is the first King. And being broken, four take their stand in his place; four Kings from a nation will stand, but not in his power. But, in latter part of their Dominion, when the transgressions are full, a King of mighty faces will stand, and he is understanding dissimulations."*

The sameness of the four beasts, who are called "four Kings" in chapter seven (7.17), are also identified here as the four Kings who come out of the "four winds of the heavens" (7.2; 8.8). Now we know to some extent the identification. The Persians and Medes were already well known by Daniel simply by being about the business of the Dominion of Babylon. Their arrival had been already prophesied by the Prophets. That they are a singular Dominion, the Medes and the Persians, is attested to in history. Cyrus was both King of the Medes and the Persians. Several Kings came after him in that Dominion until its well-known fall by the Yavanions, the Ionians, or the Greeks. These were the peoples of the distant western lands and would have been known to Daniel as well, though not as familiar as he would have been with the former.

The time line we have before us spans from the Persian Dominion to the Grecian one, ruled by Alexander the Great (roughly 550-330 B.C.E.). Daniel is seeing this vision in the year 535 or thereabouts which means he is peering down two hundred years into the future. However, Alexander's Dominion (and we are not given this name – Daniel simply sees a "horn" and calls him the "first King" – since the four horns come out of, or are a result of the Grecian Dominion after his death) does not last very long (336-323 B.C.E).

The Greeks battled the Persians for several years, being a disruptive thorn in their side, so to speak. Finally, however, and interestingly enough, Alexander marched in Susa where the Persians fell before him (330 B.C.E.). Alexander dies and this left open the famous Diadochoi (successors), the four Kings in his place. These are the four beasts of chapter seven, and from the monster-beast, one King eventually arises who will wreak havoc in the land of Israel. Daniel will have more to say about him as the vision progresses in detail to the end of the Book.

Again, this last King, the eighth horn of the monster-beast, arises at the "latter part" of the vision. The whole vision concerns the coming shaggy-goat and the four horns that arise. Concentration is focused on the last King, and this is the "latter part" of the vision (the latter time, or end). Thus, it is made clear here that the ram and the coming goat, with the breaking of its horn and the formation of four horns, is the beginning of "the vision", for "at the latter part of their (the four horns) Dominion" tells us this. The single King, the little horn, the eighth horn of the monster-beast erupts and does as he pleases in the latter part of the vision. This is why Daniel seven and eight spend the time they do on this "part". As Daniel is concerned with the fourth beast, and the little horn, so he is concerned here with the little horn

## Chapter Eight

who arises out of the four Kings. It does every injustice to understanding Daniel by not seeing the very clear and obvious comparisons here and that these visions are concerned with one and the same time period.

This also settles the matter that Nebuchadnezzar's dream-image is not at all in focus here, nor are the similarities even apparent. The complete breakdown of comparison between these two visions of Daniel and the King's dream-image in chapter two have yielded only a plethora of mind-numbing theories and special-pleadings concerned with some "four Dominion theory" of Daniel. Daniel, rather, sees far more than Four Dominions! In chapter two we witness the dream-image and its singular collapse. This was the fall of the Babylonian Dominion. During the years of Belshazzar's reign, the last King in Babylon at the time, Daniel saw four Dominions (chapter seven), and then sees two more before these four Dominions spring up (chapter eight). Thus, Babylon falls, and then comes Darius/Cyrus, the Mede and the Persian. They are crushed by a shaggy-goat, the Grecian Empire. From this "nation" (as it is called) four Kings/Dominions arise, and out of one of them comes a King who absolutely wreaks destruction on the land, trampling the remnant, making war with the saints and desecrates the Holy Place. There are no gaps in the future history Daniel is being shown by the hand of God (and we must not forget that the three beasts are given a prolongation after the little horn is destroyed- Daniel is not envisioning an end to history as popularly thought). As we progress, indeed, as Daniel sees the unfolding of these visions, which are becoming somewhat clearer and clearer as they come, we will see that this is how this Book is supposed to be understood.

Another aspect here is that at the latter part of this King's behavior, we are told that "the transgressions" are to be "finished." Daniel is given a "vision". The Holy Place will be "set right" again. Righteousness will come. Again, we ask, are these the transgressions of the people of Israel, the host? Are these the transgressions of the King who will arise?

*"And he will have mighty strength, but the strength is not his. And being surpassing he will ruin. And he will be made to thrive. And he will do. And he will ruin mighty ones and a holy people. And by his cunning also he will make treachery thrive in his hand. And in his heart he will become great. And in ease he will ruin many, and upon a Prince of Princes he will stand, but by cessation of hand, he will be broken."*

This is a long list of an amazing description of this King. The vocabulary here is very important as it is carried through to the end of the Book. The King is described as one having been given this power to do what he does. Daniel has already taught us that it is the God of the heavens that "gives" Dominion to whoever he pleases. He strengthens and empowers them. Thus, the angel is able to even speak where know historian can: this King's heart will be lifted up in himself. The issue, in terms of time, is very far off. One gets the idea here that since this King's arrival is so far off these descriptions (many we have seen used for Nebuchadnezzar) show how God will be directing him to do what he will do. This ruinous destruction of the King has not happened. It is to happen. Whoever this King is, this is how he is going to act simply because this is how God is going to direct him to act. What should come in mind to Daniel is that this ruinous, destructive little horn, the eighth horn of the monster-beast, is being directed against the Holy People! This is usually a sign that God's

## Chapter Eight

wrath is being poured out on his people for their transgressions. It is not a good thing here. I would have been absolutely terrified.

We may also observe the language of the phrase, "and none can stand", which is used of the Ram, and the Goat conquering it. The phrasing is that of total domination. It is not used of the four animals. Rather, they "stand before" the fourth monster-beast. They "remain" after the little horn is killed. These four do not "attack" the Goat, but spring from it, with the little horn attacking the Holy Land. Like chapter seven, the other horns are not said to "fall" before the fourth horn. Likewise, Judea does not "fall", even though it is ruined and attacked. The little horn dies. Judea survives, and the "remains of the animals" (7.12) live on.

*"And appearance of the evening and the morning which was said is true. Now you must shut up the vision, for it concerns many days." And I, Daniel, fell out and was sick for days. And I arose, and I did the King's work. And I was appalled about the appearance, and there was no understanding.*

Exactly. He goes about the business of King Belshazzar's administration, but this vision, and the one previous to it, form the "appearance" ("the vision"). They are directly linked, as one interprets the other and forms an underlying theme: Judgment is coming again upon the Holy People. Daniel is told to "shut up" or "seal" the vision because it concerns "many days" – the idea being that it is "far off" (even though that is not used here). Yet, he is in the third year of the reign of Belshazzar, and the ram is very near the door. Belshazzar is the last King. The ram of "the vision" is coming, but so are the four Dominions, and so is the little horn!

## Chapter Nine

*In the first year of Dareyavesh, son of Achasheverosh, from a seed of a Mede, who was made King over the Dominion of Chaldeans,*

We have already shown the issue involving Darius/Cyrus as King of the Median and Persian Dominion (chapter five and six). Here is some added information. That we know Cyrus was a Mede on his mother's side need not be discussed. That he was called King of the Medes, and that he consolidated the Medes and Persians into a single Dominion is also well attested. "Made King" simply denotes, following Daniel, that God had "given" him the Dominion. He "received" the Dominion (6.1, also in the same way the saints are to "receive the Dominon" in 7.18, that is, "possess the Dominion", 7.18,22, or "given the Dominion" 7.27 – all carry the same connotation). Some may argue that "seed" comes from the male, not the female. Cyrus' mother was a Mede, but his father was a Persian. However, in Genesis 3.15 speaks of the woman's seed (also, Genesis 16.10; 26.40; Leviticus 12.2; Deuteronomy 28.57). Revelation 12.17 also speaks of the woman's "seed".

Here, however, he is defined as a son of Achasheverosh. This is another royal title and not a name. Ezra 4.6 uses this title for Cambyses II, son of Cyrus. Cyrus' father was also named Cambyses, and so we should find no difficulty that Daniel uses the title for his father. That is, "Cyrus, son of Cambyses" is expressed here as, "Darius, son of Ahasheverosh." In the Scriptures we find a few places where seemingly odd names are used. The King of Assyria is called, "Pul" (2 Kings 15.19; I Chronicles 5.26) who is also called, Tellegath-pilneser. Sheshach is another name for the King of Babylon (Jeremiah 25.26; 51.41). Achasheverosh (Ahasuerus), is a title for the Lion Kings, of which Cambyses I was considered. The first part of the title, achash (Khsha, or "King" – from which the modern Iranian, "Shah" has come). The usages of such titles (Artaxerxes, Xerxes, Ahasuerus and even Darius) has caused considerable debate in the Scriptures (particularly with Ezra, Nehemiah, and Esther). It is a debate that I care not to enter into at this time, even though for our understanding lengthy material can be given for support (by very serious and credible scholars). Needless to say, Cyrus, who was sixty-two years of age (6.1), was the son of a Mede on his maternal side was called King of the Medes and Persians, fits the bill.

What I wish to focus on is the arrangement of the material. Chapter five marked the end of the Babylonian Dominion. It was handed over to the Medes and Persians, the ram of chapter eight. Thus, Daniel has arranged the first two visions (seven and eight) as sandwiched between the "first year" of the ram in chapter six and chapter nine. Having been given, then, the fact that during the last years of Babylon, God showed him that the ram is coming, and we now are in the first year of the ram. Daniel, then, knows that the ram will be defeated by the shaggy, male goat (the Ionians – Greeks). He knows that the seventy years are up (as we shall see). He knows that a little horn is coming as well. Belshazzar is gone, and Darius, the ram, is in his first year. This, then, sets the context for understanding all that follows. By placing the first and third year of the last ruler(s) of Babylon (7.1; 8.1) in between the first year of the ram (Persia, 6.1; 9.1) Daniel is letting us know that he is in on the fact that first year of Cyrus, great as that is, will not last. Persia will fall to another, and four will arise out that; and one ruler from those four will ravish the restored-from-exile Holy Land. The first year of Persia (6.1) followed by the last years of Babylon (7.1; 8.1) sets the context for all that is found in chapter nine.

*In the first year of his reign, I, Daniel, understood in the scrolls a number of the years, which was a word of YHWH to Jeremiah the Prophet, to complete as it regards desolations of Jerusalem: seventy years.*

Having seen the two visions and that they, obviously, concern the future after the seventy years have been "filled" (completed), Daniel, writing during the first year of the ram, is seeking understanding of his visions in terms of the what the scrolls say. He turns to Jeremiah. In Jeremiah 25.11,12 we read, "And all this land hath been for a desolation, for an astonishment, and these nations have served the king of Babylon seventy years. And it hath come to pass, at the fulness of seventy years, I charge against the king of Babylon, and against that nation -- an affirmation of Jehovah -- their iniquity, and against the land of the Chaldeans, and have appointed it for desolations age-during." And, in 25.10, "For thus said Jehovah, Surely at the fulness of Babylon -- seventy years -- I inspect you, and have established towards you My good word, to bring you back unto this place." The words here in Jeremiah are found in 9.2 of Daniel; "complete", "desolation". He is reading the scroll.

The seventy years are often regarded as the amount of years of the Exile, and that certainly includes those years. However, Nebuchadnezzar began to deport the Jews around 605 B.C.E. Babylon ended in 539 B.C.E. If we understand that Jeremiah's vision concerned the rise of the Babylonian Dominion, which was around 609 B.C.E., then seventy years is meant to include this as well. The "nations" (not just Jerusalem) will "serve the King for seventy years." It is the "completion of Babylon" – seventy years. Likewise, in 2 Chronicles 36.21, "to fulfil the word of Jehovah in the mouth of Jeremiah, till the land hath enjoyed its sabbaths; all the days of the desolation it kept sabbath -- to the fulness of seventy years." However, as that passage relates, Nebuchadnezzar ravaged the land with at least three series of raids and deportations, the last being the setting of fire to the Temple (589/588 B.C.E.). Then Jerusalem was 'desolate." Daniel hints at this when he uses the same word of desolation, but in the plural, the "desolations of Jerusalem." Obviously, one cannot count seventy years from 589/588 and arrive at seventy years to the first year of Darius (538 B.C.E.)! In the next verse of 2 Chronicles we read, "And in the first year of Cyrus king of Persia, at the completion of the word of Jehovah in the mouth of Jeremiah, hath Jehovah waked up the spirit of Cyrus king of Persia." The same "first year" we find ourselves in Daniel 9.1.

There is no mistake here in that it is not rocket science to count a mere seventy years. Babylon did not rule over Jerusalem for seventy years. The first year of Cyrus is the "completion" of those years, however. Thus, simply counting back seventy years from then (539/538 B.C.E.) we get 609/608 B.C.E., which is when the Babylonian Dominion seriously began to rear its head under Nabopolassar and his son, Nebuchadnezzar. For seventy years God "gave" the Dominion to this realm. In that seventy years, "desolations" were decreed for Jerusalem by the Prophets (as were "desolations" decreed for the surrounding nations of Babylon). Cyrus, however, ends this. It is his "first year." After seeing the event of Daniel's deliverance from the lion's pit, he is stirred up and makes the decree (Ezra 1.1-ff). Daniel, therefore, is writing, most likely, just before this decree is made. He is

## Chapter Nine

searching Jeremiah. Seventy years have been added up and are complete. The fact that Babylon is no more, and the fact that a new King has come, a Mede who is also a Persian signaled to Daniel the "completion" of the seventy years. That meant the end of the "desolations" of Jerusalem as well.

However, Daniel has seen two visions that have revealed another coming "desolation" (8.13). And, according to the Prophet Jeremiah, just after he mentions the seventy years completion, he wrote, that upon the promise of God to restore and rebuild Jerusalem, "For I have known the thoughts that I am thinking towards you -- an affirmation of Jehovah; thoughts of peace, and not of evil, to give to you a latter end and hope" (Jeremiah 29.11). From this Jeremiah launches into a beautiful description of the restoration of Judah and Israel in the terms of a "new covenant" (Jeremiah 31.31, a "renewed covenant") that will not be like the "former covenant" made with their fathers. Thus, we are, and Daniel certainly was, at a loss to explain this glorious future and latter end for Israel after we have just witnessed two horrible and appalling visions! Judah will be made desolate yet again! How can this be a glorious future? Did Jeremiah intend to convey the message that this "new covenant" would begin with the return of the people to the land? In this new covenant, God will "write" his laws "upon the heart" of his people.

*I set my face to Adonai, The God, in order to seek by prayer and supplications, by fasting, and sackcloth and ashes.*

We are at once reminded of the very beginning of the Book, where Adonai, The God handed over Jehoiakim into Nebuchadnezzar's hands. That was in the first year of King Nebuchadnezzar. Having compiled the Book, and having an understanding of all that is to happen to his people, here the Prophet signals a new phase: My Lord (Adonai), the God of the heavens, does as he pleases, according to his own will. It was his will to hand over Judah. It is his pleasure to hand over Babylon. And, it is his pleasure to rule over the Dominions of man as he sees fit, regardless if it "fits" our understanding. Daniel's stories, his key terms and vocabulary are meant to encourage the truly faithful ones, the ones who have "set upon their heart" (Daniel 1.8) upon him. These are the "people" the Dominion is promised. These are the people who must endure through the transgressions and sins (and, thus, punishments) of those who call themselves "his people" yet, in fact, they are not.

*I interceded to YHWH my God, and confessed, and said, "I beseech my Lord (Adonai), the God, the Great One, the One to be Feared, who is keeping the covenant and the loving kindness to the ones loving him and his commandments."*

Acting as a priest, Daniel intercedes for his people. God is a covenant keeping God. He keeps his covenant with those who love him (from the heart) and his commandments (to be written on the heart). It is not the case that all who are Israel are those who fit this description! Rather, because Daniel is praying in his house before his window which faced towards Jerusalem in a foreign land means that Exile has happened. Was it Daniel's and his three companions, or the Prophets like Jeremiah, and the "many", who truly did love the Lord with all their heart that caused Jerusalem's desolation? Hardly. Granted, their numbers were dim in comparison with the majority of Israelites, but it was their majority, and their sins that caused God's hand to move against them. The truly devout paid for it. They suffered as a result. A beautiful and devout follower of the Lord from the heart, Daniel, was exiled from his own land on their behalf. Yet, rather than bitterness, Daniel intercedes for them. Amazing.

*"We have sinned. We have done wrong. We have done wickedly. And we have rebelled and turned aside from your commandments and from your judgments."*

Daniel identifies with his people. He is, after all, one of them. Certainly though, and what strikes us here is that Daniel has been praised for his integrity, not from himself, but from those who he has encountered in the Book. Daniel did not sin, did not do wrong, or act wickedly. He did not rebel and turn aside from the commandments of God. We see, also, a progression of sorts. From sin, to wrong-doing, to wickedness to flat out turning aside and rebelling against what is known: his commandments and judgments. This is a heart condition, and we have a contrast between a heart that has "set upon" itself the Lord's commandments, and those who have not done this. And, the one who has set his heart upon the Lord even demonstrates the loving kindness of the Lord towards his enemies: he prays for them. A heart so transformed by the loving God of the heavens so acts as a one who has loving kindness in his heart. God has set a regenerative covenant in Daniel, and has written his laws in his heart, prefiguring the time when a new covenant would set aside the former made with Moses. Daniel demonstrates that the infilling of the regenerative Spirit was already at work under the "former covenant" of Moses. Moses' covenant did not exclude regeneration, but placed regulations upon those under the Law of Moses. However, in Daniel's case, because of the work of the Spirit upon his heart, Daniel could thrive in covenant faithfulness to God apart from the regulations of Ceremonial laws, the Land, and the Temple cultus. He could faithfully serve God from the heart in a foreign and pagan land. Or, as Ezekiel said, "I have been a sanctuary for them during their time of exile" (Ezekiel 11.16). Daniel is "my people" and God is "his God."

*"And we have not hearkened to your servants the Prophets who have spoken in your name to our Kings, our Princes, and our fathers, and to all the people of the land. To you, my Lord, the righteousness. To us, shame of the face to this very day. To any man of Judah, to dwellers in Jerusalem, to all Israel, those near and those far in all the land you have thrust out of there for their unfaithfulness who were unfaithful at you."*

Daniel does switch from "us" to "them", but designates the whole as "all Israel." Exile was the ultimate form of punishment in the curses of the law. It was one thing to be besieged by a foreign invader, and quite another to be besieged, conquered and exiled. That Daniel does not see in the visions of chapter seven and eight, or mentions any hint of another Exile under the Dominions to come, and particularly the little horn, is significant. The little horn makes war with the saints, but the saints are not exiled, and they are made victorious.

Daniel is aware (and knew) of the few Israelites and Judeans who remained in Jerusalem during the Exile period. Israel, of the northern parts, had been scattered by Assyria (722 B.C.E.). Yet, some of them even remained in Jerusalem (2 Chronicles 34.9 states that a "remnant of Israel", Manasseh, Ephraim, etc. – remained in Jerusalem after the Assyrian deportation; 34.21; 1 Chronicles 9.3). Judah, too, had been scattered in like manner. Yet, the restoration of the "house of Israel and the house of

Judah" occurred when the "remnant" returned (many, if not most Israelites and those from Judah actually remained throughout the regions which came to be known as the Diaspora). Daniel then, sees "all Israel" as those near and those far.

*"YHWH, to us, shame of the face. To our Kings, Our Princes, to our fathers, which we have sinned against you. (To the Lord our God are tender mercies and abundant forgiveness, for we rebelled against him)."*

This last sentence turns toward the reader with the word, "him" (God). As a priest, Daniel is interceding in the very same words of Jeremiah and, mainly, Deuteronomy. Curses have come from the Lord and the only reason is for sin and transgression. Yet, appealing to the covenant, God is a forgiving God, with tender mercy.

*"Neither have we heard YHWH our God's voice, to walk in his laws, which he set before our faces by the hand of his servants the Prophets. And all Israel has passed over your laws and turned aside, and have not heard your voice. The oath and the curse have been poured out upon us which is written in the law of Moses, servant of God because we have sinned against him. So he raised his word which was spoken against us, and against our judges who have judged us. To bring against us great evil which has not been done under all the heavens as that which has been done in Jerusalem. Just as it is written in the law of Moses, all of this evil has come against us. And we have not pacified the face of YHWH our God, to turn from iniquities, to be prudent in your truth. Therefore YHWH watched over the evil and brought it against us, for YHWH our God is righteous concerning all his works which he does. And we have not heard his voice."*

Daniel, in some cases, is verbatim as it concerns the laments of the Prophets, particularly Jeremiah. This is a repetitive invective against the people of Israel. It has a sad tone and feel to it. There are no excuses. There is no justification. Evil has been rendered simply because of rebellion, sin, transgression and dullness. Daniel, near his eighties if not over them, in the first year of Cyrus, is deeply confessing the sin of Israel as his own. He is not supposed to be in Babylon. He was supposed to grow up in the land God had promised, offering worship and praise in the Temple with the Priests (Princes), the King and his people. Because of sin, and only because of sin, has this horrible thing happened.

*"But now, my Lord, our God, who has brought your people from the land of Mizraim (Egypt) with a mighty hand, and made your name to this day, we have sinned. We have acted wickedly. My Lord, according to all your righteousness, turn, I pray, your anger and your fury from your city Jerusalem, your holy mountain. For by our sins and iniquities of our fathers Jerusalem and your people, all around us consider us a disgrace. So now, hearken, our God, to a prayer of your servant, and to my supplication. And cause your face to shine upon your devastated sanctuary for purpose, my Lord. Incline, my God, your ears and hear! Open your eyes and see our desolations and the city by which your name is called. For not for our righteousness do we cause our supplications to fall before your face, but for your great tender mercies."*

Intercession here involves acknowledging sin. Daniel also appeals to the very character of God, the covenant keeper who keeps the covenant when all have abandoned it and broken it, making it of none effect. Daniel is not praying in a temple. He is prostrate before God himself. As a "son of man" (8.17),

## Chapter Nine

Daniel has come before the Ancient of the days. His prayers "fall before the face" of God, before his throne. Not only his, but "we" (emphatic here), the many who serve God still from their hearts, are praying.

The sanctuary in the first year of Cyrus lay devastated. The city was desolate (except for a very few). There is no righteousness within Daniel that he himself can base his supplications upon. All good things come from God. Daniel appeals to God himself, the city he has called by his name. Daniel knows two things here: the Prophets foretold that Jerusalem would be restored and rebuilt. Jeremiah, in fact, used those very words. "This is what the LORD says: '"I will restore the fortunes of Jacob's tents and have compassion on his dwellings; the city will be rebuilt on her ruins, and the palace will stand in its proper place" (Jeremiah 30.18). And, "it shall not be plucked up, and it shall not be destroyed any more forever" (Jeremiah 31.40; which follows exactly the image-dream in chapter two). Second, Daniel knows that in his visions, Jerusalem, the city and the sanctuary will be devastated again. A "desolation" has been seen (chapter eight). Nonetheless, he prays: turn back! Open your eyes! It is a prayer for restoration and realization of the promises made by Jeremiah after "seventy years."

If our analysis is correct, Daniel has seen that Babylon will be destroyed and a rock will be established afterwards. Cyrus the Persian comes and issues the Edict to restore and rebuild. The people, not all of them, return. This answers to the rock. However, Daniel has seen that further events are to take place well after this restoration. What began as a rock must move on to growth in its becoming a mountain. That will require another blow of devastation and another desolation (chapter seven and eight). At the "time" of that "end", God's faithful stars will "receive" a Dominion of their own (7.18). But, history does not end there. Remember, the remains of the "beasts" are allowed to live for a "time and season" that has been "appointed" for them, after the eighth, or little horn is taken out (7.11, 12).

*"My Lord, hear! My Lord, forgive! My Lord, incline! And do without delay! For your own sake, my God! For your name is called upon your city and on your people."*

Daniel appeals to the "people" –the people who have the name upon them – who truly love the Lord and his commandments, who have the law set upon their hearts – and it is to "a people" that the "rock" in chapter two refers, "and it will not be left to another people" (2.44). God will "set" a Dominion when Babylon falls as a mere rock taken "out of" a mountain (the return from Exile). The Dominion, in other words, will be laid as a "foundation" – a "peoples Dominion." The restoration of Israel involves a new covenant establishment. Never before has Jerusalem been ransacked and made desolate, Daniel said. Yet, it remains as it did before the people came under the covenant with Moses; without form, void, desolate and ravished. It is to be rebuilt, restored – but this covenant is "not like the covenant I made with your forefathers" (Jeremiah 31.31). It is a "new thing". A "new beginning" so to speak. A "new people" will be "established" (foundation laid), and this people will grow into a mountain. At a time to come they will "receive" a Dominion on earth of their own, too.

Daniel entreats his God not to "delay." This is so because it often "appears" to us, in our understanding, that God "tarries" and "delays." This is a time word. Daniel is pleading for God to act now! Do not delay! The implication is that God, according to our understanding, does delay. It seems like he takes his merry own time to accomplish his word! And, God can delay if he so wants to (like a King, he does whatsoever he wills, according to his pleasure). It is not as if God reneges entirely on what he promises. It is and will be accomplished. It is that we are facing two different perspectives on the matter: the way man sees it, and the way God sees it. God's ways are not our ways. Jerusalem will be restored and rebuilt. The people will come back to the land. However, there are some other bits and pieces of the matter that need to happen, too. And God has not revealed all of those things. He is running an entire cosmos, every bit and piece, and every cause and causes of causes and their results in order that all things are made to work together. What may not look like something being fulfilled over here is being fulfilled over there so as to bring about the entire fulfillment all around – working it all together.

*And while I continued speaking, and praying, and confessing my sin and sin of my people, Israel, and causing my supplication to fall before the face of YHWH, my God on behalf of the holy mountain of my God – while I was still saying the prayer – even the man Gabriel who I saw in the beginning vision, being wearied in weariness, struck on me around a time of evening offering.*

Daniel is not praying in Jerusalem, nor in a temple. Yet, his regulatory prayer life (three times a day) rotated around temple life. This was Daniel's "evening offering" of prayer (one cannot help but to hear the Apostle Paul in Romans 12.1-ff here). His "sin offering" of prayer through confession, bringing his prayers "before the face of YHWH" directly – in YHWH's dwelling place and temple above- was heard. Gabriel shows up and the vision of the beginning (chapter eight) is directly linked. Gabriel is now going to even further elaborate on that vision – to give more understanding to Daniel, which links all of these visions together. These visions and "appearances" cannot be given in one shot. The sheer exhaustion caused by seeing them could only be handled in intervals of times. The first vision came in Belshazzar's first year. The second came two years later in his third year. This one comes in Cyrus' first year. They are, however, bits and pieces to be added together when all is said and done.

*And he gave understanding and he spoke to me. This is what happened: And he said, "Daniel! Now I have come out to cause you to consider an understanding. At the beginning of your supplications a word went out, and I have come to declare it because you are precious! Now understand in the word! And give understanding in this appearance."*

The first sentence is a summary of what Gabriel did. He "gave understanding" to Daniel by what he said. The second sentence, then, is what he gave, commanding Daniel to "understand" and "give understanding" to this appearance of Gabriel (Gabriel is himself the "appearance"). This word, "appearance" has occurred many times in Daniel. The four boys were striking in "appearance" (1.4, 13, 15); in 8.15 Daniel sees the "appearance" of a "mighty one"; he is to "understand the appearance" (8.16) – the reason the angel came –to make him understand the reason for the appearance; the "appearance" of the angel who announced the number of evening and mornings (8.26); Daniel was astonished at their appearance, that is, the announcement of they who appeared to make the announcement (8.27). Likewise, here, Daniel is told that while he was praying, causing his supplications to "fall before the face of YHWH" – his throne – Gabriel was "sent out" with a "word" from the throne! May we not see here that God hears our cries, and responds to them by sending out those armies, his host, our angels to accomplish what we ask for: thy will be done! And, yet, may we not also see that it is indeed a rare thing, hardly ever, are we placed in such a way that the angel that has our "answer" appears to us telling us this! May we not believe the Scripture, however, of the one who has, Daniel? We have been peering into the Dominion of God, the God of the heavens for a reason. If all of this is going on, if God is the King of all the land, the heavens and all therein, and does as he pleases, and none can stop what he has decreed, though he may delay (as we understand "delay"), what possible worry can we have?

*"Seven Seventies have been determined upon your people and upon your holy city in order to bring to end the Transgression."*

It is wise to take these items one at a time since so much ink has been spilled concerning their meaning. Since we are reading the words of Gabriel, the man of the vision (chapter eight), we note first that a period of time is determined: seventy periods of sevens. Are these consecutive periods? Do they run concurrently? We are simple not told. The total, of one multiplies seven times seventy, is four hundred and ninety. However, we are not told anything concerning how these periods fall out in terms of actual time (linear, successive time). Like Nebuchadnezzar's "seven times", it is clear from that text (chapter four) that seven "years" is nowhere meant, but is added by interpreters. Likewise, we must be extremely cautious here not to make any insights into this matter without first consulting the texts of Daniel itself; the immediate context.

These seventy-sevens are no doubt coined as a term so as to be tied to the "seventy years" (where "years" are specifically mentioned) of Jeremiah (Daniel 9.2). Jeremiah uttered "seventy years" – Gabriel utters, "seventy sevens". Daniel has lamented in his prayers with the terms of the "law of Moses" and the "Prophets". In Leviticus 26.18-46, the curses of the covenant, the Lord will punish Israel "seven times" for her "iniquities" and "sins." Seventy years of Jeremiah times "seven" is the idea here. To "fill up" sin, and to complete the transgression. However, in Leviticus, God never so utterly leaves Israel, his people (Leviticus 26.44). We must continue on to see if any other details are added.

One 'purpose' for this determination is so that (infinitive of purpose in Hebrew) "the transgression is finished." Since "the" is used, we must ask, "what" transgression? We are not long for an answer, for Gabriel has already announced in a vision, "the transgression": *"And a host was given in addition to the continual because of transgression" (8.12); "Until when is the vision, the continual offerings, and the transgression, a desolating one set? And holy things and host a trampling place?" (8.13); "But, in latter part of their Dominion, when the transgressions are full, a King of mighty faces will stand, and he is understanding riddles" (8.23).*

This last passage lets us know that "the transgressions" are to be "finished" in the latter part of the Dominions of the four horns, particularly the little horn who tramples, "your people and your holy city." There should be absolutely no doubt whatsoever that "the transgression" here is the exact same in chapter eight, given by the exact same angel, Gabriel. To deny this is to render all rational attempts of contextualizing Daniel's own words pointless and arbitrary. Thus, one of the reasons for determining seventy-sevens is "to finish the transgression" mentioned in chapter eight. When "the transgressions" (the transgressions that

Chapter Nine

are being committed) have reached their "fullness" places the seventy-sevens into the future. Since they concern that period of time when the little horn is raging against the land "on account of the transgression", then they reach far from the time of the fulfillment of Jeremiah's seventy years. His seventy years are to be included in the "seventy" sevens – his is but one "seventy" within the seventy-sevens, but there is more, the angels says, to come (he has already revealed that in chapter eight).

*"And to fill that concerning sin."*

Again, we are taken to the very same vision in chapter eight (8.23). Daniel was confessing the "sin" of his people which resulted in their punishment and Exile. This sin of "my people" and its resulting desolations of "my city", the punishment of God, still lingers over them after the seventy years ("seven times" in Leviticus, quoted above). Although they return as a remnant, and God fulfills the "word of YHWH spoken by Jeremiah the Prophet", all is not peachy. They are not regathered at that time so as to gain independency as they had under David and Solomon. Like Canaan, Abraham was told that Israel would not possess the land until four hundred years, "when the iniquity of the Amorites are filled" (Genesis 15.13-16). The "fullness of sin" concerning Israel and Judah reached their own as well, which led to their Exile. Their "punishment" is relieved in the return to the land. Jeremiah wrote, "The punishment of your sin is filled, daughter of Zion; he will no more carry you away into captivity" (Lamentations 4.22). "Return us to yourself, YHWH, that we may be returned! Renew our days as of old" (Lamentations 5.21). However, the Exile, as a punishment, is not an en masse return. Most stay in the dispersed regions. Israel is not returned, as

Daniel prayed, "because of our righteousness". They are allowed a return and a re-start, as it were. However, from the Exile on, Israel is never recovered as they were in the days of David and Solomon, and this must be kept in mind. According to Haggai and Zechariah, Israel is still under a curse (Haggai 1.10; compare with Leviticus 26.20-22; Deuteronomy 28.38). What Daniel foresees is a rule of foreign nations over Israel – a curse according to the Law. However, there is a remnant – those like Daniel, who have set upon their heart (New Covenant) and have the law written in their heart. It is this "rock" of people that return. It is this rock of faithful people "who love YHWH and keep his commandments" as Daniel notes. These are the ones to keep our eye on.

*"And to make atonement for iniquity."*

This phrase, "to atone" carries with it the image of the Temple. "And I have given the Levites as a gift to Aaron and his sons from among the people of Israel, to do the service for the people of Israel at the tent of meeting and to make atonement for the people of Israel" (Numbers 8.19); "But Aaron and his sons made offerings on the altar of burnt offering and on the altar of incense for all the work of the Most Holy Place, and to make atonement for Israel" (1 Chronicles 6.34), and so forth. The act of making atonement assumes a Temple by which to accomplish this. Israel has been without a Temple and its priesthood functions for seventy years (and longer, actually, because the priests before the Exile were wicked. King Hezekiah and King Josiah led the last, true reforms). Seventy-sevens have been decreed to fill up the transgression of the people, fill up the sin of the people, and to provide for atonement in a rebuilt Temple and organized priesthood.

Chapter Nine

*"To bring in righteousness of ages."*

Daniel has used this term, "righteousness" throughout his prayer to God. God is "righteous", the people are "unrighteous" (without righteousness, are not righteous). The temple, after its desecration by the little horn (and the people themselves), is to be made "righteous" or "set right" (8.14). Some translations have "everlasting righteousness", but what is here is that a righteousness will be "brought in" and established for a long duration. If the people are "without righteousness" and to blame for the Exile, to bring in and establish "righteousness" among the people would be to order them accordingly.

The verb, "to bring in" may also refer to the initial "setting up" of the Temple after the collapse of Babylon (chapter two) imaged in the "rock." Psalm 145.13 states, "Your Dominion is of ages Dominion, and your rule endures throughout all generations." Then the psalmist writes, "YHWH is righteous in all his ways and kind in all his works" (145.17). We have noted these attributes of God's Dominion throughout Daniel already. God will establish a "righteous" Dominion (not his, but one given by him), or "bring in" a righteousness that, like his, is "everlasting" or "ages" in duration (speaking in temporal aspects). Daniel, as we have elaborated elsewhere, sees the Dominion of God as over all the Dominions of man. He gives to each King his Dominion. He can take it away, too. His Dominion is not limited to risings and fallings. It is from generation to generation. It is not "set up" and it does not "grow." However, he has shown that a "rock" is coming, when he will "set up" a Dominion after the Exile (seventy years). Thus, during the times of these seventy-sevens he will "bring in righteousness."

If we follow this line of reasoning, Isaiah 41.2 speaks of Cyrus, who "from the east" is "called in righteousness". 41.3 sounds exactly like Daniel, "He hands over nations over to him and subdues Kings before him…he turns them to windblown chaff with his bow" – the collapse of Babylon is made into windblown chaff and swept away (Daniel 2.35). Again, in Isaiah 45, where Cyrus is mentioned by name (45.1), when he comes, "righteousness" will rain down from heaven and "grow" (45.8). Further, "I will raise up Cyrus in my righteousness" (45.13). "He will rebuild my city and set my exiles free" (45.13). This appears, then, to refer to the bringing in of the Exiles back to their land, to establish them in "righteousness", to atone for their sins. God does not bring his people back in unrighteousness, but, as Daniel has pleaded, "because you are righteous". His righteousness is "everlasting." By keeping these items within the prayer of Daniel (for they "concern your people and your city"), we shouldn't be far off from their meanings.

*"To fill vision and Prophet"*

The idea here is not to "seal up", but to "fulfill" (as Septuagint has it). Something that is "sealed" (and this is a different word than we find in Daniel 8.26, where he is told to "shut up" the words of the vision) is made complete, fulfilled. Some have "confirm" and others have "ratify" here. We are entirely to understand that the "vision(s)" meant here are those given to Daniel. However, not just his visions, but also the Prophet, which can only be Jeremiah. Jeremiah, "the Prophet" (9.2) has already been referenced and is the basis for Daniel's prayer: the fulfillment of word of YHWH given to the Prophet, Jeremiah. It is a mistake to understand here that "cessation" is meant. That is, that

# Chapter Nine

"prophecy" ends, as well as vision. It is also a mistake to translate the word as "prophecy", although that is included in what a Prophet does; he prophesies, gives prophecy. Daniel's visions will take place and be filled. Jeremiah's prophecy concerning the return will be fulfilled. The seventy years have come to their end (even though, for Daniel, the Edict of Cyrus has not been made – it was made in his "first year", however).

*"To anoint holy of holies."*

Another way to translate this is "most holy". The utensils in the Tabernacles were anointed and "most holy"; as were the sons of Aaron; the Tabernacle itself is "most holy." The sacrifices are "most holy" – and so this can mean anything associated with the Temple consecrations. It can also mean, as in Exodus 26.33, the "holy of holies", the inner sanctuary apart from the "holy place." Daniel has already mentioned this word in 8.14, where after the little horn desecrates the "sanctuary" it will be "made right" afterwards. Thus, after the Exile, the remnant did return and anoint the rebuilt sanctuary. Or, it may refer to the anointing after the desolation of the little horn. Either way, we will have to see if any further information is given. Gabriel's words are not over.

*"Now know and give attention: from a going out of a word to return and to rebuild Jerusalem to an anointed Prince are seven sevens."*

The "word" that has gone out, like we find with Nebuchadenezzar's word that "went out" from him in chapter two, is an utterance declaring that the people will "return", and the city of Jerusalem will be "rebuilt." Two things, then, are in this "word." First, the Exiled are to return to the land after the seventy years according to the "word of YHWH given to the Prophet, Jeremiah" (9.2). Second, Jeremiah also uttered that the Temple would be "rebuilt". This is when the word of the Prophet had been issued or "went out." "From" that issuance until an anointed Prince comes will be "seven sevens". This gives us, if we multiply seven times seven, forty-nine. This is the first "period of time" so to speak. They are divided times or intervals. If one takes this "anointed Prince" (as he is called an "anointed one" in Isaiah 45.1) as Cyrus, and Daniel is writing in his first year (538 B.C.E.) and subtract forty nine years, we arrive at the time of 587 B.C.E., the year the Temple was destroyed with fire and the final phase of the Exile implemented. Jeremiah spoke of the seventy years (which had already begun, 25.11) in that very time (Jeremiah 29.10-ff, and that God would "return" them).

It is not at all difficult, then, to see that Cyrus is the one intended here. Jeremiah wrote of this time, "The punishment of your iniquity is filled, daughter of Zion; he will no more carry thee away into captivity" (Lamentations 4.22). Yet, if we start "from" the issuance of Jeremiah which was 605/604 B.C.E. (according to Jeremiah 25.1) then we come to the early rise of Cyrus. He was King of Aswan in 559 when his father, Cambyses I died, and by revolt in 554-553 was rebelling against the Medes. In 550 B.C.E. he was the crown of Persia. The anointed Prince (which can also mean "King" in Hebrew) had come. Daniel would have known about him without doubt (news would have traveled about such a King since Media and Persia were border lands to Babylonia). Nabonidus actually allied himself briefly with others against him to no avail.

A popular view is to start the count from Artaxerxes found in either Nehemiah 2.1-8, or in Ezra 7.11-26. This, of course, is an attempt to bring us to the time of Jesus Christ. The problem, as most textual scholars point out, is that none of these "decrees" was an issue to "return (from the Exile) and rebuild." They are decrees to resume building, and the people were already returned from Exile well before 444 B.C.E. The decree is determined "in order to return the people in Exile, and to start the campaign to rebuild." It was not a decree to "resume building", which is all that Artaxerxes decreed. Cyrus' decree alone fits the bill.

*"And (from the time of the issuance of the decree) sevens, sixty and two, it will have been returned and it will have been rebuilt, a broad space and marked areas, but during tribulation of these times."*

The city will be returned to its people and rebuilt with marked out open quarters. This, of course, will take several years to accomplish, and we find this rebuilding taking place in the Books of Ezra and Nehemiah (and Haggai and Zechariah). If we compute the time here the same way above we come out with four hundred and thirty four years (if years are meant). Assuming years are meant, if we count from the "issuance" of Jeremiah, in 605 B.C.E. (Jeremiah 25.1, 11), the first year of King Nebuchadnezzar, marking the first phase of the seventy years, we come to 171 B.C.E. This is the second period of time given. Thus, "from" the issuance of Jeremiah, these two periods of "the times" (plural with the article, indicating that they are two periods of times) are to be counted. "From" the time when Jeremiah gave the word (605/604 B.C.E.), there are seven sevens ("determining" the coming of the anointed Prince, the ram in chapter eight), and sixty two sevens (determining the returning, and rebuilding of the city of Jerusalem). This last and longest "time" covers the vision of the ram (Medes/Persians), the shaggy male goat (Ionians/Greeks) and the four horns (four beasts) of chapter eight.

We base this on the word, "from". This last period will be peppered with "tribulation". There will be ups (the city and temple will be rebuilt) and downs (there are nations over Israel vying for power in her front yard).

*"And after the sevens, the sixty and two (of them), an anointed one will be cut off, and there is nothing left to him. And the city and the holy place will be ruined. A people of a Prince (the one who is coming in), and they end in the flood. But until their end, there is war, determinings, desolations."*

This "anointed one" cannot be the same as the first one. In fact, one is called, "an anointed prince" and this one is called, simply, "an anointed one". The King, a Prince, a priest, a High Priest, a Prophet and others in the Bible are called, "anointed ones." Whoever it is, and perhaps later information will surface, he is an anointed one. We may add that it is someone who, like Cyrus, is legitimately anointed in accordance with "righteousness." The words "cut off and left nothing" simply means that he is killed, banished, and has no continuation.

The city and the holy place will be ruined, and this takes us to the vision in chapter eight (8.24,25) where the little horn "ruins" the city and sanctuary. The city and the sanctuary are ruined after the period of sixty two sevens have reached their terminus in time so that we have an arrival after this period of a Prince and people for one seven. There is no "break" here. From the issuance of the word of the Lord to Jeremiah two counts of sevens are made: 49, and 62. After the 62, 7 starts immediately.

A people in league with the Prince, who is marked out with the articular participle ("the one who is coming in"), is different from "anointed Prince" already mentioned. That is clear from the text. The span of time (four hundred and thirty four years) alone lets us know this. "Its" end (the sanctuary, and the city) will come in like a flood. Until its end, wars will occur. These things are "determined." Desolations (plural) will happen (chapter eight). All of this material confirms the visions seen in chapters seven and eight. They are consistent and referring to the same periods of time, using the very same vocabulary and directly linked to Gabriel.

Like the vision in chapter eight, Daniel sees the ram (Cyrus) down to the little horn, the Prince, "the one who is coming in" to "ruin" and bring "desolations" to the city and sanctuary. This spans a time of four hundred and thirty four years. If we simply followed Daniel, we can locate the rise of the Medes and Persians. We know that the distant westerners known as the Ionians (Javanites), the Greeks defeated, eventually, this Dominion. We know, anyone can see, that four Dominions arose out of the "shaggy male goat" Dominion. And we know, for it is very well documented, that one "little horn" began a ravaging campaign against the city and the sanctuary exactly around –"from" the time from the utterance of Jeremiah – to here, 171/170 B.C.E. Who was this little horn? Antiochus IV, "Epiphanes" ("God Manifest"). He was a co-regent in 175, but became sole King in 170, and for one week (170-163 B.C.E.) ruled Judea.

Now, it is easy at this point to simply read what is recorded in history (and ancient history here is not a nice, neat pretty little package. The debates over chronologies, reports, texts, ancient historians, etc., are all over the place, but in the main there is a general consensus of sorts). That is, read the history of the people of Israel, add in the timeline and read that back into Daniel. We know these things after the facts. However, Daniel's language is not so specific. He knew and saw the rise of the Medes and

## Daniel Unplugged

Persians. He calls the "Greeks" by their ancient, Hebrew name, "Javan." A few hundred years go by (with no details at all because Daniel is not given any specific names of who these four Dominions will be. Unlike the Greeks and Persians, who would have been known by Daniel, these four future empires are vague and are not identified with any specific ethnic nomenclature) until a unique period of Israel's time, when a destructive Prince comes. An anointed one will be cut off. The city and sanctuary will be ruined, and for a time there will be wars fought in the holy land (all documented in Daniel 11). It is a brief time considering the span of the hundreds of years that have past before it from Daniel's day.

For those who believe in the God of Daniel, Daniel's God, these things have been determined; he can make them happen just as he tells Daniel they will, for he "does whatsoever he pleases in the heavens and over the realms of men." Thus, we have a witness of events to happen, and Behold! They happened! Our task is to discover if Daniel's visions can be "seen" in recorded history. They can. It is not that hard. From a theological standpoint, are these events caused by God, or are they simply seen ahead by God? If we follow Daniel, he "causes" them – for that he how he can reveal them beforehand to his servants, the Prophets. He moves the host of heavens to bring about his "purpose" over the affairs of man.

*"And he shall make the covenant difficult to the many, one seven. And in midst of the seven he will cause to cease sacrifice and offerings. And over a corner of, abominations, he makes desolation – until completion. And that which is determined is poured out on a desolating."*

The "he" that shall make the covenant difficult is the masculine referent, "the Prince, the one who is coming", the one who makes desolate. It is the little horn of chapters seven and eight and no one else. He shall cause the covenant of the people to be difficult; exert strength in a bad way ("the many" are presumably Israel, since the vision concerns them all throughout). The "covenant" is not something he enacts, for the sense is that the covenant is already in place. Throughout Daniel, "covenant" is always the "holy covenant" of God and Israel. It would be out of keeping if the meaning here is not understood as such. Some think that the "he" here is someone who "cuts" a covenant, or "makes" a covenant. But the verb here is never used for such an idea. The covenant is something being acted upon, something already in existence that is being strained, or is made to be a source of difficulty.

This will occur during, or for a short duration, "a half part" of "the seven." This does not mean "in the middle", but the "half part". Thus, "within" this seven. Within this seven period (seven years) he will also cause the continual offering and sacrifice (the daily offerings in the temple) to cease. This last period corresponds, then, to the twenty-three hundred "evening and mornings" (sacrifices) of chapter eight. It is the "latter time" or "time of an end." It is the most brutal point, focused on the fourth, eight-horned beast (chapter seven) and the little horn (chapter seven and eight). By coming in and ruining the holy city, stopping the holy sacrifice, great distress is placed upon the people who serve their God and obey his commands according to the covenant of Moses. They are stopped from doing so by this Prince. He will exert power over the holy covenant.

Basically, then, what we have here is added information as to the length of time all these visions take place. In chapter seven we are given no real time statements. In chapter eight we are given a period of twenty three hundred days, which numbers over six years into a seventh year. Here, however, we are given three sets of times that span from the rise of the ram ("the anointed Prince") down to the "the Prince, the one who is coming" who desolates the sanctuary and ruins the rebuilt city. "One seven" then, is a "time", "times" and here "half" a time from chapter seven. Daniel is given other "time" statements at the end of the Book, but we will consider them at that point. They all comport to this "one seven" time, however, that arrives "after" a considerable period of time (four hundred and thirty four years).

From what we can gather, then, from these three chapters, putting them all together, is that a ram has come (the Medes and the Persians). The seventy years has ended. Israel is regathered from the Exile and many return to the land. There they immediately began to "rebuild" the city and, mainly, the temple (Ezra-Nehemiah). Their sin is atoned for. The holy place is anointed. The Zadokite Priests and High Priests are restored. There is unrest and bumps in the road from surrounding districts in the Persian Empire, and from a Persian King (Artaxerxes, or Smerdis, an usurper, in Ezra 4.6). However, in the second year of Darius, after a lapse (Haggai, Zechariah), the temple is finally made complete. The walls are rebuilt well into the Persian Dominion (Israel is a vassal state, not an independent nation, and they have no King of their own).

Under the rise and rule of the Greeks, Alexander the Great, there is no real turmoil (and we have very little history at this point concerning the Jews). However, Alexander dies (quite young) and his Dominion is parceled out among rulers, four in particular (this material is covered greatly in chapter eleven). For a time under these Dominions, Israel is left to herself and occasions political disturbances here and there, but still under the rule of foreign Dominions. She is not her own. Her transgression is

## Chapter Nine

filling up, and several generations later of those who originally returned are deserting the covenant.

Then, seemingly out of nowhere, a great disturbance occurs. One named Antiochus IV (he calls himself that) comes to rule over the massive Seleucid Dominion (larger than the other three). For reasons that historians debate to this day, he turns severely against Israel and wages a fearsome campaign, and for a few years is triumphant. He stops the sacrifices. The daily offerings cease. The Books of 1 and 2 Maccabees surveys this period of time and records those years. Reading Daniel, looking forward from his standpoint, and being able to read back from the historical record, it cannot be more plain as to what this Prophet foresaw in the ninth century B.C.E. He is not counting down the days to the end of world history (he never says this). It is my contention that the Jews understood most of this, and that the events of the Awful King, Antiochus IV, were behind them. The Temple was not destroyed (Daniel does not say that it will be destroyed, either, but "ruined"). The sanctuary was "set right" again after its desecration. And, independency was regained – Israel had their Dominion given back to them as in the days of old (with a standing army), thus Daniel was not counting down to the destruction of Jerusalem in 70 C.E. under the Romans. For a time they had independence, but still no Davidic King.

The events that came from these decreed times, however, sets the stage for the entrance of one Jesus, bar-Joseph, bar-Miriam, of Galilee, born in Bethlehem, the Nazarene. If our interpretation of Daniel is correct, the words of Jesus towards the then standing Temple and its religion take on a much different light. These were in their minds an established People, with an established King (Herod, and Caesar) and Priestly caste. God had triumphed over the invaders, and will triumph again over the

Romans. The Exile was over, and Daniel mentions nothing about another one coming. Daniel's prophecy was fulfilled. The People triumphed. Thus, when Jesus says to them, "your house is left desolate" one can only imagine the insolence that brought. Jesus was a troublemaker. He could not be the Messiah!

The fact that Jewish interpretation has, in some quarters, seen 70 C.E. as a "fulfillment" of Daniel after the fact is telling. It is very difficult to find predictions of Jerusalem's demise on their own without Daniel being used. That is, it was acknowledged that Antiochus IV certainly "fulfilled" the visions, but that this was only a forerunner of the much greater tribulation to come. Every Jew worth his salt knew of the Maccabean Revolt and its success, and the Festival of Lights (Hannukah) arose from it (John 10.22). The Pharisees, however, certainly did not envision a coming catastrophe to the Herodian Temple. They were in progress of building it during the time of Jesus. Daniel was largely fulfilled in their understanding. They, unlike other schools of thought, did not see any "double fulfillment" of Daniel, and neither did Jesus. Thus, when Jesus speaks of a coming demise of the Temple, it would have sent shock waves through the City. We will continue to explore this as we move along.

# Chapter Ten

*In the third year of Cyrus, King of Persia, a word was revealed to Daniel (who was formerly called, Belteshazzar). Now, the word is true, and a mighty host. And he discerned the word, and understanding came to him in the appearance.*

What began as the "first year of Darius" is now the "third year of Cyrus." Likewise, chapter seven is the "first year of Belshazzar" and chapter eight is the "third year of Belshazzar" – same King. Since the names Darius and Cyrus are the same person, one can see the obvious parallel of their first and third years. It would be quite odd to speak of a virtually unknown King in his first year, followed by a known King is his third.

Daniel is no longer called "Belteshazzar" (past tense is used here). It has been three years since he was called that name, the last year of Belshazzar, when Darius, who never referred to Daniel except by his proper name, took over in chapter six. It is, I believe, another indication of the cryptic play on Darius' name. Daniel was called Belteshazzar and Cyrus was called Darius. However, in the third year, Cyrus is called by his universal name, and so is Daniel (who used to go by another name). Why would Daniel place this descriptive addition of his former name in the third year of Cyrus? He does so because he no longer uses "Darius", but "Cyrus" and adding, "Belteshazzar" indicates what Daniel's name used to be, and using "Cyrus" instead of what he used to be called by Daniel, "Dari-vash." Name change.

The "word" is revealed to Daniel and it is of a "great host". A "host" is an army(ies) of the Lord, or of nations. His "word" that was "revealed" is of a "great host" – a vision of massive armies (chapter eleven). It appears that this may be written by an added hand for the pronoun, "he" is used. We must not think that Daniel spent his entire career in that Province without aids and faithful servants. In the next verse, however, it switches back to "I" in the first person.

*"In those days, I, Daniel, was mourning three sevens of days."*

This phrasing of "three weeks (sevens) of days" shows how Daniel qualifies the word "seven". In chapter four, Nebuchadnezzar was under "seven times" (unspecified). In Daniel nine, there are "seven" seventies – unspecified (though most understand "years" simply from the context). It is on the last of the seven "times" that Nebuchadnezzar confesses his weakness. It is in the last "seven" that major atrocities occur.

*"I did not eat desirable bread, or meat, or wine did not enter my mouth, or anoint myself. I did not anoint myself until the three sevens of days were complete."*

Why Daniel is in this state we are not told. However, it has been offered that being in the third year of Cyrus, well after he has given his Edict to return to the land of Israel (his first year), the setting up of the Dominion has not occurred as he had thought. However, I find this a bit odd. Daniel knows that coming Dominions are on the horizon. He knows that he has seen a coming "abomination of many desolations." It may be that "in those days" (the third year of Cyrus) his mourning was connected to the regathering (which he would have been witness to). He may have witnessed the many pack up and head off to the Promised Land. But, many stayed. Rather, having seen what is ahead

Chapter Ten

for his people and his city, and the fact that a coming catastrophe is determined, the joy and happiness of those who were returning is not shared by Daniel entirely. It is a lonely place for Daniel, knowing what he does. He is fasting (as in chapter nine) and in deep prayer. He is in lamentation.

*"On the twenty and fourth day of the first month, I was upon the hand of the great river that is Hiddekel."*

The old word, "tig" means "sharp". The Tigris was fast flowing, swift, sharp. Hidekkel means, "rapid river". It ran with the Euphrates (40 miles apart). Nisan/Abib (March-April) in the Hebrew calendar was the month of Passover. If Daniel fasted for three sevens, he began on the third day of Nisan. However, he is not celebrating the Passover (and hasn't for the whole time he was there in the Exile). It may also be that Daniel began his fast on the first day of the month, lasting until the twenty first day (Passover on the 14th, and Unleavened Bread ended on the 21st). Prayer and devotion replace the ceremonial (New Covenant ideas). On the twenty fourth day he has eaten and is out and about his affairs. He did not eat "desirable bread" but may have eaten "bread of affliction" (Deuteronomy 16.3).

*"And I lifted up my eyes and I saw, Behold! One man having been clothed in white linen and his loins girded in fine gold. His body was like beryl, his face like an appearance of lightning. And his eyes were like torches of fire. And his arms and his feet like a sight of burnished brass. And voice of his words like a voice of great rumblings. And I, Daniel, only saw the appearance. The men who were with me did not see the appearance. Truly, a great trembling fell upon them and they fled and hid. And I was left alone. And I saw this great appearance,*

*and there was no strength left in me, even my splendor turned from me to ruin. And my strength was not retained.*

Daniel uses a few words to denote certain things that he has seen. Here, in connection with angelic beings, he often employs "appearance". It is an actual being, an actual appearance. He is using earthly terms to describe the indescribable. He is literally, physically, emotionally overwhelmed and overpowered by the appearance. The men with him (assistants) heard the sound of what sounded like a thunder collapse. They fled and hid, but Daniel remained looking at this heavenly being. It opens the reader to what is going to be announced. We are dealing with heavenly powers here that rarely show up, if ever, in the life of an ordinary believer. These are powers that are of the invisible Dominion of God. They are very real. If in any common church service God would open our eyes to give a glimpse of what is also there in attendance, I do not believe that we would be able to retain our strength, either. It is one thing to have an encouragement in these stories that God saves from burning flames, or from the lion's pit. Those are miraculous accommodations that the vast population of believers do not experience. Daniel does not often experience them, either.

Most of Daniel's life is spent going about the business of the King – ordinary and mundane. His whole span of life (here in his late seventies, early eighties) only has three visions, two interpretations to dreams and one miraculous deliverance from the lions. What did he do for the rest of those years in between? He lived a life of faithfulness. He prayed regularly (three times) a day. He served the Lord while living in the world of "appearances", but emboldened by a life that has "seen" the invisible. I have not seen it. I have never had such experiences or visions.

## Chapter Ten

Yet, I am reading the account of one who has. And I believe this account. My experiences or lack thereof do not nullify the facts of the invisible Dominion of God. Nor am I to be discouraged because I have no such miraculous deliverances. How many times have I even known of those rescues from danger, accidents, tragedies that could have occurred were it not for a being directing them otherwise?

*I heard voice of his words, and when I heard voice of his word sleep came over my face, and my face was on dirt. And Behold! A hand struck me and shook me upon my feet and palms of my hands. And he said to me, "Daniel, precious man, understand about the words which I speak to you. Now stand upon your place for now I have been sent to you." And when he spoke with me this word, I stood trembling. And he said to me, "Do not be afraid, Daniel, for from the first day that you set your heart to understand and to humble yourself before the face of your God your words have been heard. And I have come to you because of your words."*

The "first day" that Daniel set his heart upon understanding of his visions and humbled himself refers to the "three weeks". That is, Daniel, in spite of what he has seen and recorded in his visions, is still troubled by them and was seeking from the God further understanding. He is still trying to understand what 'the word' of the vision and "appearances" mean. Thus, this mighty angel has been sent.

*"But, a Prince of the Dominion of Persia was standing opposite of me twenty and one day. Behold! Michael, one of the Princes of the Leaders came to help me. And I remained there beside the Kings of Persia."*

That is, for three weeks the angel contested with the "Prince of the Dominion of Persia." It is at this point we are being revealed something entirely out of the ordinary. Although, as we have seen, many functions of the King's court mirror the invisible Dominion of God, here we are being told that these Dominions of man have over them invisible "principalities" and "powers" of their own. That Cyrus is the current visible King there is no doubt. However, over him is a Prince. They, too, have been placed there by the hand of God and this angel has to contest with these beings – but God's will is accomplished. The Prince of Persia is not at all to be thought of as a being that is friendly to Persia. It was God's will to "set up" Cyrus as King, and as we shall see, set up others as Kings. There was considerable infighting after Cyrus died (530 B.C.E. – just five years from the time of this chapter). His son, Cambyses II came to power with his brother, Smerdis (who was appointed as a Satrap), to follow. There are varying accounts here, but it appears that Cambyses killed his brother (or, Darius I killed him), but an imposter named Gautama ruled in his stead (who was certainly killed by Darius I). Either way, there was considerable turmoil within the Dynasty. The mighty angel, however, stands with the future appointed "Kings" – appointed by God according to the "writing of the truth" as we shall see.

*"And I have come to make you understand that which is to befall your people in the latter days, for a continuance of vision concerning the days."*

Daniel has been shown two visions (chapter seven and eight) and each vision is an enlargement upon the other. This demonstrates our thesis throughout that these visions are of one thread.

## Chapter Ten

Chapter seven was simply of four Dominions. Chapter eight elaborates on the four Dominions that come after the shaggy male goat (Greece). Out of them comes a little horn (both in seven and eight). In chapter nine Daniel is told that Jeremiah's seventy years is not the whole of the "times of distress" as it concerns the sin of Israel and her Exile. They will return, and the city and temple will be built. However, "seventy-sevens" expand the time of Israel's misfortunes, culminating in the rise of a Prince who is to come. He will desecrate the sanctuary. An anointed one will be "cut off" and left with nothing. Abominations will occur. In the following, final "words" of revelation, more details are coming that tie in all these visions together (10-12). As such, we will begin to make a detailed sketch as to what the previous visions meant, for they are explained, finally, for Daniel.

However, Daniel has also been told that a small beginning of a Dominion will be "set up" after the fall of Babylon (chapter two). This will be like a "rock" from a mountain that will grow to become a mountain itself. In chapter seven the saints will be trampled upon, hardly left with anything, but will "receive" and "possess" in those days a Dominion of their own. Yet, in chapter eight some of the "people" of Israel are not at all "saints"! Many that return to the land after the Exile are not all "saints" either. The idea here is one of growth (Jesus' parable of the Mustard Seed explains the "secrets of the Dominion of God"). Israel is a vineyard (Isaiah 5.1-ff). Daniel has singled out those who belong to the Lord as ones who love him and love his commandments – who, like him, have them written in their hearts.

The phrase, "the latter days" are linked to the "time of the end" (8.17, 19), concerning "the transgression" of Israel. The same phrase is used in 2.28 concerning the "latter days" of the King's image-dream. The phrase has come to mean, quite apart from the text of Daniel, as "the final days" of earth's history as we know it. However, Daniel is clearly not using it in that fashion. Daniel is not envisioning an end to history. The "remains of the beasts" (7.12) continue on after the "little horn" is killed (7.11). Further, a "son of man" at some point is to appear before the Ancient of Days, and this vision is strangely left out of what we are getting ready to read. This is a word that is explaining more of his previous visions. It itself is not a vision, but an "appearance" that dictates a "word of understanding."

*And while he was saying these words to me I set my face to the earth and was silent. And Behold! One as like similitude of sons of a man, striking upon my lips! And I opened my mouth and I spoke and said to the one standing opposite of me, "My Lord, because of the appearance my pain is turned upon me. I cannot retain strength. For how is a servant of my Lord able for this? To speak with my Lord as this? That is, I now have no power to stand. And breath has left me." The one like an appearance of a man struck me again and strengthened me. And he said, "Do not fear, man of desire. Peace to you. Be strong now, be strong." And when he was speaking to me I was made strong. And I said, "Speak, my Lord. You have made me strong." And he said, "Do you know why I have come to you? And now I will return to fight with the Prince of Persia. And I am going out. And Behold! A Prince of Javan will come!"*

That he has told Daniel that he is going to give him further information has been made known. He must return to the fight against the one opposite him, the Prince of Persia. A Prince of

Greece will come. This is not an earthly Prince. Greece and Persia waged various wars and scuffles under Darius I, Xerxes on up to their last King, Darius III. Xerxes waged one of the largest campaigns against them. Things are busy in the heavenlies! But Daniel has already been shown that the ram will eventually fall to the goat. Centuries will pass, though. Although God's power and knowledge of all things is secure, it appears that the angels, for and against God, are not at all aware. After all, they are not omniscient. They only know what they are told. They do not have psychic powers, either. They know what's in a man's heart if God tells them, who does know. Satan believed that Job would curse God if God took away all his amenities. This was false, and Satan was wrong. It may be, also, worthy of noting that the angel that stopped Abraham from killing Isaac declared, "Now I know that you are faithful." Thus, it was for their benefit, not God's (who already knew), to know these things; to know who they were protecting. Angels are fierce creatures of God, ready to punish wicked men at a moment's notice. They have to be "restrained."

These "watchers" carry out the orders of God, as the angels of Satan carry out his. God is not at "war" with these beings. Rather, they war against each other in their own strength. God's army, however, is more powerful than they are, and certainly more powerful than any human army, which he can snap in a blink. Although the forces that stand opposed to God's angels do so on the basis that they think they may win (they are not omniscient, either), and for a time they may "win", these skirmishes "in the heavens" and movements of human armies "on the earth" are directly linked. This account, then, sets up the reading of the words from the "writing of Truth" – a snippet from a page of one of the "books" that are "opened" on the Ancient

One's Judgment Desk. The Plan of God for the Future, interacting with human beings who "think" they are in charge, and to whatever degree of freedom they have, they are. However, as Nebuchadnezzar learned, God rules over the mastery of men and has the ultimate say as to what occurs in history, down to the signing of a pen.

## Chapter Eleven

*"Truly I declare to you the Writing in the Writ of Truth. And there is not one who is strengthening me against these ones except Michael, your Prince. And I, in the first year of Darius the Mede, stood to strengthen and to protect him."*

Michael is here called the Prince of yours ("yours" is plural). Michael is the Prince of your people, Israel. He is their guardian Prince (as there are Princes for Persia, and Greece in the invisible world). "These" is plural also which would refer to the plural and "Prince" of Persia, and when he comes, the Prince of Greece. This mighty angel stands and contests with these other malevolent principalities, and Michael stands with him as well. Also, this mighty angel stood and protected King Darius the Mede (and is still protecting, for we are in the third year of Cyrus/Darius). Thus, in the opening, this angel is fighting against the Prince of the Persian domain, but this Prince is not out for the good of King Cyrus but to topple his government through whatever means. The mighty angel "strengthens" and "protects" King Darius against this malevolent Prince of Persia (a Prince assigned to disturb Persia). Thus, his duty is to strengthen and protect the Kings of Persia so that the plan of God is accomplished. What we are to gain from all of this while we worry about the influence of elections, is that elections are influenced! By God! His plans are carried out in the heavenlies and these created beings are moved by his thought (decree from the throne).

Thus, Cyrus is here is called "The King of Persia" (10.1), and the first year of Darius (9.1) is mentioned, which hearkens back to 6.1-ff. An angel was sent to protect Daniel (6.22), and this may be the mention here, standing to protect Darius (and Daniel) from his accusers. It is another indication that Cyrus is Darius, that Cyrus, the King of Persia (10.1), who is being protected by an angel assigned to Persia, stood with the same, Darius the Mede, in his first year. He is Darius, the Mede, and Cyrus, the Persian, but the writing on the wall (by the hand of an angel) stated that Babylon will be divided and given to the Persians – "Medes" was not written on the wall. It was added by Daniel (reading Jeremiah).

All these things that have been shown to Daniel are "written" in a "writing of truth." Pre-written history. The affairs of men, on the surface, appear to be randomly and haphazardly going about their business, but behind the scenes God and his myriad and host are "sent out" of his Palace. His "strong ones" make sure the plan is carried out by directly contesting anything that stands in the way of their marching orders – what is written. Man does indeed have a will, and his thoughts are his own. He is one to be contested with by the powers above. The message here, though, is that the powers above always win. Several were in line for the death of Cyrus, but it was most important that the Kings that have been appointed be protected so that the following "word" (chapter eleven) is carried out.

*"And now, truth I declare to you: Behold! Three Kings are standing regarding Persia, but a fourth King will become rich, greatly richer than them. And according to his strength of riches he will stir up the whole Dominion of Javan."*

These three Kings are the ones the angel protects. They were, in fact, in the third year of Cyrus' rule over Babylonia, alive. Cambyses II (son), Smerdis (son) and Darius I, brother in law of

Cambyses II were all alive in the third year of Cyrus. The fourth King was the son of Darius I named, Xerxes who "will become", but at this time was not born (b. 522 B.C.E). And he waged a massive campaign against Greece (Javan/Ionians). His rule was from 485-465 B.C.E. and Persia lasted until 330/329 B.C.E. to the last King, Darius III. The Javanites gained the Dominion. It is simply fascinating that the angel refers to Cyrus as "Darius the Mede", when in fact several heirs of Cyrus would be named, Darius. I believe God has had fun with this ever since.

*"And a great King will stand. He rules a mighty reign. And he does as he will."*

Skipping over the later Kings of Persia (who are not alive at this time) we come to the shaggy male goat of chapter eight who "will stand" in the distant future. Although he is not named, we know that this is Alexander the Great, one of the most powerful Kings, and controversial. He does not at all stir up the Israelites and enters into no conflict with them. Israel, particularly Jerusalem, is enjoying a time of peace (thanks to Michael?). However, from Haggai to Malachi, the last Prophet until John the Baptist, complacency and lethargy set in. Malachi, writing somewhere in the late fifth century (433 B.C.E. is the terminus?) denounces his people. The Jews have largely settled in Alexandria, Babylonia/Persia and in and around Asia-Minor/Greece. There is a settlement in Jerusalem and the surrounding areas and the priestly functions are in operation.

The High Priest of the line of Zadok from the time of his sole appointment over the House of the Lord by David and Solomon on through the return from Exile where they are restored is attested to in Nehemiah and Ezra. We know of their uninterrupted line up to Joshua and Jaddua (350-320 B.C.E.) to Onias I (died in 290 B.C.E.). Israel has no King of the line of David and has not had one since Zedekiah, who was killed by King Nebuchadnezzar. This is critical information.

*"And while he is standing his Dominion will be broken and will be divided to four winds of the heavens, but not to his latter part, nor according to a similitude of his Dominion which he ruled, for his Dominion is plucked up, that is, for others, these beside each other."*

The visions are all coming together now. In chapter seven four Dominions/Beasts are seen reigning simultaneously ("together", "beside each other"), yet "different from one another." They are also, as stated in the vision of chapter eight, "different" from the previous mighty horn of the shaggy male goat (Alexander). These are the four that come out of "the four winds of the heavens" (7.2; 8.8 and here). In each vision four Dominions come out of the "four winds of the heavens" which is their identity marker. These four, then, are the same "four" in chapter seven and the same "four" in chapter eight – the same four that come out of the four winds of the heavens. The four winds are a judgment sign. They are being stirred up for Israel and the people of Judah and are setting the stage for a coming catastrophe; the "little horn", the "Prince who is to come", the vile King.

The identity of these four Dominions is readily known from history: the famous Diadochoi ("successors") of Alexander's Empire.

*"And the King of the Negev will grow powerful, but from his Princes even grows stronger over him. And he shall rule a great Realm, his Dominion."*

## Chapter Eleven

Daniel has no history books to consult. We do. The King of the Negev ("south" – Egypt) was Ptolemy I, Soter, which means, "savior" (323-285 B.C.E.). He was a trusted General under Alexander. Another Infantry General under Alexander was Seleucus I, Nicator. He was appointed as Satrap over Babylonia. For a brief time, he and Ptolemy Soter worked together. However, from Babylonia, Seleucus began a massive campaign and dominated what became the largest Dominion of all of them: the Seleucid Dynasty.

*"And at an end of years they are joined together. And a daughter of a King of the Negev will come to the King of the north to have a right life. But she will not retain the power of her arm. And he does not stand, nor his arm; and she is given, and those who brought her, and the one who begat her and strengthened her in the times."*

Ptolemy and Seleucus did fight in alliance with each other against Syria in the Battle of Gaza, where Demtrius I of the Antigonid Dysnasty (which arose from the Grecian Empire after Alexander) was defeated. Lysandra was the daughter of Ptolemy I, Soter. She was married to Alexander V and the son of Lysimachus, King of Thrace, who enjoyed high favor from Alexander the Great, being one of the four Generals ("Kings") that succeeded Alexander. She does seek the arm of King Seleucus I towards the very end of his life. Nothing becomes of her. Her father, the one who begat her (Ptolemy I), also dies. Lysandra was married previously to Agathocles, who was son of Lysimachus (who killed him). Seleucus I and Ptolemy I both eventually pass away, but they leave powerful successors in their stead.

*"And he will stand, one from a sprout, one from her roots, in his own right. And he comes to the army and comes to a place of the King of the north. And he will press among them and will be strong."*

"One from her roots, a sprout" is not Lysandra's child. Her "roots" are from her father who "begat" her, that is, her brother, Ptolemy II Philadelphus, son of Ptolemy I Soter. In what is known as the First Syrian War, he pushed and maintained Ptolemaic control of the regions in Syria vied for by the second Ruler of the North, Antiochus I Soter, son of Seleucus.

*"And also their gods with their libations, with articles of desire, silver and gold into captivity. He will go (back) to Mizraim. And he stands for years longer than the King of the north."*

As with any spoils, Ptolemy II takes what is needed to continue to finance the war efforts. His reign was from 285-246 B.C.E. Antiochus I ruled from 281-261 B.C.E. There were no further skirmishes between these Dominions for some years.

*"And he shall come into the Dominion of the King of the Negev. And he will return to his own ground."*

Antiochus II Theos (261-246 B.C.E.), the third Seleucid King, launched what is known as the Second Syrian War. He aligned himself with Antigonus II who knocked out a fleet of ships belonging to Ptolemy II. This second war lasted for about seven years ending with Antiochus marrying Berenice, the daughter of Ptolemy II (though most commentaries see this as the events in Daniel 11.6, I have not followed that line of interpretation). Antiochus II returns afterward to his own district. He

Chapter Eleven

divorced his first wife, Laodice, in order to marry Berenice. However, he does later leave Berenice and returns to Laodice, who kills him. Berenice and her son, Antiochus, are also killed. Laodice proclaimed her son, Seleucus II Callinicus to be the fourth King of the North, which he became (246-225 B.C.E.). Meanwhile, Ptolemy III Euergetes ("the Benefactor"), who also came to power in 246 B.C.E. was outraged by the death of his sister Berenice and her son. This launched the Third Syrian War. We may note, too, that Antiochus, son of Berenice, was a legitimate heir to the throne. He would have been Antiochus III, but Fate stepped in.

*"And his sons stirred themselves and amassed a strong army, but he will certainly come, and he will flood, and he will pass and he will turn back. And they will stir themselves to his place."*

Antiochus II had two sons, Seleucus II Calinicus and Antiochus Hierax. Ptolemy III came against Seleucus II and overwhelmed him. Laodice wanted Hierax to be a co-regent with his brother, which did not happen. Instead, Hierax turns against his brother. Ptolemy III came like a water swell and overwhelmed the Syrian Dominion all the way to Babylonia. Seleucus II eventually arrived. Daniel is standing in the vicinity where he is receiving his word. Seleucus II attempts to save the city of Babylon. However, Ptolemy III "turns back" all of a sudden to Egypt. From what we know, Seleucus II remains in the city, as well as his son, Seleucus III Soter and his brother, Antiochus III during the year 222 B.C.E., Nisanu 8th for a religious festival. "They stir themselves to his place", that is, following the first part of this verse, Seleucus II two sons "stirred themselves." They wanted vengeance.

Thus, the sons of Antiochus II, Seleucus II and Antiochus Hierax, were stirred themselves (against one another), and each one amassed their armies, but Ptolemy III will most certainly come and advance against the northern Dominion and will pass through it, but he will turn back. Before he turns back, though, his passes through the Dominion of the Seleucids. From Babylon, Seleucus II's "sons stirred themselves", Antiochus III and Seleucus III.

*"And the King of the Negev will be embittered. And he will go out and wage war with him – with the King of the north – and he will cause a great multitude to stand, but the multitude will be given into his hand."*

The King of the Negev here is Ptolemy IV. Seleucus III Soter (the fifth Seleucid Ruler), who briefly rules from Babylonia (225-222 B.C.E.), attempts to reconquer areas in the east (Anatolia) lost by his father, Seleucus II. He is not successful. However, his brother, who visited him in Babylonia, was Antiochus III, the Great, just eighteen or nineteen years old. Antiochus III does regain parts of the Seleucid Empire shortly after the death of his brother. Ptolemy IV wages a great campaign against him and is successful. Antiochus put up a great fight, but the victory was given to Ptolemy IV at Raphia. This was the Fourth Syrian War (221-217 B.C.E.).

*"But when the multitude is lifted up, his heart shall become exalted. He will cause ten thousand to fall, and he will not remain strong."*

Ptolemy IV reign was marked by pleasure and avarice. Many mark the slow decline of the Ptolemies from his rule onward.

## Chapter Eleven

Antiochus III, the Sixth Ruler, comes to be called "The Great", following the titles of Cyrus and Alexander. What follows from here is a concentration on Antiochus III and his son, Antiochus IV, Epiphanes. Antiochus III ruled from 222-187 B.C.E. In 198 B.C.E. he solidifies his reputation as the Great and after many battles regains the now dominant Seleucid Empire, covering the regions from India to Egypt and Asia Minor. Judea had been under the thumb of the Ptolemies until then.

Concerning the history of Judea up to this point is necessary. Under the Ptolemies, who heavily taxed their regions including Judea, there were no major skirmishes. Ptolemy I Soter did relocate Jews to Egypt in the early third century. Under Ptolemy II, Philadelphus the Jews constructed synagogues. Alexandria takes on an important role in the history of Judaism from this point. From all accounts, although sketchy and filled with variations, this King commissioned a translation of the Hebrew Bible into the Greek language, known as the Septuagint (the Alexandrian Version would be a better title). There is considerable debate as to when this was formally completed, however (ranging from this time all the way to around 125 B.C.E. for its completed form). Ptolemy IV, according to 3 Maccabees, committed an act of sacrilege in Jerusalem, but this story has been largely demonstrated as referring to Ptolemy VII, Physcon (the date and composition are highly vague, although Daniel is mentioned in 6.6,7).

We have to remind ourselves that Daniel has absolutely no idea who these Kings are. He is not given any indication of the few centuries ahead in terms of time. All that he knows is that Cyrus is in his third year over Babylon. Three more will follow him, and a fourth one will come and stir up the distant Javanites. A Javanite King will come and he will be broken and four will come from that. After this, he hears from the angel that Kings of the Negev region and Kings of the northern region fight against each other, and, on occasion, make truces. "Several years" occur (left entirely indefinite). As for Daniel, he knows that the land of Judea is caught in the middle of all of this fighting. There is no King David, no Branch of the House of Israel and Judah. The Kings here are not Davidic Kings, but foreign Kings who fight constantly with each other. Judah, the "beautiful land" is not mentioned at all so far. Even writing this down after he heard it must have left him in the dark (which is intimated in chapter twelve). Where is Judah in all of this? Why does this matter about who these Kings are, or a daughter of one who goes to another? I certainly would have been thinking this!

This changes, however, in the following verses. We know from the previous visions of chapter seven and eight that a "little horn" is coming. We know from chapter nine that he will commit an act of abomination. Daniel knows that somehow his own people are involved, and not for good. However, there are "saints" as well – true followers of the God of the heavens, Most High. God has already brought them from Exile and has established the foundation-stone under Cyrus. His people, albeit not all of them, but those "who love YHWH and love his commandments", are still active. God has not failed them. He is keeping his covenant of love. Yet, a great calamity is coming against the wickedness of his people, their sins, and the righteous among them will be caught up in it. The composition of Daniel is written to them, for their sake. The return from Exile, in spite of there being no Davidic King that brings about worldwide unity and peace, was fulfilled. God does whatsoever he pleases in the heavens and on the land. His purpose stands, and the promises are being fulfilled, in spite of what is seen. When understood from the viewpoint of the Ancient of days, the righteous have all things in heaven and earth, for they belong to the One who has Dominion over all things.

*"And the King of the north will return. And he will set up a great multitude unlike the first one, even to end of the times – years – he will certainly come in a great strength and large fortune (But in the times, those times, many will stand against the King of the Negev. Even sons of violent men from your people shall lift up themselves in order to establish the vision, but they will fall) – Now, the King of the north will come and cast up a mound and capture the city of fortifications and arms of the Negev. They shall not stand, nor his best people. There is no strength to stand."*

Antiochus III, the Great, is the King here, who after thirteen or fourteen years returned his attention to the Negev region. Ptolemy IV was dead (203). His son, Ptolemy V, Epiphanes received the throne at the age of four! During these years Antiochus III conquered the regions of Persia, Bactria (northern Afghanistan) and Asia Minor. This makeup of his Dominion will last up to the "end of the times" – a phrase we have encountered in chapter eight. The vision of the little horn concerns the "time of end" (8.17). From Daniel 9.25 the city will be restored and maintained during "distress of the times". In 11.6 "the times" are mentioned as well, where it appears that "the times" spans the remainder of the decreed seventy-sevens – these are "the times." In the same verse, "at the end of years" denotes how the author is clear to make distinctions. "To end of the times" is not the same as "at end of years" in 11.6 (as the context dictates). Daniel reserves the phrase "the times" or "end of the times" or "appointed time of end", "time of the end" for a specific end in mind (chapter eight). What is gathered from here is that Antiochus III and his greatness sets the stage for the appointed time of the end – but he is not the little horn, the "Prince who is coming" (Daniel 9.26). These words of the Writing of the Writ of Truth concern "the latter days" – the end of the times – not the end of history.

This passage directly relates to the previous "vision". Chapter ten is an "appearance" of the might angel that utters "words" – Daniel is not "seeing" any images here as in chapters seven and eight. He is "hearing" the word of truth spoken from the "appearance" of the angel. Thus, to "establish the vision" means that a vision has already been announced in connection with "your people", the Judahites. In the same way – same word – that the hearts of Kings were "lifted up" in themselves, here these violent Jews (not all of them) lift up themselves. The rule of the Ptolemies is over under Antiochus III. His allies stood with him against the Egyptians. However, they would have to now align themselves with this new King – and many of them do and violate the laws of God in the process (breaking the covenant). Thus, one of the items in the determination of the seventy-sevens was "to confirm", "seal", or "establish vision and Prophet" (9.24), and it is here that the stage, due to this act of violence (whatever it was) has been "set". "The transgression" against God has been put forth. His "indignation" against their "sin" will have to be quelled with "great wrath." They will fall.

There is a break in these verses that predict the coming King, Antiochus III, and then, as I have placed in parentheses, notes the setting of the rebellion of Daniel's people (which is here still to come). It then resumes the discussion of the "coming of the King of the north" in what is called the Fifth Syrian War. Antiochus formed an alliance with Philip V, King of Macedonia and decisively defeated Ptolemy V's best troops in the Battle of

Panium (Caesarea Philippi in the Gospels). This defeat is before the violent men of Judah do what they will do.

*"(Now, 'the one who comes in to him' shall do as he pleases. And there is none that stand before him. And he will stand in the beautiful land, and completion (will be) in his hand).*

This verse, too, is parenthetical of the "the one who comes in" (found in Daniel 9.26). It is to make the distinction that the one who is to come, the little horn, is not the King (Antiochus III) here. Antiochus III does not invade Egypt. He wanted to, but was more or less "encouraged" by the growing power of Rome to cease (196 B.C.E in Lycimichia). However, for "the one coming in" no one will stand in his way and he will invade Egypt and take it, but not conquer it. It survives. Antiochus IV, Epiphanes, was the son of Antiochus III. He was born around 215 B.C.E. Antiochus III never launched an invasion of the Negev, but did take large portions of the Greek west. Thus, "the one who is coming in" (the same phrase in 9.26) is the one with "completion" in his hand – a term that again takes us to Daniel 9.24, "the completion of the transgression." The words of the angel then resumes back to Antiochus III. Judea becomes his possession around 198 B.C.E. which would make his son, Antiochus IV around eighteen years of age. In the Treaty of Apamea (188), Antiochus IV was sent to Rome as a political hostage. He was around twenty eight when that happened. Did young Antiochus IV travel the land of Judea under his father's possession in his formative years? We are left to wonder.

*"Now he will set his face to him to come into strengths of his whole Dominion, and uprightness is with him. And he will do. And a*

*daughter of the woman he will give to him in order to ruin it. And it shall not stand, but it will not be his."*

Antiochus III sets his campaigns against the territories of King Ptolemy V, Epiphanes. And, as noted before the parentheses, he invaded the Dominion of that King. "Dominion" is a feminine noun in Hebrew and stand for the pronoun, "it" (feminine) in our translation. Thus, a daughter of the woman he will give to Ptolemy V, in order to corrupt his "Dominion". That is, Antiochus sets his face to him (Ptolemy) and comes into his (Ptolemy) Dominion. "And he will do" is common in Daniel for "it will happen". Ptolemy loses a good deal of territory in Syria and Asia Minor, but the Negev (Egypt) is not gained by Antiochus – it will not be his.

"Uprightness" is with the King, which is meant to assert that his actions are following the "Book of truth". God's determined decree is with him. Antiochus III does, indeed, give his daughter of his wife, Laodice III in 196 as a peace agreement. Her name was Cleopatra Syra – Cleopatra I. She was only ten or eleven, and Ptolemy V was around sixteen or seventeen. They were married in 193, being a little older. It is a strange phrase, rare, "daughter of the woman" and would refer to Laodice III, who was the cousin of Antiochus III, her husband (she was called, "sister-Queen"). Ancestral unions were not uncommon. However, "the woman" is emphasized because she is the mother of Antiochus IV, Epiphanes, the coming terror.

*"And he shall turn his face to the coastlands and captures many, but a Commander will put an end to his scorn. Rather, he will turn back his reproach to him!"*

## Chapter Eleven

This again relates the events of the peace agreement (196 B.C.E.) and Antiochus' continued efforts until the Treaty of Apamea (188). He lost considerable territory in the famous Battle of Magnesia. Although Daniel does not identify the "Commander", there is one who fits the bill: Lucius Cornelius Scipio Asiaticus a very able bodied General in the Roman Army. Rome was a growing threat in the west, but nowhere near the power that would become of them towards the later end of the first century B.C.E.

*"Then he shall turn his face to his own place of land. And he will stumble. And he will fall. And he will not be found."*

Such is the ending of the life of Antiochus "The Great." He died in Persia, in Elymais, plundering a temple of Bel. He was killed by a deeply offended mob.

*"Then one will stand in his place, causing one to pass, one who extracts adornments of the Dominion. And in those same days he will be broken, but not in anger, and not in battle."*

Seleucus IV, Philopater, son of Antiochus III, gains the Purple (187-175 B.C.E.). Seleucus IV is the last son what has been a successive line of fathers and sons (and add, mothers/wives/sisters – forming a dynastic chain. For even though Antiochus IV is his brother, the son of Seleucus IV, if the proper, royal pattern of this Dominion be followed, would rule after him. This pattern is broken after the death of Philopater. He is the Seventh King of the Seleucid Dynasty.

His death, it is generally agreed, came by the hand of a very high ranking and trusted official named Heliodorus. A stele was discovered with Seleucus addressing him courteously as "brother", and that in the address the monetary affairs of the Dominion are "our" concern. Thus, Heliodorus was from all accounts the King's right hand man. He is mentioned in the ancient Greek historian, Appian, and in an amazing story in 2 Maccabees 3.1-ff (where also Seleucus IV is mentioned in connection with taxes).

The Hebrew text comes the final days of the King, the "same days" he sent out this "extractor of adornments". The Seleucid Dynasty, as with all of them, was funded by taxes and donations. Temples were often a depository of such extra revenue, including gold and silver. This Heliodorus, according to the story in 2 Maccabees 3, is sent out on the instigation of one Simon, who was an overseer of the Temple in Jerusalem (Onias was High Priest who was in the direct line of Zadok, the appointed High Priest of David and Solomon). Heliodorus is sent by the King and attempts to take "ornaments" or "adornments" from the Temple. He is met by an epiphany of horses from heaven which scourge him. Reporting back to the King that he was unable to gather any tribute, there is nothing more to be done.

It is not my contention to debate the accuracy of this story, or whether or not this Heliodorus is the same mentioned by Appian who killed the King. Nonetheless, one named Heliodorus did, in fact, kill the King, Seleucus IV, and attempted to usurp his throne with the son, Antiochus (who was but a boy) by acting as co-regent. Now, before all of this, Antiochus IV, the brother of Seleucus IV, was hostage in Rome, given to them by treaty mentioned above. However, Seleucus IV, for whatever reason (Rome made the demand), is given the release of Antiochus IV in exchange for his other son, Demetrius who would

Chapter Eleven

have been the direct heir before his younger brother, Antiochus (which is most likely why Rome wanted Demetrius instead of Antiochus IV). Antiochus IV spends his time in Athens. Upon the assassination of Seleucus IV and the very brief co-reign of Heliodorus, Antiochus immediately swings into action and takes the throne of his brother Seleucus IV – a throne that did not belong to him, technically, but belonged to Demetrius (who Rome refused to release) and the boy Antiochus. Antiochus IV's coming into power, then, literally knocked out three Kings – Demetrius, Antiochus (who he later kills, and who would have been crowned as Antiochus IV), and Heliodorus, co-King.

In fact, Antiochus, the son of Seleucus IV, was minted on coinage as King (175 B.C.E.). Antiochus IV, Epiphanes (who assumed this name, for his real name was Mithridates) become the sole King in 170, when, from all accounts, he had the young nephew Antiochus murdered by an official named Andronicus. Antiochus IV was away in Cilicia at the time, and apparently claimed innocence of the plot, putting to death Andronicus. This is the stuff of great political cunning and intrigue! This may, too, have been part of a greater plot of Mithridates to rule the Dominion of Seleucid, yet remain friendly to Rome (they never warred against each other, Antiochus IV always gave in to them). We must also include Eumenes II of Pergamon who appears to have had a hand in the ousting/assassination of Heliodorus, paving the way for Antiochus IV. Thus, Seleucus IV, the seventh King of the Seleucid Dominion, died not in anger (his anger), nor while he was in a battle. He was assassinated. Heliodorus steps in as prime caregiver to the heir, Antiochus, then five years old. Demetrius, the true next-in-line heir was kept by Rome. Mithridates sees an opportunity, and takes it.

*"And in his place shall stand a despised person. But the royalty of the Dominion is not set upon him. So in ease and he will seize the Dominion in slipperiness."*

We understand from all that we know that this is the Little Horn of chapter eight, who "with ease" (8.25) comes to the Dominion. He is a monster, a vile man, cunning and crafty, deceitful. He usurps the throne from his brother through craftiness. Though his arrival and ousting of Heliodorus does not officially make him King, he is the co-regent with Seleucus IV's son, young Antiochus (and marries Ladodice, his brother's wife). Mithridates does take this name for himself later, and proclaims himself Antiochus IV instead of the young nephew. He is the eighth horn of chapter seven, bringing low three horns. He is the eighth King of the Seleucid Dominion. And he is vile. Like the other visions of chapter seven and eight, the rest of the text centers in on this Little Horn of the fourth Beast, this Little Horn that grows out of the four Dominions of chapter eight. This Eighth Horn of which three are plucked up before him; Demetrius I, Antiochus, and Heliodorus, the "extractor of ornaments", who killed the seventh horn and paved the way for the Eighth. The linkage and connections of these visions are now all together in a continuous stream. The seventy-sevens can now be correctly calculated so that there is no mistake: 49 years to Cyrus; 434 years til Antiochus IV; 7 years of his Sole Rule; In the midst of that 7, total hell floods in, but in the end of the time, in those latter days of his rule over the people of God, he will come to nothing.

*"And the arms of the flood will be swept away from before him. And they shall be broken. Moreover a Prince of the covenant."*

The previous details, particularly of Daniel 9.25, 26 confirms for us that the same character there is our man here. The "arms" (metaphor for armies) will be swept away by "the flood" of Antiochus. In 9.26 he brings in the "flood", and comes against a "Prince of the covenant", too. This would be the death of Onias, the High Priest and last High Priest of the Zadokite lineage from the time of David to serve as such in Jerusalem. Now we know "and understand" that from the issuing of the word of the Lord given to Jeremiah til the rise of this little horn was sixty-sevens, or four-hundred and thirty four years. That would bring us right to the time of 170/171 B.C.E. when Antiochus the Nephew was murdered, and Antiochus IV is sole King of the eight horned Seleucid Beast, the fourth beast of chapter seven, one of the Four that will arise when the shaggy goat's horn is broken. It all now makes sense and adds up.

Now, what happens here, since we are speaking of a High Priest of the covenant (priests and High Priests were called, "princes" in the Scripture), is an amazing story of wickedness within the ranks of Daniel's people, the Jews.

*"And from uniting to him, he will practice treachery. And he will ascend and be made strong by a few of a nation."*

That is, through cunning, Antiochus comes to power by an alliance with a few from another nation (an alliance with Pergamum). Antiochus IV, as we have noted, was a co-regent and was not sole King until the death of his young nephew, Antiochus. There is plenty of evidence to suggest that his ascendency to power was gained by establishing himself before 170 B.C.E. (the death of his nephew Antiochus, the boy) with Judea (making a covenant with them). Antiochus IV came to power in 175 B.C.E., but was sole King in 170. He was totally committed to Hellenism, the Greek gods and the Greek way of life, even though he dressed as a Roman (with whom he had alliances). From 175-170 this mastermind consolidated his relationships in Asia Minor and Syria, and Judea. What is sad is that many Jews went along with it, and decried the "pious" Jews who abhorred the Greek world and lifestyle. The gymnasium was introduced to Jerusalem, where naked athletes displayed their strength (gymnos is the Greek word for, "naked"). To the pious, this was outrageous.

In short, what unfolds in Judea is a civil war between the Progressivists/Liberals and the Conservatives/Orthodox. Blood would be shed between them. From the standpoint of the covenant of Moses, the everlasting covenant, it was transgression and wickedness. The nation of Judea had once again desired to be like the other nations. But, there was a remnant, a few, who understood what was going on and cried out to their God for mercy. All of this is recorded in 1 and 2 Maccabees (and other sources). Judea, with her civil inner turmoil, was now under a vile King who would suddenly turn against them in great ferocity – to complete the transgression, confirm the vision and Prophet, to fill up her sin (Daniel 9.24). The confirmation would be in this King's hand. The vision would be fulfilled by this people, and this King.

*"In ease and in a district rich with booty he will come. And he will do that which none of his fathers had done, nor fathers of his fathers. Spoil and plunder and property he will scatter to them. And against fortified places he schemes his schemes – that, for a time."*

This is further description of his plotting towards ascendency. "For a time" (175-170 B.C.E.) he plots, rewards, distributes and schemes. He wants the throne to himself. The atrocity to the sacred lineage of the Seleucid Dominion he is willing to forgo. Killing his nephew is an atrocious act that violates everything the Seleucid Family stood for. This King was not of the "royalty" of the Seleucids. He usurped the throne through intrigue and vice. When the time was right, young Antiochus, just nine or ten years old was slain. With Demetrius in Roman hands (and their compliance to keep it that way), nothing or no one stood before him to oppose him.

Of our concern, however, are the actions of this King towards "your people and your city, Jerusalem" – for which the seventy-sevens had been determined. He installs the brother of Onias, Jason, as High Priest (174 B.C.E.). This was a bad move. Jason kills his brother, Onias, and Antiochus, in reaction, kills him and sets up Menelaus, who has no relation at all to the Zadokite Prince. "An anointed Prince shall be cut off, and have nothing" (Daniel 9.26). The Zadokite line is forever abolished in Jerusalem (171 B.C.E.), four hundred and thirty four years from the proclamation of Jeremiah (sixty-two sevens).

With the installment of a foreign High Priest that violated the laws of Moses, and having made a covenant with the pro-Hellenist Jews (173/2 B.C.E.), the events to follow began to deteriorate in Jerusalem into a civil and bloody war. Meanwhile, as Jerusalem's King, Antiochus set his eyes on Egypt, and in 170/169 B.C.E. launched a massive campaign against Ptolemy VI, Philomater. For the first time a King of the Seleucid Dominion invaded the Negev/Egypt. As Daniel was shown in the vision, the Little Horn set his eyes on the "Negev" (8.9). This was the Sixth Syrian War. "And wars will continue to the end" (Daniel 9.25). Desolations have been decreed. The Transgression has come.

*"And he will stir up his strength and his heart against the King of the Negev in great force. And the King of the Negev will stir himself to do battle with a great and mighty force. But he will not stand for they will scheme schemes against him."*

The year is 169 B.C.E. The region of Syria and Palestine had been in the hands of the Ptolemies. Yet, with his ascension, a threat was seen and war was declared by two under officials, Eulaeus and Lenaeus. Ptolemy VI, Philomater was King of the Negev. Now, remember the treaty where Antiochus III sent his daughter, Cleopatra I to marry Ptolemy V? That was Antiochus' sister. Ptolemy VI, then, was his nephew. Thus, in the fashion he took the throne with his nephew Antiochus (who is dead now), Antiochus IV sees the same opportunity for co-regency in Egypt. He invades the land and takes strategic cities. A peace treaty was made with Antiochus ruling as co-regent over Egypt. This did not last, however, for there were two others, Cleopatra II and Ptolemy VIII Physcon (later to rule), brother and sister to Ptolemy VI. These siblings scheme their schemes.

*"(Now the ones who eat his portion of food will break him), but his army will overflow and they shall fall. Many are pierced. Two Kings, both hearts are meant for evil. And at one table they speak a lie, but it will not prosper, for yet is the appointed time."*

Again it appears, as we have seen before, that the words of the angel jump ahead, and thus we have a parenthetical statement here. Antiochus will successfully invade Egypt. For over a year the treaty is honored. But, the very ones who schemed the treaty at the one table (treaty table), will plot against Antiochus. Antiochus will be broken, eventually, but not yet.

On his way to Egypt, Antiochus visits Jerusalem and is welcomed by the wicked priest, Jason, and the people with him. He takes Pelusium of Egypt and forges ahead to Alexandria, but stops short. The treaty is made. Now, Jason, hearing that Antiochus IV was dead, a rumor of course, sought to reinstate himself over the hand picked Menelaus. This outraged Antiochus and he joined forces with the Hellenizers of Judea and his own forces and ransacked the city. The slaughter was notable. Meanwhile, Cleopatra reconciled the two Kings, Physcon and Ptolemy VI, Philopater, breaking the treaty, thus eating at the same table of Philomater and Antiochus. All of this quite confusing political intrigue takes place. But the words of the angel are certain: this is not yet the appointed end.

*"Now he does return to his land with great booty and with his heart against the holy covenant. He will do and return back to his land."*

That is, after his campaign in Egypt, having Philomater ruling with him, for him, in Egypt, Antiochus IV returns. This is 168 B.C.E. He has not yet heard the news of the broken agreement in Egypt, and after Jerusalem returns to his own land. Menelaus is reinstated as High Priest, who is also a wicked, worthless man. Jason is driven out. Antiochus IV entered the Temple and he did plunder it. As we have it, Onias II was murdered, the last true High Priest. Jason ruled as High Priest for three years, but is deposed because of the murder. Menelaus was placed as High Priest, who was not even a priest! Jason, while Antiochus IV is away in the Negev, plots against Meneleus and take the Sanctuary. Civil war and bloodshed ensues in Jerusalem. Antiochus IV returns, outraged, plunders the city and also inflicts a slaughter. Menelaus is positioned back in place and Antiochus IV goes to his Syrian homeland. What a mess. But, "the appointed end is not yet." Another desecration is coming.

*"At the appointed time he shall return and go into the Negev. But, it is not like the first, that is, the latter part."*

We now move into the phase of "the appointed time". The first invasion of Egypt will not be like the latter part, where "the latter" hints that "the latter time" has begun with this second expedition. This is "the time of the end" in 8.17; "the appointed time of the end" (8.19); "the latter of the indignation" (8.19); "in the latter part" (8.23), which is "when the rebellion" occurs in Jerusalem, when "the completion of the transgression" is commenced (8.23); when the Little Horn "shall do" (8.24); and shall make war against the covenant, stand up to the Prince of princes (the High Priest; 8.25) and kill many saints (8.25). The words of the angel are now tying in the vision of Daniel in chapter eight, given several years earlier. It all relates in a seamless patchwork, progressing in terms of expanding the "knowledge" that Daniel must "understand" so as, when these things happen, "many" – the truly righteous among the pathetic of Israel, will know what to do, and how to respond. The Lord is with them, as he was with Daniel in the lion's den, and with the three Jews in the fiery furnace. God is the King of Kings, and rules over the affairs of all men, doing as he pleases according to his plan. And Daniel is hearing the words of the book of what is true; true and trustworthy words that will most certainly come and take place in the fashion as they are written. History is written, dictated by God who moves the affairs of Kings, nations, men and daughters, women and sons, Kings, Princes, Armies, and treaties. He does as he pleases with those who are lifted up in their own heart, whose wickedness soars to great lengths. He does as he pleases with the will and heart of man bent on destruction and chaos. He does as he pleases, even with those who are called by his name, but whose hearts are far from him and do not know him. There are some who do know him, who have the law written in their hearts. They have come back from the Exile and have lived peacefully from generation to generation, faithfully following the Lord from their hearts and his commandments. Yet, at this time, in this generation, are those who follow the world of Hellenism, who have aligned themselves with an evil King and an even more vile pretender of a High Priest – and yet bear the name of God. The time has come for them to be exposed, to reward the saints, and destroy the wicked among them, due to their sin and transgression. The Indignation of God has decreed it.

*"And ships of Kittim come in among him, and he will be disheartened. And he will return. And he will be indignant against the holy covenant. And he will do. And he will return. And he will discern on behalf of the ones who are forsaking the holy covenant."*

It is now obvious that the previous words of the angel Gabriel, given to him in the first year of Darius/Cyrus (9.1), are meant here. There, the "Prince, the one who comes", greatly exerts the covenant over the many, that is, makes it strenuous to bear. That we are now in the "middle part" of his reign of Terror, "the appointed time" of the "one seven" is evident.

However, before this, what sets him off, is that he is forced to turn back in Egypt. The "ships of Kittim" (the Septuagint has, "Romans"), are usually taken as referring to the Roman fleet.

Notably, in Numbers 24.24, the ships of Kittim will ransack the kings of Asshur (the Syrians?) – an ancient prophecy. "Kittim" is a son of Javan, which in Daniel, Javan are the Greeks (Genesis 10.4); this reference should not surprise us since Daniel has also called Babylon, "Shinar" in 1.2 (which see). "Cyprus" appears to be the referent (translation) of "kittim" in Isaiah 23.1. Ezekiel 27.6 also makes a reference. In a sad denunciation of Judah, Jeremiah tells them to consider "Kittim" – do they do the things of Judah to their gods the way Judah does to their God? That Kittim, in apocryphal literature, was code for Rome is well known. However, at this time (167 B.C.E.) Rome was a growing Dominion, but only in its earliest stages.

We must not, however, totally press the term here to mean, "Romans" – but, like "Negev" and "Javan" – "Kittim" are those of the west – ships from the West – who were undoubtedly Romans, but in Daniel's time (sixth century) this would have been impossible for him to associate – "Kittim" are ships from the west (Cyprus was a mid way port), the isles of the Great Sea (the Mediterranean). Kittim has also been found in the Arad Letters, where, in the 6th century B.C.E., around the time of Judah's collapse, they are more or less Greek mercenaries. Kition was the main city on Cyprus and associated with Greeks in ancient literature. The reference here would simply designate "from the West". Of course, the son of Javan is Kittim (Genesis 10.4, 5), associated with the Greeks and western peoples.

What this relates to is that Antiochus IV, initially, makes a successful push into Egypt, and is within miles of taking Alexandria. However, Popilius Laenas, a Consul of Rome, appears in Eleusis and demands Antiochus IV to withdraw. Now, this is interesting. How can this one Consul, without a shot being fired, demand Antiochus Epiphanes, God Manifest, Zeus Most High to withdraw? This would get back to the fact that he was once a hostage in Rome, and treated however as a Prince. When Demetrius, the true heir, was demanded, Antiochus IV was freed. However, the Romans knew they had an ace card here. Antiochus IV came to power probably through conspiracy by design with the help of the Romans, since he would then be an ally of sorts. However, holding Demetrius, the true rightful heir, they could simply order a coup – a legitimate coup – and Antiochus knew this. He is "disheartened."

There was nothing he could do; trapped by his own schemes. Thus, in a rage and fit of indignation ("the indignation" of Daniel 8.19, where the noun is used), and because Jerusalem is simply rebelling against itself between the Hellenists who were loyal to the King, and the Orthodox "saints" who could not stand him or his Greek, worldly, god-hating philosophies and culture, his usurpation of the High Priest, his previous desecration and looting, his deifying himself and everything else abhorrent about this "vile" King, he has had enough defeat for one day!

Here we are specifically, and sadly, told that a good multitude had "forsaken" the Holy Covenant. Will Judah ever learn? The King is "discerning" of those loyal to him, and stirs them up for what happens next (the Little Horn "discerns dissimulations" – riddles – and now we know that he discerns the enigma or mystery of the disloyalty of the Jews to their God and covenant – and used it to his advantage – 8.23). Thus, against the backdrop of Daniel nine, and the intercession of him concerning the wickedness of his people, that their Exile was due to their sin, that God's wrath had been poured out upon them because they "forsook" the covenant and laws of God, and turned their backs on him, we are to understand what happens within this "one seven" period, and in the middle part of the seven (it is often thought that middle part means a clean severing of three and a half, thus leaving three and a half, but this is not demanding by the phrase, found in Daniel 9.27. Rather, if seven years are meant, the years in between, the middle part, are meant. Thus, if we have, say, 1-10, the middle part would not be 5, but 4-6).

*"And arms out from him will stand, and they will pollute the holy place. And they will take away the continual. And they will set the abomination, the one that is desolating."*

Thus, upon the King's return to Jerusalem, in the midst of their civil infighting, those who are aligned with the King change the law of God and cause a cessation of the continual (daily) offering. This is exactly what was said in Daniel 9.27 and the abomination that brings desolation. Also, in Daniel 8.11-ff the actions of the Little Horn are described as we find them here. There can be no doubt that all of these visions (chapter seven and eight) and the words (chapter nine) and the word here are all pointing to the same desolation. He makes the covenant of the Jews strenuous by seeking to "change the appointed time and law" of the Jews. From what we know, Antiochus IV made obedience to the Law of Moses a crime punishable by death. No King had ever done this. His armies and generals were ruthless and the slaughter was numbered into the tens of thousands. This, we are told, happened in December of 167 B.C.E. If we understand that Onias II was murdered (170 B.C.E.) after the "sixty and two sevens" of Daniel nine, and that another "seven" would happen (the period in which the two thousand twenty-three hundred days would occur, from his reign to the setting the sanctuary "aright"), then we can see that "in the middle part" of that "seven" he would make the covenant of Israel strenuous (difficult to obey). So strenuous

Chapter Eleven

that many of Judah simply "forsook" it. Thus, now we are in 167 B.C.E. – the middle part. Also, the "times, time and half a time" are in reference in chapter seven which also refer to the entire seven year run from 170-164 B.C.E. Antiochus IV succeeds in having his nephew, the King, murdered (170). He campaigns against the King of the Negev twice. On his second (his latter end) invasion, he is disheartened and returns to find that the people of Jerusalem are in an upheaval. Their own sin and rebellion stirs Antiochus IV to issue a Pro-Hellenist pogrom to wipe out the Jewish religion once and for all.

For three years the temple is in shambles. Antiochus IV sets up a statue of Zeus in its walls. A pig is actually slaughtered on the altar ("the wings of the altar" in Daniel 9.27). Orgies occur. Desolations. Profanation galore (all recorded in 1 and 2 Maccabees; Josephus and other sources). Murder, wars, death, needless bloodshed. And this all begins to take place in the Winter of 167 B.C.E., and one of the worst massacres happens on a Sabbath, where the Jews refused to fight because of that law, and were crushed, trampled on, broken in pieces. All of the visions of Daniel up to this point apply to this point of time, the "appointed time" – the "time of the end". There are no gaps. No mystery periods to be inserted. No other fulfillments to be had. Daniel is not envisioning the "end of time", but a "time of the end", and we will do well to note this fact.

*"And the condemners of the covenant he will pollute in the hypocrisy. But, a people, the ones who know their God, will make firm and they will do."*

What we have here is division between the people of Judah. There are those who are evil, condemners of the covenant (a term used for the sin and transgressors of the Exile in Daniel 9.5,15). Antiochus IV has polluted them, and they have sided with him. However, the "people" who know their God and love his commandments, singled out in Daniel 9.4, their God "keeps his covenant and loving kindness" towards them. There is an Israel within an Israel – not all Israel is Israel – but there is always a "remnant" within a remnant that has the laws of their God on their heart; those who are truly his, and he is truly theirs. Daniel was written for their benefit and no others. God dwells with them, and they dwell with him. He has renewed the covenant (Jeremiah 31.31) with them, and overshadows them. From them, a 'people' has been 'set up' after the Exile (Daniel 2.44). They rebuild the city and the temple.

They maintain their righteousness in accordance with the law of God written on their hearts. In short, they are the Daniels, the Hannaniahs, the Azariahs and the Mishaels of the covenant people of God. They are the Ezras, Nehemiahs, Zerubabbels, Joshuas and Esthers of the Dominion of God. God returned them to the land – he set them up as a Dominion, a nation, a people, and this Dominion, this nation of priests redeemed of the Lord shall not perish, nor shall ever be overrun or removed. They are the true People of God that operate within the hypocrites and despisers of the covenant who claim they know God, but are wicked in heart, easily drawn away, easily enticed into the world of pleasure and sin, easily made to fall away and forsake their God. These lovers of God, on the other hand, will give their very lives to the flame of the furnace, to the lion's pit, to the hand of a wicked tyrant in death before they forsake their religion.

*"And the wise ones of the people will make the many understand, even though they will stumble by sword and flame; in captivity and in spoil – days."*

## Chapter Eleven

And here our point is made even stronger. "The many" (the remnant, the true people) are singled out from among 'the rest'. Of course, we know that a righteous uprising occurred in the days of Antiochus IV, and we notice here, too that the shift comes off him for a bit and focuses on the true saints, "the many". "The many" are trampled on by the fourth beast (7.7, 19, 'the many' in Aramaic); the covenant is made strenuous over "the many" (9.27); the Little Horn wages war against the many (8.25). This becomes a key term in the following words as well.

*"And when they stumble, they will be helped – a small help. And many will be joined against them in the hypocrisy."*

Again the stress is laid on the fact that within the people of Judah, there are the Righteous, and there are the Wicked. This is a civil war, and Antiochus IV "perceived" it and with flattery and offerings of treasure allured a good number of Jews to his cause. The emphasis is on "small" – like the rock in the dream of Nebuchadnezzar. It is the word of Prophet Zechariah and the days of "small beginnings". The Exile scattered the people of Israel throughout the world – all throughout – and their subsequent generations in Egypt, Persia, Babylonia, Asia-Minor, and in Greece, populated those areas that maintained, even if nominally, a connection to the Jewish covenant (the Diaspora). There was a divine reason for this. Jerusalem is not yet let go of in this plan, and a righteous remnant of Spirit filled Jews maintained the faith (as witnessed in Zechariah and Haggai). Even though the covenant is once again broken (it was broken before the Exile); it was nonetheless the center point of the faithful few, with Jerusalem as the capital city of David, and the temple as the center of worship.

Israel never regained her place as she had in those days of David and Solomon – never, but something arises out of the slaughter in the days of Antiochus IV that brings her into Independence – with a standing army (under the Maccabees and later Hasmoneans). She "receives a Dominion" (7.18); they come to "possess a Dominion" of their own (7.22); But, is this is an everlasting Dominion (7.27) which is closely, yet from Daniel's point of view, somewhat enigmatically linked to "one like a son of man" receiving the same Dominion (7.14)? The "one like a son of a man" is interpreted to mean that the "saints" shall receive a Dominion after the trampling of the Seleucid King – a furtherance of what was "set up" in the following years after the Exile. From that time, stretching over to 170 B.C.E.

Israel populated the Middle East and its surroundings and flourished. Judea, in the time of Jesus, was a vassal nation, having lost her gained independence in 63 B.C.E. During the time of the remaining beasts (7.12), well into Roman solidification and consolidation of their empire, Jesus announced that the Dominion will be taken from the current rulers of Judea and "given to another nation that will bear fruit" (Matthew 21.43). Indeed, in Daniel 7.14 the son of man is "given a Dominion" by the Ancient of Days. Is this a reference to that action, when the Son of Man ascends to the heavenly throne, and is given the covenant "nation" obligation? If he is given a Dominion, then who was it taken from? Nebuchadnezzar was "given" the nation of Judea and gave it to his own people. Likewise, the Son of Man is given the nation, who in turns gives it to his people, making them a "nation of priests" (Revelation 1.6). For Paul, this is concluded when he "delivers up" this kingdom/nation to God (1 Corinthians 15.24), having finally brought the people of God who love him to their destined inheritance: a new heavens and a new earth.

## Chapter Eleven

The blow received here from this King is not a blow that wipes out the people of God and their renewed covenant, but a furtherance in their establishment towards the goal of the Prophets and the covenant: so that the nations would come in and worship at the true Mount Zion, in the true Temple of the Lord. Thus, from the Return to this point, a ground work is laid for a much larger enterprise of God – a foundation is being laid for a much more grand complex that will eventually include the worship and obedience of the nations (7.27, which see).

*"And from the wise ones will fall – in order to refine in them, to purify, to make white up to a time of end, for yet is the appointed time."*

Here we have the infinitive of purpose. This decree of God, these seventy-sevens for "your people and your city" is in order to further refine, to further purify and to further make them white by their allegiance and faith to God. God's purpose for his people is to bring about an everlasting righteousness – a whiteness – among them. It is a whittling away of the dross that is brought about by the smelting furnace of God's refining fire. It is a pruning of the branches of the tree, leaving the good, and destroying the bad. It is a reduction of the people of God, the true people of God, from the hypocrites who claim God, but have nothing really in their hearts that make them his.

"The appointed time" of course, comes through the actions of Antiochus IV, as it is stated in 11.29. The "appointed time" concludes with the "setting right" the holy place, as was made known in 8.14 . The "rebellion" amongst the Judeans commences the "time of the end" leading to when the "sanctuary is cast down" (8.11, 12) and a few years of tribulation and turmoil ensue. They are to endure these "times" and the "half times" (the whole of the "one seven" which includes the middle part). The angel is asked "how long" will be the "vision" of this, and he is given the answer of two thousand and twenty three hundred days (a little over six years) "and then the holy place will be set right" (8.14). The whole vision is the "time of the end" (8.17). Antiochus IV, "at the appointed time" (11.29) commences this "latter end" of the "appointed time", and the saints must endure until the whole "time of the end" – when the Temple is once again, "set right". It is not that hard to follow when it is understood that all of these visions and words given to Daniel concern the same time-frame as marked out by the divisions of the times in the seventy-sevens. The fact that 1 and 2 Maccabees records these very times, using Daniel (mentioning him), and the vocabulary of him confirms our interpretation here.

Even Josephus mentions Antiochus IV in fulfillment of these times, as does other Jewish literature, including an excerpt from the Dead Sea Scrolls. Daniel is not envisioning the end of the world. He is not predicting the restoration of all things for the second century B.C.E. faithful. Antiochus IV is not the last King (and is never called that). Rather, as we have shown, that while the line of the Seleucid Dominion is radically broken after the death of Seleucus IV, this eighth horn is destroyed. The Seleucids never regain full recovery, even though one of the horns plucked before Antiochus IV, Demetrius I, the true heir who was brought low, did come to power. He killed the young son of Antiochus IV (also named the same), and also defeated and killed Judas Maccabaeus. However, Jonathan, his brother, defeated Demetrius in 150 B.C.E. with the help of a rival Seleucid king, Alexander Balas. Civil strife continued until finally, under the Roman Pompeii, the Seleucid region came under full Roman power.

We should see the obvious here in that the fourth beast is survived by one of the horns, and that the three contemporary beasts (most likely being the Ptolemies, the Antigonids, and the Attilids – the three other Dominions that arose from the four horns after Alexander the Great) are not destroyed, but survive the beast with eight horns (7.12). It is the eighth horn of the beast that is destroyed (the line is altered). Antiochus IV was the eighth King of the Seleucid Dominion, knocking out three: Demetrius (hostage in Rome); Heliodorus (usurper of the throne, but a co-regent); and Antiochus, the young son of Seleucid IV who was ordered to be killed by Antiochus IV). He is not at all envisioning the end of the world in some sort of great Apocalyptic Holocaust.

*"Now, the King shall do according to his will. And he will exalt and magnify himself concerning every god; even concerning the God of gods he will speak wonderful words. And he will prosper up to the completion of the indignation, for that which is determining is done."*

Having ended the war with the saints and emphasizing their role, the angel now turns again to the King of the North, Antiochus IV with a string of descriptions that have already been stated in the previous visions of chapter seven and eight. In other words, this is a summary of the King so that no mistake is made concerning what "has been determined" (this word is in Daniel 9.26). He will prosper and bring about the fullness, or completion of the indignation (9.24; "when the transgression is filled", 8.23; the time of "the indignation", 8.19). He will prosper (8.24). He will magnify and exalt himself (8.25). He will speak words of flattery concerning God, seducing words that will draw away the people into a condemnation of the covenant itself (7.8, 11).

*"And concerning the gods of his fathers, he will not perceive them. And concerning a desire of women, nor concerning any god he will not perceive for he will magnify himself over them."*

This was certainly true of Antiochus IV, who had no real affiliations with the gods of his fathers, and broke protocol after protocol with them. Antiochus named himself "Epiphanes" – as God manifest, and claimed on coins printed under his rule an image of himself as Zeus! This image of Zeus is the statue of the same set up in the Temple. From the Jewish point of view, this was an exaltation of himself over God himself – acting as a god and murdering the saints simply because they followed the covenant. He set himself up in the temple and by that very act made himself a god – to the Jew. As far as the angel who is giving Daniel these words, Antiochus IV is an abomination. He doesn't even have concern for the desire of women – he is not a man. He is wrapped up in himself, in love with himself.

It is interesting that the word "perceive" is used here. It is frequently employed in Daniel (for Daniel) in the sense that Daniel "perceives" knowledge, has "insight" in visions and mysteries. Various times Daniel is told to "understand" ("perceive" – same word) what the words of the angel(s) mean. In 8.23, however, the Little Horn is described as one whose "perceiving" (participle) is enigmatic riddles. This could mean that he is just not like the other Kings in terms of his depth perception; he doesn't operate according to how things are supposed to operate. He has a lack of perception when it comes to the ordinary because he is so wrapped in his self interest. It is not that he does not know of the gods, but that he does not "perceive" them – he is not devoted to anyone or anything other than his own interests.

*"And to the God of fortresses, in his place he will weigh down – that is, to the God who his fathers did not know – he will weigh down with gold and with silver and with precious stones, and with the desirable things."*

I stick with the way certain terms are used throughout Daniel, and here, following the previous forms, Daniel uses the article "the" for God. And so here. God is regularly called the God of refuge or fortress (2 Samuel 22.33). "Here now is the man who did not make God his fortress but trusted in his great wealth and grew strong by destroying others!" (Psalm 52.7). This psalm captures, I believe, what is intended here. Antiochus IV denied the God of Judah and, in his place, magnified himself and through seeking riches he weighs down his constituent lands – burdens them. The parenthetical clause further delineates that "the God of strongholds" is "the God unknown by his fathers."

That is, they were just as in the dark as he when it comes to "perceiving" God. Then, the sentence continues by repeating the same verb, "he will weigh down" after the parenthetical interruption. So, following the last clause of the previous verse, "he will magnify himself, and as regards the God of fortresses, in his place he will weigh down…" Taking the place of God, he brings about a burden to the people in terms of hoarding their wealth. This certainly fits what we know of Antiochus.

*"And he will do concerning the fortification of fortresses. With a strange god, who he has acknowledged, he will make honorable, and he will cause them to rule over the many. And the ground he will divide for a price."*

Again, all of this concerning the actions of Antiochus IV is well recorded in the historians. Antiochus was not an atheist, and the idea is not that he was irreligious, but that he eclectically assimilated them into his narrative and life. Antiochus identified with Zeus, so much that his image as Zeus appeared on the coinage at the time. Some thought that he was quite mad (instead of Epiphanes, they called him Epimanes, "mad man"). He built several cities throughout his time, garrisons, fortifications, and mainly, one in Jerusalem where his people and troops worshipped and sacrificed to "strange gods" (a common Hebrew expression for foreign gods, unknown gods). "The many" here is with the article and refers within the larger context as the Judeans. Antiochus' garrison (fortress) can be viewed in Jerusalem. For the pious, orthodox Jew this was simply a bad situation that had gone insane.

The above verses are simply describing this King with terms already used throughout Daniel and adds a few more specific details about him. This is what he will do when he is made King over the many. He will be completely indignant towards Jerusalem. He will rule with an iron hand. He has no regard for Seleucid protocol, and he is a rewarder of those who side with him in his campaigns, doling out land, wealth and honor.

*"And in the time of end, a King of the Negev will thrust with him, but the King of the north will storm against him (the King of the Negev) with chariot and horsemen and with great ships. And he will come in the lands, and overflow and pass through."*

These terms have been used in 11.10 concerning the campaign of the King of the Negev. It is known that a few short years after Antiochus took to recover the Purple of his killed brother,

## Chapter Eleven

Eulaeus and Lenaeus declared war on the King, vying for the Coele-Syrian area, which included Judea (remember, Antiochus III took that from Ptolemy IV). This is simply repeating what had already been said.

It is often thought, indeed assumed, that the words here predict a third invasion of Antiochus IV upon the region of Egypt. However, the period is marked as the "time of the end" (170-164 B.C.E.). There, in 170 B.C.E., Antiochus IV responds to the campaign against him and secures Coela-Syria and marches to Egypt with all his arsenal. We are told in Daniel 8.17 that "the vision" of the Little Horn and all that he does when it comes to "your city, and your people" is "the time of the end." This whole period commences in 170 when the King invades Egypt for the first time, and civil unrest comes to the people of Judea. After a few years, the King returns to Jerusalem after his failed campaign and this commences "the appointed time" (11.29), which lasts until the "vision is fulfilled" (8.13), when the sanctuary is "set right" (8.14). It is the last "seven" of the seventy sevens, and this whole "seven" is "the time of the end." In the middle part of the seven, the "appointed time" – the latter time of the end – commences. Here, then, we are told that "at the time of the end" (the beginning of the seventh "week" in Daniel 9.27), the King of the Negev will push against Antiochus, and Antiochus pushed back. This is the first entrance into Egypt. Antiochus was successful – "but the appointed time is not yet" (11.27) during this campaign. When this is understood, there is nothing at all strange in the angel reiterating this period and the first success of the King. It has been repeated a few times already, bringing further clarity so as to prepare the "wise" among the condemners of the covenant. We find this same sense of repetition in chapter 7 concerning the "little horn".

*"And he will come into the beautiful land, and many will stumble, and these will escape from his hand: Edom, and Moab, and the Chiefs of the sons of Ammon."*

And so he does, and it is repeated, "and many will stumble" (11.33, 34, 35); that is "the many" of the righteous will stumble. Of course, forming the borders of the Seleucid Dominion (Arabia), and just outside the Coele Syria are the regions, as Daniel would know them, of Edom, Ammon and Moab – virtually left untouched (remember, in Daniel's thinking, "Javan" is Greece, Negev is "south", Shinar is Babylon – and so these lands are designated not how they were named in Antiochus' day, but in Daniel's time). Jeremiah often repeats these three regions together as well (9.26, 25.21, 27.3).

That we know that he will enter the glorious land is told to us already in 8.9, that this vision belongs to the "time of the end" (8.17). It is repeated again in 11.16. This is the focal point of the conclusion of the visions and the words: a King, a little horn, is coming, the coming one, and he will enter the glorious land, and when he does, mark from that time "one seven". "Days" will ensue, but the appointed time is not yet. In the middle part of that time, there will be a "latter part", the "latter days" (10.14). These final days will end "at the appointed time" of the whole "time of the end", when the sanctuary is "set right" again.

*"And he will send his hand among many lands, even the land of Mizraim, and it will not escape."*

In comparison with the neighboring regions east of the Jordan (Ammon, Moab and Edom), the invasion of Antiochus IV gobbled up the western coastal areas and moved into the Negev region. Mizraim, of course, is the biblical name for Egypt. It is important to repeat the war with Egypt for it is the marking point of the "time of the end". When it is seen that Egypt and Antiochus go to war, know that it is near. Thus, in 11.13 we are told that Antiochus III launched into Egypt, and this phrase, "to the end of the times" is noted. But, the appointed time is not yet. Antiochus III's invasion is not to be confused, then, with the invasion to come. Antiochus III will push through towards the end of the times (the Hebrew phrase), but it is not the end of the times – yet. The similarity of the language, thus, could cause a misunderstanding, hence the repetition: The King will do as he pleases, he will shower his friends with gifts and land, and they will oppress and trample on the righteous many. He will invade Egypt and take it. He will come to Jerusalem and oppress it. This is the determined time of end meant for the purging of the righteous from the unrighteous in Israel. He will come, and they will stumble. He will arise and exalt himself with blasphemies against the Most High God and his people.

*"And he will rule in hidden stores of gold and silver, and over all the desirable things in Mizraim – even in Lubim and Cushim will be within his steps."*

During the first invasion of Egypt, Antiochus secured the coastal regions along the Mediterranean, including the taking of Cyprus, or Kittim (hence, Ammon, Edom and Moab are not the focus of his invasions in the Negev. Moab, incidentally, under the Persian Dominion fell out of any substantial meaning in terms of a "nation". Thus, Daniel's usage of "Moab" is for "the land of Moab" – what was once called Moab). Antiochus, as we have seen, took Pelusium, which was a key entrance city to Egypt. His armies also attacked Alexandria, which places him within the area of the Lubim (modern Libya), and he also secured his rule in Memphis, placing him in the area known biblically as Cush (modern Ethiopia). He did not hold these places but a couple of years, having Ptolemy IV as a vassal King. His second campaign (second attempt at securing what he started) ended in 168 B.C.E. at Eleusis, just four miles or so from Alexandria. Lubim and Cushim were much more broad in terms of the geographical lines we see on today's map. Lubim, in ancient Greek, was Libue, or Libua and covered far more land overflow into Egypt than we see today. Like "Moab, Ammon and Edom" – spoken of in terms of sixth century Daniel – the word of the angel who was giving Daniel these vicinities, is not at all out of keeping with the extension of Antiochus IV and his Dominion. As noted, it was not long held and was a tenuous operation.

What is surprising, however, is that Lubim and Cushim are not at said to be "over ran" "passed through", "ruled over" or conquered. The phrase is, "within his steps" (literal Hebrew), and this is open to meaning (see the various translations). Also, Daniel has not used this term in any military sense, whereas he has used frequently repeated terms of campaigns and defeat throughout this chapter. It is exaggerated then, to suggest that this verse envisions the regions of Libya and Ethiopia as under the Dominion of Antiochus IV. They were not. However, as far as the ancient regional boundaries at that time, Antiochus marched towards the south (Memphis) and east (Alexandria), wherein the people of Cushim (south) and the people of Lubim (east) were "within his steps" (see 2 Chronicles 12.3 – the plural ending is attached which mean "Libyans" and "Cushites" – people). The word, "feet" is not a frequent word. It may simply mean, his feet were marching (a derivative meaning in Hebrew for this term)

## Chapter Eleven

towards the east and the south. Nothing more is said. It is not a military term, and we would, rather, expect to find the other word for feet which has been used for the "trampling under his feet" in chapters seven and eight. Thus, these regions are within his steps, but not under his feet. Daniel qualifies this distinction. "And one from the others, from them one horn came out, a little one, and grew exceedingly great toward the Negev, and to the sunrise and to the glorious (8.13). 11.43, then, is simply a reiteration of what has previously been revealed concerning "the King." His Dominion will take Mizraim, and within his steps are the Libyans to the east, and the Cushites to the south – marching towards these ancient lands.

*"And reports will trouble him from sunrise and from north, and he will go out greatly hot with intent to exterminate and to destroy many. And he will pitch tents of his palace between seas towards a mountain of beauty of holiness. And he will go to his end, and there is none helping him."*

Antiochus' capital city was Antioch, appropriately enough. According to history, he left there sometime in 165 B.C.E. because of disturbances he was hearing from the eastern ("sunrise") Parthian region, Armenia and the "high lands" of the north. Plus, the Dominion was slowly evaporating. The Roman Dominion was closing in, and within a hundred years would solidify the Diadochoi (the Seleucid, Ptolemaic, Antigonid and Attalid Dominions) into one Realm. Antiochus needed funds. He is known to have gone as far as Elymais, just east of the Babylonian region. Leaving there because of a revolt against him, he planned an incursion into what is now modern Iran. He died sometime in late 164 B.C.E. in a manner left with little clues, and no known grave site to this day – unsung. It is said that he died in the place called Tabai (or Gabai) located in or around the Persian border with Media (modern Isfahan, Iran – where, interestingly enough, it is reported that after the Edict of Cyrus to return the Israelites to Judah, many migrated to this place, calling it, Yahudiyah.

The text does not say he died, or was expected to die in Jerusalem. The phrase, "between the seas" (plural) is quite open in terms of location. Of course, "the seas" we know, the Red Sea, the Caspian Sea, the Black Sea and the Mediterranean, were very well known in the ancient world. Babylon saw itself as the in the center of the lands, surrounded by the seas. That Antiochus died in the Persian area designates the remoteness expressed here. That is, somewhere "between the seas" (unknown) with his tents pitched in the direction of the west. The striking thing that should be noticed is not any expected return to Jerusalem, but that his "tents" are compared to the "mountain" of the saints. The mountain is still there. Tents are pitched, they move, and have no stability.

It is true that the sanctuary was restored and cleansed before Antiochus IV died (December 25th, 164 B.C.E.). The eighth horn of the fourth beast was destroyed (7.22). The saints possessed the Dominion once ruled by him with an iron fist (7.18). Although he trampled them for a time, times and half a time, they emerged victorious under tremendous leadership (Mattathias and Judas Maccabeus). In Daniel 7.26 we are told that judgment was rewarded to the saints and the little horn's "power" was taken away. 11.45, then, is the fulfillment of that vision. The Seleucid Dominion was never the same after his death. The chain had been broken in terms of the proper succession of Kings. Antiochus V, the son, was weak and was not the legitimate heir. One of the horns usurped by the little horn – Demetrius I – the proper heir, overthrew him.

## Chapter Twelve

*"And in that time, Michael will stand, the great Prince, the one who stands over the sons your people. And it is a time of distress which has not been since there has been a nation to that time. And in that time they will escape, your people (all the ones who are found having been written in the book)."*

We are immediately tagged with the same phrase in 11.40, "And in the time of end" – at that time. The "time of end" as we have seen encompasses the "one seven" of the seventy sevens of Daniel 9.25-ff, the last seven (170-164 B.C.E.). "In the middle part" of that seven there will be years of great turmoil, which lasted, from the historical record, a little over three years (167- 164 B.C.E. – when the "sanctuary is set right" – 8.14). Thus, Michael is over them during that time, as was already stated in 10.21, and we are clued into the "behind the scenes" peek. The amazing turnaround of Mattathias and Judas Maccabeus is, of course, well known (recorded in 1 and 2 Maccabees). Literally, they throw off the Seleucid yoke and restore the sanctuary and fortify an army – no such undertaking had been done in Israel since the days of her Kings.

However, the distress of the time, such as has not happened to Israel since she was found as a nation, was an epoch marking event in her history. The phrase, "such as has not been since..." is a common one in the Prophets, (see Joel 2.2; Daniel 9.12!). This makes plain the idea that not all Israel is Israel. A distinction is made. There are those who are called "Israelites", and then there are the ones "written in the book." The "rebellion" that brings on the wrath of God through Antiochus against Judah is that many forsook the covenant of

God – they are wicked ones among the Israelites – their names are not written in the book! The mark of a true saint, a true Jew, is one who is "circumcised in the heart" (Deuteronomy 10.16; 30.6; Jeremiah 4.4; Leviticus 26.41; Isaiah 52.1; Jeremiah 9.26; Romans 2.27). Thus, more than ever before, Daniel is being shown what the mark of one who loves God and keeps his commandments is.

The "book" referred to here is found in Exodus 32.32, 33; Psalm 69.28. There is another "book" here as well, found in Daniel 10.21, the book of truth, which appears as preordained history. Psalm 139.16 refers to this as well. However, this book is one in which the names of the saints are recorded, and not all the names of the Israelites are in it.

*"(And many from those sleeping, from out of ground of dust they will awake. These to full life of age, and those to reproaches, to abhorrence of age)."*

The parenthetical is continued from the first clause that mentions "the ones who are written in the book". Of course, during the time of the end Daniel has been shown that many saints will be trampled and killed. In fact, many are ruled over and killed. But, not all of these who die during this time are written in the book. Not all of "your people" who fall asleep in the ground of dust are written in the book. The ones who are promised resurrection, "these" who are found written in the book who are of the "many" (Israel) will awake from the ground of dust to full life ("life" here is plural). This is an explicit reference to what resurrection is as spoken from the word of truth given by the angel. It is a full recovery from that which has been laid to rest ("sleep") in the ground, the body.

## Chapter Twelve

However, out of the many of Judah that die, not all of them will receive such a resurrection. Some of "your people" will be raised to an "age" of reproaches and abhorrence. A terrible fate. Their names are not written in the book. This is as stern a warning to those who "forsake the covenant" and "reject God" as one could have. Not only will your life on earth be filled with terror, but you will raised from the earth to face an age of terror! Fear the Lord!

It is commonly and erroneously thought that the promise of resurrection here is attached to the "time of end" under Antiochus. This is only done because these two events, the "time of end" and the resurrection are placed alongside each other. What many fail to understand, however, is that grammatically, textually, this verse does not say, "at that time many who sleep in the ground of dust shall awake." The "time" clearly refers to the "time of end" in 11.40, which, of course, ended when the sanctuary was "set right" (8.14), marking the end of the two thousand and twenty-three hundred days of chapter eight (as we are explicitly told). This is, rather, (and as many scholars have noted) a promise to those who maintain the Faith truthfully during that time. They are promised a future reward of resurrection to a full life. They have their names written in the book because of their steadfastness towards God. They ("these") will receive the crown of life. Thus, Daniel's "time of end" is not the resurrection time. That time, when that happens, is not mentioned (it is mentioned later, as we shall see). What happens, however, "at that time", the "time of end", is that Michael will be over them, protecting them and making sure that some will escape from the clutches of the claws of the fourth beast. At that time, they will be delivered. They will come through. And who are "they"? They are the ones whose names are written in the book and who are promised a future reward of full life when they are raised from the dead (whenever that is). The forsakers of the covenant, they are promised retribution. They may have died with the wealth of Antiochus being showered upon them, but they will be raised to reproaches and abhorrence from God!

*"And the ones who have insight, they will shine like the brightness of the firmament. And the ones who make righteous the many like the stars to an age and beyond."*

The first clause is almost a duplicate of 11.33, "they that have perception shall instruct the many". These righteous souls will instruct many "even to time of end" (11.35), or during this time, and here, since we know that 11.33-35 concerns the events of Antiochus IV and his ravishing of Judah, we clearly see that the same are being addressed. These righteous souls are the ones who hold the fort and rally to God and purge the wickedness. They will shine, even as many of them will be trampled and rejected (8.10, where the "stars" are trampled). Their lives were not given in vain, and their commitment to God is not lost. They will shine in the firmament like the stars. It is most probable that Saint Paul had this verse in mind in Philippians 2.15, "so that you may become blameless and pure, children of God without fault in a crooked and depraved generation, in which you shine like stars in the universe." The Greek Version of the Hebrew Bible known to Paul is verbatim here. Those who have the Light of God in their hearts shine in the midst of the wicked around them. They are endowed with glory and honor and their names are written in the book that are open before the Ancient of Days.

The "stars" of "the firmament" is found in Genesis 1.14-18. The reference is surely meant by the words of the angel since "the firmament" and "stars" were made in the "fourth day." The stars are made to "rule" creation "in the firmament" of the heavens. Hence, we have a remarkable comparison ("like") here. The wise saints shine in the Dominion of God. They are like stars that have been given the authority to rule over the affairs of men in terms of time. The days pass by as the events of the book of truth unfold in history, and the stars, the ones who have understanding, rule during the darkness of night. What is meant here, then, is that these stars are "shining" (Genesis 1.15) the light in dark places. They rule in the firmament and oversee the contests of men. It is by their understanding and their love for God that they rule – even when they are being trampled and fall. Such is the paradox of the Dominion of God for his people. In Luke 21.16-18 Jesus warned that some of his followers would be put to death, yet concludes with, "but not a hair of your head shall perish" (perhaps referencing the three Jews in the fiery furnace). That the Dominion of the saints is here meant is confirmed by the fact that they are to "possess" and "receive" a Dominion from God. They are counted worthy of resurrection life and their names have been written in the book. They are a nation of priests and a kingdom to the Lord their God. They have the law in their hearts and understanding in their minds. These are the true saints who reign with him on earth in the exact same manner that Daniel has demonstrated in his life. Like the "son of a man" who was enthroned before the Ancient of days, they, the saints of the Most High, are too exalted before him. They are marked and separated out from the rest of their nation as that true and holy nation with circumcised hearts.

*"But you, Daniel, close the words and seal the book until time of end. Many will wander to a fro, but the knowledge will increase."*

Daniel is now told to close the book ("book of truth", 10.21) and to seal it. It is for the "time of end" as in 8.17, where he was also told to "seal" the vision of the time of end (understanding that Daniel is writing down these things as indicated in 7.2). Thus, Daniel has been shown two visions (chapters seven and eight) and has seen two "appearances" with "words" given by an angel (chapters nine and ten through twelve). "The knowledge" is the knowledge of understanding that is given to the wise ones, the many, whereas the others who do not have understanding wander to and fro. It will grow, as the rock that will become the mountain that will become the Dominion that will never be uprooted. It is "the knowledge" of God's inner workings that have been revealed to Daniel in the book. The understanding of it will be "perceived" by those who keep close attention Daniel's words. By hindsight they will see the fulfillments come true. The knowledge will grow as the fulfillments of the words come to pass – those who are wise will understand them.

*And I, Daniel, saw and Behold! Two others were standing, one there on the lip of the stream, and another on the other lip of the stream. And one of them said to the man clothed in the white linen who was above the waters of the stream, "Till when is an end of these marvels?"*

Suddenly Daniel sees two other angelic beings on the sides of the Hiddikel river where the first mighty angel clothed in white linen appeared to him (10.4,5). He spoke of one Michael who helped him (10.13), and is the one who tells Daniel the words of the book of truth (10.21). Now that he has finished these words, two other angels appear and one of them asks this mighty angel, "How long?" This is reminiscent of 8.13 where one of the angels asks the other, "how long" – and we should take this to mean that they are asking the same here since the vision there "concerns the time of end" (8.17). There he was given the answer, "two thousand and twenty three hundred days" till when the sanctuary is "set right" (8.14). Even the angels inquire about these things. However, we should note that the "setting right" of the sanctuary is not mentioned in the words that have been given to Daniel by the angel. The words end with the death of "the King." It is the same in the vision given to him in chapter eight. The sanctuary is cleansed on the last day of the two thousand and twenty three hundred. But, the death of the King is mentioned in 8.25. When is that fulfilled? When does he die?

*Then I heard the man who was clothed in the white line, who was above the waters of the stream. And he raised his right hand and his left hand to the heavens and he swore by the Living One of the age that, "After an appointed time, appointed times, and a half, that is, at the completion of the scattering hand of the holy people – these things will be completed."*

The phrase, "time, times and half time" was used in 7.25 for the time when the people are under the domain of Antiochus IV. When this is finished, when "the transgression is complete" (9.24), the events of the words in chapter eleven are done. It is interesting to note that the rededication of the sanctuary is not mentioned in chapter eleven. Like chapter eight, Daniel was shown a vision of a little horn that would come and desecrate the sanctuary. That was the end of the vision. However, one of the angels asks the other, "How long?" It is then that the "setting the sanctuary to rights" is given in the answer – not in the vision. So here the setting right of the sanctuary was not given in the words – and so it is asked again, what is the end, the termination, of these words? The answer is akin to the one given in chapter eight: when the scattering by hand of holy people is completed, i.e., when they are no longer scattered and the sanctuary is set right, and the hand that scatters them is terminated (11.24 where his scattering is mentioned – also, I am following the rendering of the Septuagint here, as well as other commentaries – compare Judges 7.19).

That this interpretation follows is seen in the word "hand." It is not the hand of Judah, but the hand that scatters (or "shatters") Judah – the hand of the King. In Daniel 1.1 Judah was given into the "hand" of Nebuchadnezzar. Then, Judah is given into the "hand" of the Medes and Persians (8.4). Then, the Dominion of the ram (Medes and Persians and all in their hand) was given to the "hand" of the shaggy male goat (Greece, 8.7). There is an exchange of "hands" between the Kings of the north and the Kings of the Negev (11.11, 16, 41, 42). Likewise, in the Aramaic portions of Daniel, the three boys "escape from the hand" of Nebuchadnezzar (3.15-17 – where Nebuchadnezzar says, "who is the god that will deliver you from my hands? Their reply is, "he will deliver us out of your hand"); Daniel is "rescued" from the "hand" of lions (6.27); the saints are "given into the hand" of the little horn (7.25), and he "shatters" them (7.23).

The stories in chapters three and six, then, are illustrative of God's power to "rescue" and "deliver" his people, to "save" them from the "hand" that oppresses them – a hand that they have been given into by his decree in order to demonstrate his power. Thus, these things (the things in the words of the book of truth) are completed when the scattering/shattering hand of the holy people is finished by the hand of the King. "And he will be broken, but without hand" (8.25); "And he will go to his end, with none helping him" (11.45).

## Chapter Twelve

"...until the completion, and that which is decreed is poured out on him" (9.27).

*And I heard, but I did not understand, "My Lord, what is after these things?" And he said, "Go, Daniel. For shut and sealed are the words till time of end. Many will purify themselves and make themselves white and will be refined. And wicked will be wicked and none of them will understand, but the wise ones will understand."*

Daniel is pressing the question he heard answered by the mighty angel a bit further. He knows the time, times and half will come and the King's hand will be broken. However, according to the vision he was given in the first year of Belshazzar, the saints are to be given a dominion. That has not been mentioned here, so it seems. When is that? What will happen after these things – the things said in the words? In other words, when is this glorious Dominion of the saints received? Is it when the hand is broken? Is it when these things are completed? It is when the sanctuary is set right? What comes "afterwards"?

The angel responds with the same: the words are shut and sealed. No more is revealed. The sanctuary will be set right. The King will be destroyed. The sense here is that the wondrous reception of the Dominion, the Dominion that was "set up" like a rock that is to become a mountain (chapter two), the Dominion that is given to the "one like a son of a man" who stands for the "saints" who "receive the Dominion" (chapter seven) is left out of the words of the Book given here. They are shut up and sealed from Daniel. The words of the book of truth from which the angel has been saying to Daniel follow from the eruption of four Dominions. Two of these battle against each other between the north and the south. The vile King of the north does come and does what the vision in chapter eight and the words in chapter nine say he will do. And, then, the words end with his death. Therefore, Daniel is pressing for more information: what is the outcome of all of this, what comes after his death?

The answer is that the many who survive the time, times and half will purify themselves, and continue in righteousness. They will continue to be refined. The wicked will continue to be wicked, but they will have no understanding. In other words, the true saints will continue and the wicked will continue – life will go on. He does not specifically answer his request. This has interesting implications when Jesus is pictured opening a seven sealed scroll – evidently relating more "history" to come that was "sealed up" to Daniel. In other words, the "book of truth" is how history plays out, in detail, and Daniel is given a brief glimpse, but only up to a time. Then it is sealed. This does not mean, however, that there are no further words in this book. History is indeed planned out to the time of resurrection (the last day) – each Dominion, each King, and each true and false followers of God, with each eruption of tribulation and distress in the world. These are the "times and seasons known to the Father" (Acts 1.6; Daniel 2.21). Daniel is shown a few "times" and a few "seasons" – but he is not shown everything to happen in the history of the world. The book is sealed.

*"From the time the continual is taken away, and to set the abominable thing, the desolating one – days – one thousand two hundred and ninety. Blessed is the one who waits to the days – one thousand, three hundred, thirty and five."*

Here the angel refers back to the words of the book of truth verbatim (11.31). The King will "take away the continual and set

## Chapter Twelve

the abomination, the desolating one." This, of course, is also the vision of chapter eight. In chapter eight a rather long number is given (2300), ending with the sanctuary being set right. That was done from the time of continual offering being stopped (somewhere in June, 167 B.C.E.) and the appalling setting up of the Olympus Jupiter idol within the sanctuary (December 25th, 167). If we follow what has been reported to us, three years or so of outrageous afflictions and slaughter occurred from that time to December 25th, 164, when the temple was set right. Antiochus IV came to power in 175 B.C.E. but was sole King in 170 with the murder of his nephew, and the murder of Onias, the last, true High Priest (thus begins the "one seven" of the seventy sevens). Two thousand, three hundred and thirty days ensued (a little over six years), and within the middle parts of that time, the "times, time and half a time" marked the "latter part" of that time. This latter part ends with the "appointed time" of setting the sanctuary right. However, it is further revealed that "the King", the little horn, the eighth horn of the fourth beast, is destroyed. But, he was not destroyed when the sanctuary was set right. He was destroyed within a few months later, in 163 B.C.E. His exact date, and even his tomb, is unknown.

Thus, that Daniel's further pressing is related to what he has already seen and heard is made clear. The horn is destroyed (but remains of the beasts live on for a time and season). The people, the saints, are supposed to be given a Dominion. And it is precisely here that he is pressing. And it is also precisely here that he is told that time will continue. The saints will be given victory and the King will come to his end. The sanctuary will be set right, and the true saints of God will be refined, made white and purified – and they will continue to be made white and purified after the "appointed time" has come. Thus, these numbers extend beyond the sanctuary being set right and up to the death a few months later of Antiochus IV. At this time we have recorded the amazing successes of Judas Maccabeus and his armies over the surrounding regions. These pious Jews make a name for themselves all throughout that region in the year (163 B.C.E.) that followed. A Dominion has been established – but Judah continues to face wickedness and even war. And there is another large nation growing in the West – the Roman Dominion. Where is this Dominion of the saints that shall never be destroyed? Where are the words of the book of truth ended with "and they shall receive the Dominion and the nations shall obey them" (7.27)? Doesn't this come after the "time, times and half time" (7.25)? When the sanctuary is set right, and the King is finally killed, is that when, after these things the Dominion that shall never be destroyed comes? The Dominion that was set up concerning a people, and that this Dominion would be left to no others?

*"Now you, go to the end. And you will rest. And you will stand to your lot in the last day."*

This is the last word of the angel to Daniel. And it is loaded. Daniel's book begins with Exile and defeat. The Dominion of Judah has been handed over to the Babylonians (1.1). It is not recovered for several hundred years. The people return from the Exile and certainly rebuild what was crumbled. But, the glory days of the past appear to be long gone. Only a handful, a remnant, returns and even among them there are the wicked. The next centuries bring about one Dominion over another, with Judah being under them all. There is a time of peace for a few hundred years, but it was revealed to Daniel that a terrible, terrible time is coming. A King will come that will scatter the people and

## Chapter Twelve

trample them, and even throw down the rebuilt sanctuary and sack the rebuilt city. But not only this, from Daniel's own people there will arise wicked ones who join with the King! These will forsake the covenant! Daniel's people were divided in the Exile, the House of Israel from the House of Judah. And the remnants of these Houses returned, albeit without great international power as with David and Solomon. And, at this time, Daniel's people will fight among themselves, between the wicked ones and the righteous ones. The stars of the firmament against the darkness. A remnant is even further whittled down – a remnant within a remnant of those who truly have the love of God in their hearts.

Nonetheless, the people of God were promised by the Prophets that they would be established after the Exile and never again uprooted. The vile King does come and scatters them, but they do remain in the land – and the sanctuary is restored. But, where is the "lot" – the inheritance? The term "lot" here is specifically used in Numbers and Joshua for the divvying up of the Land of Promise. It is the "lot of the inheritance". The Dominion. The "lot of the inheritance" is "given" to the people ("given" is used throughout Numbers and Joshua in this context). It is their "possession".

Daniel is told to go to his end, the end of his life (obviously not "the end" as it concerns the visions!). He will rest. Daniel was an old man at this time. Thus, he is to join with those who have "fallen asleep" in the ground of dust (12.2). And he will stand again (the Greek version has "rise again" – what becomes the main word for "resurrection") in order to receive his lot, his inheritance at the end of days – the last day. Again, this cannot be in reference to the "days" discussed, for quite obviously Daniel would not be alive in those days! This is the end of Daniel's days on earth. He will die and rest and he will awake with the many "in the last day". From Exile to Resurrection!

**Summary**

One thing is striking to me and stands out. In the first vision, Daniel is shown one like a son of man, and this appears to be interpreted by "the saints of the Most High." And, there, in chapter seven, it is repeated that they shall rule and reign and be given dominion, honor and glory. In chapter eight, however, there is no mention of this glory. All that is mentioned in a positive sense is that the sanctuary, after it has been trodden down, will be "set right." Chapter nine, which is the first "appearance" (not a vision) with "words" spoken, mentions the catastrophe brought on by the little horn in chapter eight, and it mentions that the wrath of God will be poured on him. Chapters eleven and twelve again mention the terrible plight Jerusalem will face at the hand of the King of the north, but only mentions that they will be "delivered".

However, we must not downplay the significance of the fact that the ones "delivered" are the very ones whose names are written in the book. They are the wise ones who are compared to the rule and reign of the stars of creation in the firmament – a specific reference to the fourth day in the Genesis account. Thus, their deliverance, afforded by their insight and understanding (their faith), is to be seen as their receiving the Dominion – with glory and honor. They rule in the firmament with the Ancient of Days – but this rule is not like the Dominions of the land. It is a heavenly rule, for God's Dominion is a heavenly Dominion that is not of this world.

The stories of the "rescue" and "deliverance" of the three "sons of Judah" from the fiery furnace is most illustrative of this point. The boys rejected King Nebuchadnezzar's command. They maintained their faith in God – to the point of death. They were delivered as a result from his "hand" (which is explicitly stated). Daniel, likewise, was delivered from the "hand" of the lions. Daniel is a star in the firmament with understanding and insight, and awarded with "power" (2.23). The Three sons are stars in the firmament, having insight and power, obeying God above all else. These "deliverance" stories, then, are meant to illustrate how the saints rule and reign in the world in the Dominion of God that is not of this world. Their deliverance comes through their resistance to the end of their lives, whether they fall by the sword, are captured, burned, trampled or slain. If they survive and remain on the land, they are stars. If they die, they are stars. All of their names are written in the book, and they are promised resurrection, where they will receive "the lot of inheritance" - a new land and a new heaven – restored and given to them.

Thus, Daniel has effectively transcended the mundane and the earthly Dominions that come and go, that change and are here today and gone tomorrow. God sets up these Dominions and passes them down. His Dominion is forever and his people, "a nation of kings and priests" is a Dominion in and of itself. Thus, from the fall of Babylon, a small rock shatters that Dominion and is resettled in the land. From a very few who are known of God and who know their God, many centuries pass. But, there is coming, so Daniel saw, another wave of terror over the people and the city. A further refining takes place, whittling away the sons of God from the sons of darkness. The stars, as they are called, shine for they have the light of God as their lamp, and he overshadows them and delivers them. However, there is a further act of deliverance to come for all those whose name is in the book: resurrection to inheritance. The stars on earth who shine and who are shined upon not only reign in this life, but are promised a continual reign in the next by resurrection over death itself. The promises of God are met, fully, in the resurrection of the dead.

Thus, we may have a cryptic understanding, not very clear, of the "one like a son of man" that comes before the Ancient of Days. How can a mortal approach God? Only if he is made immortal. The same applies to the "saints of the Most High". It appears, then, that Daniel is not entirely informed about the relation between this "one like a son of man" and the "saints of the Most High." But, they both come together in the exaltation of the son of man.

That the New Testament picks up on Jesus and calls him the son of man repeatedly, and he even calls himself that, must have reference to Daniel's vision in chapter seven. In other words, the parousia in 7.13 is applied to Jesus' enthronement and ascension to the right hand of the Father. Second, Jesus is, in fact, raised from the dead as was promised to Daniel – who is not raised from the dead. Jesus is the "firstborn" and is called the "first fruit" of the resurrection promised in Daniel (and to Daniel himself).

I say this because even though Judah gained massive success and even independency, that was lost within a hundred years when the Romans made Israel a vassal state. Herod, who was no King in any accordance with the Law of Moses, or the Promises of God, and the High Priest was not of the line of Zadok. That line was broken under Antiochus IV, when Onias was murdered. Daniel says nothing concerning a coming Messiah who will be crucified and raised from the dead. But, he does see a vision of one "like a son of man" that the NT authors pick up as Jesus.

Daniel nine, it is thought by very many within Christian theology, supposedly predicts the death of Jesus, but as we have shown, this is far from likely and simply does not remain consistent with the way history unfolded within the historical framework Daniel is shown (and, again, this is understood by a good deal of scholars, too).

Deliverance, then, comes to the people of God in time and space. They are the sons and daughters of his Dominion, and are a Dominion on earth in their own right. They are stars in the universe, who rule and reign with his angels, and the myriads at God's call are on their guard for the people of God, moving history for them, for his purpose. This is power, honor, glory and dominion. However, ultimate fulfillment is when the lot of inheritance is received when the resurrection of the dead occurs "at the last day" – as Daniel is told. It is the "last word" of the book! If the people of God are delivered on earth, in terms of enduring evil Kings and fearsome Dominions, then how much more is the deliverance of resurrection of the dead over all the powers times powers to infinity?!

With the message of Jesus, who is persecuted for his faith in God, and killed at the hands of the rebellious within his own people (those who forsake the covenant), and by the hand of King Caesar, represented by the Pontus, Pilate, he is delivered by resurrection of the dead. He is exalted at the right hand of God as a result, and given all power, dominion and honor (Matthew 28.18; Revelation 5). In fact, he is called, "one like a son of man" in Revelation 1.13. The connection is not made clear in Daniel, but it is in the NT.

If our interpretation is correct, then we have to re-look at the NT and the way it treats of Jesus as the son of man. The fourth beast is not the Roman Dominion as is often stated by many. The similarities are far less than their dissimilarities. Revelation 13.1-ff has hardly any resemblance to the beast in Daniel 7, except one peculiar item that actually confirms our interpretation. In John's vision, his beast is made up of three images of Daniel's: the bear, the eagle and the leopard – forming one beast. If these three represent the "remaining" of the Diadochoi who are allowed to "live for a time" (Daniel 7.12), then we can clearly see that these three Dominions are now consumed, absorbed, or consolidated into one beast: Rome, who ruled over Egypt, the east and the north. John's vision, then, is not Daniel's. John's vision is a new beast, that of Rome, which Daniel did not see. This has fresh implications for interpreting Revelation.

Likewise, Daniel nine is not at all envisioning the destruction of Jerusalem and the temple (Daniel nowhere mentions the destruction of the temple – the sanctuary is made desolate, and will be set right afterwards). He is not foreseeing the coming of Titus in 70 C.E. He is not seeing the rise of some super "anti-christ", either. This has, then, implications for the way Jesus viewed, and the way the more nationalistic Jews understood the city and the temple. If, in fact, God delivered the city and the people, and even a feast day was originated as a result ("The Festival of Lights" or "Hannakah" – mentioned in John 10.22) of resetting the sanctuary (December 25th, 164 B.C.E.), then to speak against the city and the temple, or more to the point, to prophesy the destruction of the city and the temple, was downright blasphemous. The Jews in Jesus' day did not entertain the notion that God was coming to pour out his wrath upon the city and the temple! Daniel was fulfilled, and the People were victorious –or so they thought. Yet, Jesus, alluding to Daniel (Matthew 24), states that the city and the temple will fall. Wrath is coming. And it did under the Roman legions who, like the civil strife in the

## Chapter Twelve

days of Antiochus IV that was among the Jews, squashed the city. They continued a bloody campaign throughout until 135 C.E. Jerusalem was never the same. This was not at all "foreseen" in the Prophets. Jesus is, then, not foretelling what the Scriptures foretold, but is prophesying his own word – a fresh word of God. If this is the case, this would have implications for the way we view Jesus' antagonism against "King" Herod, and the "High Priest" family that was, according to the promises and the law of Moses, illegitimate and defunct.

In fact, one could go so far as saying that by the time Jesus arrives with his message, the covenant with Moses was broken in its most fundamental sense. When Jesus said he has come to "fulfill" the law and the prophets, he means that he has come to renew the covenant, a new covenant, bringing out the fullest meaning that were in them – the meaning that we have seen Daniel enacting in his life – a man after God's heart, who has the law "written upon his heart", who is "circumcised in the heart" and follows God from his heart. Daniel had no land, no priests, no temple, and no sacrifices. There was no altar, no King from David's Seed. Yet, he ruled and reigned with God and received power from God – powerful angelic beings stood by him. Michael watches over those written in the book. They are the stars of the Dominion of God, the Most High, whose rule never ends, and is never plucked up from the land. It is this Dominion that God established as small rock, that grows into a mountain, that is delivered from the hand of Antiochus IV. The son of man has come and has been exalted before the Ancient of Days, fulfilling the Prophet Daniel, and has made " a nation and kingdom of priests" in the world that will never be destroyed and never uprooted, but will be raised from the dead and inherit all things that have been given to the son of man.

Even though the Exile ends and the city and temple are rebuilt, this still does not account for the great mass of Israelites that remained within the outer regions of the land of promise. These were not all irreligious gatherings, either, but established what became the channels of Judaism throughout the world: the synagogue. It was upon the basis of the Diaspora that the "good news" of the preaching of the disciples could spread abroad as rapidly as it could, surviving Rome and even toppling it. It was in the Divine purpose that the Exile, although ended, fulfilled many prophecies found in the Seers concerning the spread of Israel's God to the nations. After all, it was the followers of one of David's son, the son of man named Jesus, that preached the promises of the God of Abraham, Isaac and Jacob, which is the basis for the Christian Gospel.

In the NT witness, as mentioned above, Daniel 7.13 is directly taken from in Matthew 24.30, where the "sign" of his fulfilling Daniel 7.13 is the fall of the city of Jerusalem. Daniel 7.13, then, is picked up as the "parousia" of the son of man, being exalted in the heavenlies before the Father, the Ancient of Days. That the destructive forces of Antiochus IV took place in the winter, and that a slaughter happened on the Sabbath (as we have recorded in 1 and 2 Maccabees), drives home the point that Jesus alludes to Daniel and those events that transpired under that King (Matthew 24.15; 20). There, Jesus hopes that this does not take place in the winter, or on the Sabbath, as it did for them in 167 B.C.E. By using Daniel and its separating the true saints from the false, and by noting that he is forecasting similar destruction (though far more devastating than Antiochus IV), throws light on the fact that Jesus is acting as his own Prophet, speaking the word of God in a fresh and unheard of way. It would require great faith to follow him – true faith from heaven itself – in order to go the whole way with him. There was no verification afforded in Daniel or in any other Prophet that directly stated in so clear terms that this Jesus, son of Mary and Joseph, the carpenter's son, the Galilean, was "the Christ" that the Prophets and Moses heralded. If Daniel were so easily understood, why not just count down the years of the seventy-sevens until you get to his birth year in the Jewish calendar? Wouldn't that have been an easy task to accomplish? How hard could it have been by a people who were ferocious about time keeping? What would have been shocking to them if Jesus simply said, "Look, Daniel clearly says that in the year I was born, thirty years ago, the Temple was going to be destroyed by a Prince of the Fourth Beast, which is clearly Rome. Do the math!" But, strangely, we do not find such an appeal to Daniel as we do today by Christians who remain so confident that Daniel predicts with great detail, even to the year, of Christ's birth, his crucifixion and the destruction of Jerusalem! If it was so easy now, what prevented it from being so easy then?

The fact is, the text of Daniel, his visions predict that the "people" of God, the truly devoted, will return from the Exile. The city and sanctuary will be rebuilt. For many centuries, however, Israel will remain under the Dominion of other nations and Kings. However, as it is powerfully demonstrated throughout Daniel, God's Dominion is unaffected by the scattering of his people – which is the display of his wrath (Daniel nine). God's Dominion is eternal, from generation to generation and remains unaffected by this King or that King. In fact, it is God who "gives" these Kings their sovereign power! He rules over them all, and is the very Cause of their being and their falling. His Dominion works through history, in spite of history, and his purpose stands and none can stay his hand. His Dominion has no end, and has no beginning, and it sets above all other Dominions that he has established by his host. God is not Exiled. God is not punished. God's temple does not suffer collapse, nor does his sanctuary allow for pollution of any sorts. It is never desecrated nor defiled. No unclean thing ever enters into his Courts.

This is precisely the point that Daniel ties together. It is said that God will "establish" a Dominion on the land (2.44). This is not his Dominion – the Dominion that is from generation to generation – his Dominion has no need of being "set up." This is a "Dominion and nation" of "priests" (Exodus 19.6). God is their King. God, after the Exile, renews the people and renews the covenant, although it will not be like the covenant made previously (Jeremiah 31.31). Jeremiah saw the return from Exile as God re-establishing his people – his faithful people – and setting them up in such a way that they will never be removed again (Jeremiah 31.40). This is word for word in Daniel 2.44. "It will not be left to another people."

Thus, one can now begin to appreciate the tie in with the "son of man" in 7.13 and its interpretation being "the saints of the Most High" – It is the people that are given power and glory – those who do not forsake the true heart understanding of the everlasting covenant and the Everlasting God who is tender in mercy and love "to those who love him" (Daniel 9.4). There were true saints filled with the Spirit in the days of Joshua and Zerubabel (Zechariah-Haggai). There were true saints who lived their years faithfully and in peace during the rise and fall of Persia and Greece. There were true holy ones filled with insight and understanding who maintained their love to God, even over death, during the vile King, Antiochus IV.

The NT picks up on this when we encounter the very old Simeon (Luke 2.25-ff). He was but a generation or two away from the time of Antiochus IV and the coming in of Rome. "This child shall cause the rising again and falling of many in Israel" (Luke 2.34). Compare this Daniel 12.2 and 13! Jesus steps into the unfinished business of God that had apparently remained dormant for some time. And then, Behold! One who is the son of man appears! Israel is about to be whittled and separated down to the true Jew, the true Israelite – this time marked by following Jesus, the one who the Ancient of Days has sent. With the same earnestness, Spirit, and faith the saints of the past followed hard after their God, so also will the true saints follow hard after the one who God has sent. Jesus is about to take the vision of Daniel's rock-becoming-mountain-becoming-a Dominion into heights and growth and depths it has never seen before. And it is precisely on the 'scattered ones' (the Diaspora) that he does so, bringing in all peoples, languages, nations and lands and making them his "nation, Dominion of priests" as far as the sun is to the east and west, wherever land may be trod, over whatever sea or stream can be crossed (Revelation 1.6; 5.10). Just when the light appeared to be flickering out, "at just the right time" says Paul, "God sent forth his son."

The promises of God, then, in Jesus, who fulfills all righteousness, are met in him and shall be accomplished in him for all those who are now called into this Dominion that shall never perish. The promise of resurrection, given explicitly and directly to Daniel (12.2;13) are for all those who call on God during this time of expansion. "And they shall all be raised at the last day" – echoing Daniel 12.13. They will be raised from the dead to "receive the lot of inheritance" – a fully restored Dominion of the nation of people/priests in new heavens and a new earth, where Abraham and all the faithful Israelites will "stand again" in the land of renewal and everlasting endurance – fulfilling the promises. For Paul, it is through Jesus, who is the firstborn of the new created man – the man made from heaven – of whose nature believers are also being conformed to in the same manner God has conformed his faithful all along. Every true Israelite, and every true believer from all the nations who are made partakers of Israel's promises, who are equally called, "children of God", inherit the true Temple above, the heavenly city whose builder and maker is God – the Dominion that can never be destroyed – on earth as it is in heaven.

Daniel's book, then, is a book for all generations and ages and its message is plain and clear: God does whatsoever he pleases. He changes the times and seasons (which are not for us to know – Acts 1.6). He sets up Kings and deposes them. In Jesus, the son of man, the seed of David, who sits at the right hand of God, this power of God has been given to him – to a man. This man, Jesus, rules from the heavens, shaking the nations and the heavens, separating as he is gathering together the nations before him in the call of "Today! If you hear his voice!" Jesus, by the sent Spirit, is calling all to repentance, pouring down blessings from the Spirit, and at the same time, wrath and indignation towards the nations. These are his "all" – his people – who have been foreknown, called, and will be made justified in the generations of men and women to come – until that last, unknown day. The saints must endure the same persecution and death he suffered, realizing that God is not finished calling those who are his and who have been given to the son of man. As long as God calls, his people must suffer and live "in the world" even though they are not "of the world." They must put up with the unfinished business of sin in their own lives, their "old man" as Paul puts it, until one of two things happens: death (at which time they enter into the "house of God" in heaven – 2 Corinthians 5.1-10), or the son of man suddenly descends from his abode and raises the dead at the last day (John 5-6); effectively ending history. Until such time, the saints, like Daniel, are charged with: "Go your way, dear one, until your end. You shall rest, and you will stand again and receive your inheritance."

The continuance, then, of sin and death in the life of the believer, the sin and the death that has been overcome by the man, Christ Jesus, is not because it has not been removed. All things are yes and amen in Jesus. There is now no condemnation for those in Christ Jesus. Slugging it out with the old man, the sinful nature, and facing the wage of sin, death, is the very vehicle by which God conforms the believer to his son's life. Because the believer has been forgiven and justified, his wrestling against principalities and powers, against darkness and against sin is a battle that has been won already. It is because of seeing Jesus, who won the battle on the cross, that we are able to see our own future in the redemption of all things. It is the same faith that the saints had in the time of Antiochus IV, the time of Exodus, the time under Joshua, or in the time of the Judges. Daniel suffers for his faith, and he is delivered. Yet, he does die, but is promised resurrection – it is his, he will have it. It will happen because of what has been done in Christ – as Simeon said, "God has kept his promises." Sin does not have the last word, and neither does death for the Saint.

# Bibliography

This is by no means an exhaustive Bibliography of the works I have used and read throughout my studies over the past decades. These are some of the more important works that I have found to be indispensable, and even here, I have not listed all of those.

Anderson, Steven D., *Darius the Mede: A Reappraisal* (Ph. D. Dissertation, Dallas Theological Seminary, May, 2014).

Bickerman, Elias. *Four Strange Books of the Bible*, (Schocken Books, New York, 1967) 61-ff.

Bulman, J. M. "The Identification of Darius the Mede." WTJ 35:3 (Spring 1973): 247-267.

Calvin, John. *Commentaries on the Book of the Prophet Daniel*. Translated by Thomas Meyers. Vol. 1. Calvin's Commentaries. Edinburgh: Calvin Translation Society, 1852. Reprint, Grand Rapids: Eerdmans, 1948.

Collins, John J. *Daniel with an Introduction to Apocalyptic Literature*, Volume XX *The Forms of the Old Testament Literature* (Eerdmans, Grand Rapids, 1984), 51

Collins, John J. *A Commentary on the Book of Daniel*. Hermeneia, edited by Frank Moore Cross. Minneapolis: Fortress, 1993.

Colless, Brian E. "Cyrus the Persian as Darius the Mede in the Book of Daniel." Journal for the Study of the Old Testament 56 (Dec 1992): 113-126.

Davis, P. R. 'Daniel, Chapter Two,' *JTS* 27.2 (October, 1976) 392-401.

Dougherty, Raymond Philip. *Archives from Erech: Time of Nebuchadrezzar and Nabonidus*. Goucher College Cuneiform Inscriptions, vol. 1. New Haven, CT: Yale University Press, 1923.

Dougherty, Raymond Philip. *Nabonidus and Belshazzar: A Study of the Closing Events of the Neo-Babylonian Empire*. Yale Oriental Series, vol. 15. New Haven, CT: Yale University Press, 1929.

Driver, S. R. *The Book of Daniel.* Cambridge Bible for Schools and Colleges, edited by A. F. Kirkpatrick. Cambridge: Cambridge University Press, 1900.

Frye, Richard N. "DARIUS ii. Darius the Mede," *Encyclopaedia Iranica,* VII/1, pp. 40-41, available online at http://www.iranicaonline.org/articles/darius-ii(accessed on 30 December 2012).

Fuerst, Julius. *A Hebrew & Chaldee Lexicon to the Old Testament,* Translated from the German by Samuel Davidson (Leipzig: Williams & Norgate, 1867), 260. Fuerst translated Dan. 9:27 as, 'he will make the covenant difficult for many'. That is, 'he' (Antiochus IV) shall cause (*hiphil*) a strong burden, where *gbr* is taken in a transitive sense.

Gressmann, Hugo. *Der Messias* (Gröttingen: Vandenhoeck & Ruprecht, 1929); I am grateful for this reference from John Bright's *The Kingdom of God* (Abingdon: Nashville, 1978 [org. 1953]) wherein he mentions Gressmann and his interpretation, with which he concurs, of the Four King-doms as the *Diadochoi*. Gressmann is also mentioned in *The Interpreter's Bible Commentary* Volume 6 (Abingdon Press: Nashville, 1956), 453.

Jeffrey, Arthur and Gerald Kennedy, 'The Book of Daniel', *The Interpretor's Bible Commentary* Volume 6 (Abingdon Press: Nashville, 1956), 453. Here mention is made of translation *Dn* 9.27, 'he shall make burdensome the covenant for many' (498). See *Fuerst*.

Kraeling, Emil G. "The Handwriting on the Wall." *Journal of Biblical Literature,* vol. 63, no. 1, 1944, pp. 11–18. *JSTOR.*

Kratz, Reinhard 'The Visions of Daniel,', pp. 91-113, *The Book of Daniel: Composition and Reception,* Vol. 1, Eds., John J. Collins, Peter W. Flint, Brill, 2001

Law, George R. *The Identification of Darius the Mede* (Pfafftown, NC: Ready Scribe Press, 2010).

Lucas, Ernest C. *Daniel,* Apollos Old Testament Commentary, ed. David W. Baker and Gordon J. Wenham, vol. 20 (Downers Grove, IL: InterVarsity Press, 2002), 134-37

Miller, Stephen R. *Daniel.* NAC. Nashville, Tenn.: Broadman and Holman Publishers, 1994.

Rowley, H. H. *Darius the Mede and the Four World Empires in the Book of Daniel: A Historical Study of Contemporary Theories.* (Cardiff: University of Wales Press Board, 1959).

Schmitt, Rudiger "DARIUS i. The Name," *Encyclopaedia Iranica*, VII/1, p. 40, available online at http://www.iranicaonline.org/articles/darius-i (accessed on 30 December 2012).

Seow, C. L. *Daniel* (Westminster John Knox Press, Louisville, 2003), 44-ff.

Shea, William H. "Darius the Mede: An Update." Andrews University Seminary Studies 20 (1982): 229-247.

Steinmann, Andrew E. *Daniel.* Concordia Commentary. (Saint Louis: Concordia, 2008).

Stuart, Moses. *A Commentary on the Book of Daniel*, (Boston: Crocker & Brewster, 1850).

Whitcomb, John C. Darius the Mede: A Study in Historical Identification, (The Presbyterian and Reformed Publishing Company, 1973).

Wiseman, D. J. "Darius the Mede." In *Notes on Some Problems in the Book of Daniel.* (Eugene, Ore.: Wipf and Stock Publishers, 2000).

www.ingramcontent.com/pod-product-compliance
Lightning Source LLC
Chambersburg PA
CBHW050312120526
44592CB00014B/1883